Logistics:
an Integrated Approach

Professor Michael Quayle BSc, MLitt, PhD, FCIPS, MIMgt, MIPD

and

Bryan Jones BA, MCIPS, MILog

© Michael Quayle and Bryan Jones 1999

First published in Great Britain by Tudor Business Publishing Limited, 1993

A CIP catalogue for this book is available from the British Library

ISBN 1 872807 67 4

The right of Michael Quayle and Bryan Jones to be identified as
the authors of this work has been asserted by them in accordance
with the Copyright, Designs and Patents Act 1988.

Typeset by PACE Typographics Ltd, Bromborough, Wirral
Printed and Bound in Great Britain by
Athenaeum Press Ltd, Newcastle upon Tyne

Logistics:
an Integrated Approach

Preface

This is the second edition of "Logistics: an Integrated Approach" and has been produced in response to market demand. We have continued to develop and reinforce the conception of logistics as a dynamic and managerial process, and have added material which reflects the now more general view of logistics as a strategic function. We have also attempted to reflect the emergence of supply chain management as an activity recognised as key in the public sector and in service organisations generally.

We have retained the basic structure of the previous edition but reorganised the material to suit the millenium environment. We hope that the text will continue to be found useful by a broad range of students and practitioners, and that we have not lost the practical style that made the first edition so popular.

Thanks are due to colleagues and friends who have contributed their ideas and advice, and to the business concerns and copyright holders of included material. Specific acknowledgements are, of course, given in the book where appropriate.

This book is about decision making and actions which determine whether an enterprise excels, survives, or dies. This process is called "logistics management". The job of logistics managers is to make the best use of an organisation's resources in a changing environment.

Because this book focuses on top-level decisions, you may have a problem with the relevance of the subject matter for your short-term career interests; but several reasons can be given why the knowledge you can gain in the study of logistics management is practical and useful for your early career stages:

- You are likely to perform better, regardless of your level in the organisation, if you know the direction in which the organisation is going. As the manager of a subunit, you would like to know how your function fits into the broader picture. If you know how you contribute, you should be able to do a better job of helping the organisation reach its objectives. If your unit is successful and higher level managers realise how you contributed to this success, it will reflect positively on you. Furthermore, lower-level units often interpret strategies and policies set at higher levels. If you understand why those were established, you can implement them more effectively. Finally, if you understand how your job relates to others in the organisation, you will be in a better position to work effectively with peers when cooperation is called for and compete for resources when the time comes.
- In your study of the logistics management process you will begin to identify factors which may lead to significant changes in the organisation. Some of these strategic changes could be positive or negative to you personally. For instance, a major divestiture could eliminate your unit! A new market thrust or product development could make your unit more critical for organisational performance. If you understand what factors may be pushing the organisation in certain directions and how your job fits in, you might decide to change or keep your job. Foresight about critical organisation changes can be a real asset to your career.
- If you are aware of the strategies, values, and objectives of higher-level managers, you are in a better position to assess the likelihood of acceptance of proposals you might make. As you consider offering your suggestions, tying the reasons to your assessment of the interest of higher-level managers is likely to enhance their acceptance and your visibility.

Thus we believe that an understanding of how and why logistics decisions are made can be helpful to you in terms of securing resources beneficial to your subunit, improving your job performance, and enhancing your career development. This book's purpose is to help you make sense of the logistics management process while you are a first-line manager or a middle manager. It is also designed to help prepare you to become a successful top manager. Its goal is to show you that if you understand the business policy and logistics management process before you get to the top, you will be a more effective manager.

The book also is designed to fulfil a teaching function at postgraduate, professional and undergraduate level in schools of business management and administration. The material is designed to help you integrate the functional tools you have learned. These include the analytical tools of physical distribution, logistics and purchasing management which provide help in analysing business problems. The text and the materials in it provide you with an opportunity to learn when to use which tools and how to deal with trade-offs when you cannot maximise the results or preferences of all the functional areas simultaneously.

Most importantly – enjoy it!

Professor Michael Quayle

Michael Quayle is a fellow of the Chartered Institute of Purchasing and Supply, member of the Institute of Management, and member of the Institute of Personnel and Development. He has a Doctorate (PhD) in Procurement, a Masters degree (MLitt) in Industrial Relations and a first degree (BSc) in Business Management.

Michael holds the Bosch Chair in Purchasing & Supply at the University of Glamorgan UK. He earned his PhD from University of Lancaster UK, his Masters from University of Glasgow UK and his Bachelors from University of Maryland USA. Formally the Dean of Business Management & Technology at University College Suffolk (Ipswich) UK, he gained significant procurement and project management experience in the European electronics and defence industries prior to entering academia. Michael is a registered purchasing and supply management specialist with the United Nations and has been published extensively in the fields of management development, purchasing and materials management.

Bryan Jones

Bryan Jones is now the principal of Supply Chain Projects, an independent organisation specialising in Logistics and Supply Chain Management, Training and Consultancy.

Bryan has had a progressive career having worked in several industrial and service sectors, then moving into local government, private sector purchasing and NHS Regional Supplies. The core professional element of his career has been based on Supply Chain Management practice and latterly he was a General Manager in a £multi-million Operational Service Directorate with a Metropolitan Authority.

In parallel with his career he has always taken an active part in professional training and presentation with a number of organisations. Recently this has included writing and delivering course material and programmes in the UK and overseas. In 1994 Bryan was appointed as an external examiner for CIPS at professional level and continues to undertake that role to date.

The current work as a registered freelance Supply Chain Consultant has grown considerably by recommendation and results, and today Bryan is working with clients both nationally and internationally. He is equally interested in developing Supply Chain Skills at SME and local level and works with such organisations as the Chamber of Commerce and TECs to this end.

Contents

CHAPTER 6: MANAGING THE LOGISTICS FUNCTION

- Directing the function; staff; resources; job description, motivation, professional and supervisory staff.
- Management and implementation of change; impact of change on people and jobs; effect on performance; scope for more creative work and decision making.

CHAPTER 7: OPERATING ENVIRONMENTS

- Logistic action planning; manufacturing, public services and utilities, the armed forces, construction, retailing and distribution; integrated logistics support; logistics information systems.
- Co-ordination of physical control; contribution to overall profitability and service capability.

CHAPTER 8: PROVISIONING AND INVENTORY CONTROL

- Stores links in the chain; the need to hold stock; provisioning; pareto analysis; use of computers.
- Coding and inventory systems; related effects on standardisation and variety reduction; accounting methods; stores vocabulary; price analysis.
- Economic order quantity.
- Liaison with sales and production.
- Application of JIT concepts, MRP and MRPII.

CHAPTER 9: STORES MANAGEMENT

- Warehouse, storehouses, stockyards, depots: location and distribution networks.
- Premises: determination of handling requirements in relation to products eg perishables, fluids, gases; design and layout; movement patterns and volume throughput; cost factors; environmental factors.
- Operational requirements: automation, security, hazardous stocks, preservation, packaging, housekeeping, accounting.
- Personnel: development of teams; health and safety; training.
- Equipment: degrees of automation, applications of robotics; static and mobile equipment.
- Surplus, scrap and obsolescent stocks; treatment and disposal.

CHAPTER 1

Development in Supply Chain Management and Logistics

Procurement, Purchasing, Outsourcing, Supply Management, and Supply Chain Management

The purpose of this section is to provide an overview of the differences between procurement, purchasing, outsourcing, supply, and supply chain management. Supply Chain Management is not a fashionable set of words for supply, purchasing and procurement, et al! Understanding the differences is crucial to the development of a world class culture.

Procurement

Compton and Jessop (1995) define procurement as "the obtaining by various means (eg loan, transfer, hire purchase) of supplies and services with or without consideration". Arjan van der Weele (1996) defines procurement as including "all activities required in order to obtain the product from the supplier and get it to the place where it is actually used". It encompasses the purchasing function, store, traffic and transportation, incoming inspection, and quality control and assurance. Some firms also include salvage and management of environmental issues (as they are related to materials) in procurement .

Another definition might be that procurement is purchasing, contracting and logistics where logistics is taken to be inventory control, warehousing, transport, quality assurance and control. The distinction between purchasing and contracting is that contracting is usually the purchasing activity associated with major works.

Often the term procurement is used where government purchasing is involved. The specific activities of purchasing are, as described by Dobler (1990): "Participation in the development of requirements and their specifications; managing value analysis activities; conducting supply market research; managing supplier negotiations; conducting traditional buying activities; administering purchase contracts; managing supplier quality; buying inbound transportation".

Purchasing

Dooley (1995) argues that purchasing and supply management has emerged as an important strategic area of management decision making. Porter (1982) refers to the "value chain" as fundamental to the performance of an organisation. In this value chain, inbound and outbound logistics, and management of the manufacturing operations, are prominent. Deming (1988) dealt with "supply chain" concepts as crucial to the successful introduction of TQM. Other references to the growing significance of the functions of purchasing and supply include Crosby (1976), Schonberger (1986), Womack et al (1989), and Lamming (1993).

Purchasing has two main purposes: firstly to purchase for resale and secondly to purchase for consumption or for conversion (Dobler, 1990). Purchasing for resale is carried out by merchants and speculators, and their task is mainly one of knowing the final market for commodities so that, almost regardless of the cost of purchase, the on-sale can be made at a profit. Purchasing for consumption or for conversion involves a far more difficult decision. Firstly, it is often a long-term decision, for example the decision to use gas as a source of energy. Secondly, although there are many different such purchasing decisions, each one is not repeated so often that a mistake can have long-term damaging effects, such as the decision to use a particular make of alternator in the assembly of a motor vehicle engine (Dooley, 1995).

The clear definition of purchasing is the one given by Steele and Elliott-Shircore (1985) who argue it is the process by which a company (or other organisation) contracts with third parties to obtain goods and services required to fulfil its business objectives in the most timely and cost-effective manner.

The terms purchasing and procurement are often used interchangeably. However, there might be a distinction in that purchasing is more concerned with establishing and managing a commercial relationship, whereas procurement is also concerned with the more physical material or service delivery control aspects after the contract has been let or the order placed.

Van Weele and Rozemeijer (1996) suggest that a possible model for future purchasing organisations to make simultaneous improvements in both increasing functional expertise and horizontal synergy, and in improving focus and flexibility at the business unit level, could be the hard core/soft core organisation. In this organisation a small centralised hard core of corporate purchasing professionals is surrounded by a rather fluid soft core of business specialists. The hard core is responsible for the purchasing process, the strategy, professional development, and the recruitment, training and development of the people involved in the purchasing process. Van Weele and Rozemeijer also use the term "the virtual purchasing organisation" to describe their vision of what is now required. I see absolutely no reason why a group of small and medium size enterprises could not develop a "core" purchasing activity.

Indeed much has been written about what is now required of suppliers. Myer (1989) was an early proponent of supplier change and argued that if suppliers hope to regain a measure of control over their destiny, they must assert themselves and take responsibility for managing their customers. In doing this, suppliers face challenges in two realms: reallocating resources in the company and redesigning programs to better serve outside customers. This should be small and medium size enterprise philosophy.

Purchasers, suppliers and customers are inevitably involved in sourcing strategies and decisions – the genesis of obtaining goods and/or services in both the public and private sectors. Clearly they need to work together to secure competitive advantage and/or world class status.

Outsourcing

Hendry (1995) suggests that one of the strongest and most sustained trends within business over the last ten years has been the trend towards outsourcing. With increased fervour and conviction, corporations have sought to reduce costs by contracting out services and activities traditionally provided in-house. The rationale of this movement is simple and compelling. If contracting something out is cheaper than doing it yourself, outsource. That way you not only save money through greater efficiency but also gain effectiveness by focusing more clearly on those things you can do better in-house. The benefits are obvious. Hendry argues that, supported by political ideology, management fashion and short-term responses to recessionary pressures, the benefits of outsourcing have become so obvious that they have hidden the very real associated costs. It is the purchasing and supply function that "generically" carries out the role of outsourcer.

Supply Management

The term supply management is often referred to as material management. Materials management is described by Dobler (1990) as: "procurement activities; inventory management; receiving activities; stores and warehousing; in-plant materials handling; production planning scheduling and control; traffic and transportation; surplus and salvage". Whilst these descriptions are useful it is important to realise that the practice of purchasing and supply management is changing rapidly.

Supply Chain Management

Supply chain management appears in current dialogue as a new(ish) terminology but definitions of what it encompasses are at best vague. New (1997) suggests that the development of an idea of the supply chain owes much to the emergence from the 1950s onwards of systems theory, and the associated notion of holism (Cavinato, 1992). This may be summarised by the observation that the behaviour of a complex system cannot be understood completely by the segregated analysis of its constituent parts (Boulding, 1956). However, New suggests the use of this idea in regard to supply chains is neither consistent nor straightforward. New also argues that the supply chain metaphor is used in many ways, but three meanings dominate discussion: the supply chain from the perspective of an individual firm; a supply chain related to a particular product or item (such as the supply chain for beef, or cocaine, or oil); and "supply chain" used as a handy synonym for purchasing, distribution and materials management (New, 1994). Supply chain management can mean any one of these but one aspect is certain: purchasing and/or outsourcing activity is being undertaken (CIPS 1997).

Macbeth et al (1989) and Ellram (1990) suggest supply chain management is an integrative philosophy to manage the total flow of a distribution channel from the supplier to the ultimate user. Another definition is the management of a chain or operations and centres through which supplies move from the source of supply to the final customer or point of use (Compton and Jessop, 1995).

In essence, the supply chain starts with the extraction of raw material (or origination of raw concepts for services) and each link in the chain processes the material or the concept in some way or supports this processing. The supply chain thus extends from the raw material extraction or raw concept origination through many processes to the ultimate sale to the consumer of the final product, whether goods or services. Some environmental thinkers have suggested that it should also cover the disposal of the waste associated with the consumed product.

The recognition of the supply chain as a key and vital area both in the public and private sectors has focused attention on its effectiveness. In a number of organisations, cost-effective supply chain is a matter of survival as purchased goods and services account for up to 80 per cent of sales revenue, whilst in the public sector there is an ever-increasing demand for savings in the procurement process. The globalisation of some sources makes it essential that the professional practice is improved and regarded as a key element in the preparation of company or organisation strategies.

Figure 1: Interrelated Strategies Framework

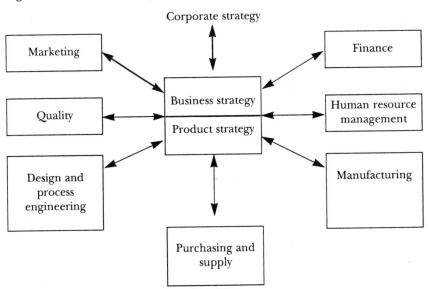

The linchpin in connecting functional strategies to the business strategies, whose intention is to provide competitive advantage and competitive scope, is that of the product strategies. Figure 1 illustrates these connections in relation to the basic functions of a manufacturing firm (Saunders, 1994, "Strategic Purchasing and Supply Chain Management", Pitman).

It is possible to break out of the conventional functional differentiation between purchasing (used generically!) and manufacturing and consider a more integrated perspective, which links both together in a framework for supply chain strategy. This is illustrated in Figure 2 (Saunders, 1994).

The phrase "supply chain" is inadequate to capture the full complexities of the interconnections between different organisations. The idea of a network with various nodes might be a more appropriate analogy and description. However, perhaps the most popular convention is the term "supply chain".

Figure 2 Supply Chain Strategy Framework

Product strategies establish the basic task for the supply chain which, therefore, encompasses both internal and external activities. They include the determination of priorities, with regard to product objectives, needed to meet customer requirements and to beat the offerings of competitors. Differentiated strategies, with regard to quality, cost, time and product innovation, impose different requirements on the supply chain. They should play an important part in the design and development of both the structural and infrastructure features of the supply chain.

The primary function of the supply chain might be said to be the provision of goods and/or services required by customers and to provide appropriate form, time, place and quantity utilities in the package offered. However, the chain also acts as a medium for the exchange of information and the communication of orders or instructions. As well as providing for the flow of products, it provides a channel for the flow of money from customers, which is the normal reward for the supplier. There is a fourth object of exchange and this incorporates social values which are involved in the interpersonal relationship between suppliers and customers (Saunders, 1994). There are clear buying links in the supply chain and this is shown in Figure 3.

Figure 3 Buying Links in the Supply Chain

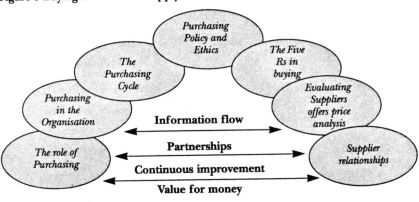

The structure of the supply chain is undergoing rapid transformation. Consumer pressures for lower prices and higher quality of service are forcing retailers, manufacturers and distributors to achieve greater cost efficiencies and improve lead times making supply chain efficiency a key factor in gaining competitive advantage. As a result both retailers and manufacturers are increasingly looking across the supply chain, beyond their traditional logistics boundaries, to form partnerships with the aim of creating a seamless flow of goods and information from the raw materials supplier to the end consumer.

The message here is, I feel, that there is a supply chain of events to be managed the art perhaps is recognising there is one and where it can be influenced in one form or another.

The incentive for purchasers is clear: they need to develop a consistent approach to supplier performance and development, they should obtain an improvement in supplier performance and hence their own; indeed purchasers may learn something about their own performance in terms of relationships with both suppliers and customers. Arguably companies and organisations learn best from each other and this is illustrated in Figure 4.

Figure 4 Supply Chain Solution

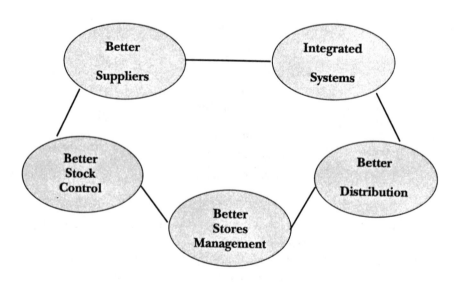

Companies learn best from each other, therefore supply chains and other networks are crucial

Supply chain management is the management of all activities in order to satisfy the ultimate consumer. It covers, therefore, almost all business activity, including marketing, manufacturing, purchasing, logistics and, more generally, such activities as finance and personnel. Supply chain management is arguably the holistic approach and it is this approach we need to take to create a world class culture.

Logistics Into the Future

Logistics is changing at a rapid and accelerating rate. It is changing for two sets of reasons.

The first set is the pressure for change arising from managerial and technical development from within the logistics system itself. These include:

- The increased speed and intelligence of computing systems for the control of the information flows in logistics. This has given rise to what is called "time compression" in logistics. High speed computing and data transmission can transmit and react to user demand almost instantaneously over any distance.
- Distributed data terminals coupled with "real time" data processing makes logistics planning and control both more flexible and more accurate. When this is the case "intelligence" can replace "investment": for example, a computer system which can effectively plan inventory needs will reduce the necessity for holding contingency inventory levels. "Just-in-Time" logistics is also dependant on fast data-handling systems so that assets deployment outcomes can be improved.
- The availability of flexible computer facilities enables logistics companies to engage in "dynamic simulation" of problems. There are many variables in the majority of logistics problems. Real time interactive computer systems enable logistics undertakings to explore a variety of inventory level, transport mode warehouse location and other problems. This increases the accuracy of logistics decisions.
- Lastly, the realisation of the systems nature of logistics and of the potential importance of "trade offs" within the total system. These trade offs require an awareness of total cost measurement and sophisticated management accounting.

However, all these pressures for change will only take root with a sophisticated management process and, in particular, a willingness to manage across functional barriers in the organisation to meet particular organisational goals. This is sometimes described as a "missions" approach. The key to the introduction of this managerial culture in organisation lies in a strategic management informed on logistics issues.

The second set of pressures for change comes from the wider economy and these include the following factors :

- Trends in the economy suggest a future uncertainty in the growth of consumer markets. This will require manufacturing and retail organisations to deal with markets which may vary in size at fairly short notice. The basis of effective business and logistics strategies in this context must be effective flexible options to enable organisations to compete in this tough global market place.
- Market structures are changing with the expanding EC and East European Market, a slowing rate of exports to the USA and fast growing global and high technology markets. There is increasing fragmentation and specialisation in markets and a growth in specialised retailing. This puts pressure both on the marketing and, in turn, the logistics functions.
- Life cycles for products are shortening with more selective and critical customers. As a result, logistics systems are necessary to promote shorter product lead-times and faster and more flexible distribution provisions.
- In the production function, a move is occurring away from mass production towards flexible manufacturing systems (FMS). These systems enable a company to switch production quickly from one product to another. In the marketing function a variety of changes in distribution channels, for example the growth in large, out of town supermarkets, has led to a concentration of buying power and an emphasis on improved distribution service levels especially Just-in-Time delivery. Producers and retailers are sharing information systems to promote Just-in-Time delivery. This philosophy continues to evolve. The principle of "lean production" was first promoted by the Massachusetts Institute of Technology. World Class Factories of the future will be lean producers and are characterised by teams of multi-skilled

workers, lower batch volumes, greater product variety, a total quality ethic, production flexibility and a very high responsiveness to customer needs. This principle obviously extended itself into the supply chain and created the concept of "lean supply" to support the whole process. The process demands continual review of the organisation, management, suppliers and the flow of information at every stage.

● Competitive pressures in markets are also growing. In static markets competition becomes more aggressive. The growth in international marketing has made such aggression more acute. This, in turn, places pressure on logistics systems to support production and marketing initiatives. It is especially true since so much competition in both consumer and industrial goods is now fought on dimensions of customer service.

Logistics Education

Logistics has been an important feature of industrial and economic life for many years, but it is only in the relatively recent past that it has been recognised as a major function in its own right. Distribution and logistics activities make extensive use of the human and natural resources which affect a national economy. Recent studies have attempted to estimate the impact of distribution and logistics on economic life.

One such study indicated that about 30 per cent of the working population in the UK is associated with work related to physical distribution. Another study estimated that up to 40 per cent of the UK gross domestic product was spent on distribution and logistics activities. A further study has indicated that, using a fairly broad definition of distribution, the associated costs in the UK were approximately 17 per cent of company sales revenue.

Need for Education and Training

It is now accepted by both the academic and the business world that there is a need to adopt a more formal and global view of the many different logistics and distribution-related functions. The appreciation of the scope and importance of distribution, especially with respect to new technology, has led to a more scientific approach being adopted toward the subject and to a recognition of the importance of managing the new technology and the changes that it can bring about. This approach is aimed at the individual sub-systems but especially at the overall concepts of the distribution and logistics function.

One of the major features of logistics in recent years has been the speed with which the industry has advanced. Technology has developed, demanding a good knowledge of both physical and information technology, and the jobs span a much greater area of responsibility, requiring a good overall logistics perspective together with the traditional demands for management and communication skills. Logistics is therefore now recognised as being a vital part of the business and economy of a country. In recent years in the UK, for example, the industry has set out to develop a distinct profes-sionalism to reflect this new found importance. In doing this, it has recognised the need for established career structures and good education and training programmes.

Lately there has been a number of initiatives to provide education and training opportunities for those seeking to develop their career in distribution and logistics. These opportunities include:

- Correspondence and various distance learning courses
- Professional NVQs
- Diploma and first degree courses
- HND in Distribution
- Higher degrees most notably Masters degrees
- "Tailor made" company/organisation programmes

A New Concept In Logistics Education

How does the busy distribution or logistics manager keep up to date with new ideas in a rapidly changing environment? How can he or she learn about new techniques and how to apply them? How can this be done whilst also obtaining a recognised educational qualifi-cation? One way is to embark on an advanced course of study which provides relevant education and training without significant periods away from the workplace. It is for this purpose that the Executive Masters Degrees which have programmes in Distribution and Logistics have been set up.

Relevance of Part-Time Study

The programmes are designed to cater for distribution managers and executives, enabling them to continue in a full-time job whilst participating in postgraduate education. For young graduates who are just beginning their careers, the course provides an opportunity to receive a solid grounding in all major aspects concerning Distribution and Logistics. For more mature staff who have already spent some years in industry or commerce, the course allows them to consolidate their existing knowledge, update themselves in the latest concepts and techniques in a more formal environment and broaden their experience.

This initiative is aimed at enabling companies to pursue an active management training programme in Distribution and Logistics which also provides an internationally recognised postgraduate qualification. There are opportunities for companies to attract and keep high quality distribution and logistics staff by using the Executive Masters Degrees to enhance their own management training course. Companies will also be attracted by the work-based content of the programme. In the second year the major input to the course is a company-based thesis, which will be of immediate relevance to the company.

Programme Outline

The courses are based on the core elements of Distribution and Logistics, covering logistics strategy, distribution system design, the planning and management of transport and warehousing operations and the design of appropriate operational systems. Emphasis is given to the impact of information technology and the development and use of distribution information systems and planing tools. Relevant analytical and management techniques and methods are covered, including modelling techniques, statistics, operational research, management accounting, materials and inventory management, human resource management and the interface between law and business activity. Time is also given to developing personal effectiveness and communication skills.

A selection of options and electives are available to allow participants to study particular aspects in greater depth, or to broaden their scope they selecting new topics. Typical areas of specialisation include:

- Distribution Strategy and Planning
- Distribution and Transport Management
- Warehousing and Materials Handling Systems

- Distribution Information Systems
- Information Technology and Logistics
- Logistics System Design
- Materials Management
- Advanced Warehouse Design
- Supply Chain Management

The course programme has been structured to fit within a full-time working environment. Attendance in the first year consists of long weekends, single days and a summer school. Of necessity the teaching programme is intense and requires a full and active commitment. A certain amount of reading and support work will be undertaken on a homestudy basis.

Year two, which is concentrated on a company-based thesis, requires some work days as well as sessions held at the individual's work place with a tutor for the planning, discussion and review of the individual project.

Some useful facts summarised below, based on those who are currently undertaking the course, indicate those managers and organisations who are participating in courses of this nature.

- Ages range from 23 to 48 years, with the average at 34.
- Qualifications vary from those with some type of diploma (plus many years of relevant management experience) to others with a First at degree level.
- Positions vary from Distribution Analyst to Distribution Director, and include a number of different job titles: Distribution Development Manager, European Logistics Manager, Distribution Consultant, General Manager, Quality Control, Distribution Information Systems Manager, Distribution Services Director.
- Different industrial sectors and interests are well represented: there are manufacturers, retailers and third party companies. Industries represented include brewery, clothing, pharmaceuticals, leisure, telecommunications and food.

This demonstrates the importance of logistics education and its overdue recognition in the academic world.

Professional Competence – Food for Thought

It is a sad fact that the level of understanding in the field of materials management is often low or not well-balanced across the whole purchasing/production control spectrum. It is more worrying that we do not have a common yardstick by which to recognise the limited numbers of professional practitioners. Without effective materials management a business which markets fine products and which is supported by excellent manufacturing facilities and purchasing skills cannot survive. We are well aware of the impact materials management has on business performance and cost control. To achieve professional performance we must measure capability and ensure that it is obtained.

We have internationally recognised professional and technical standards to declare the ability and potential of accountants, engineers, metallurgists and even our shop floor workers. Until now, materials management staff have been handicapped, only half equipped as it were. Admittedly the purchasing side of their professional responsibilities has been well supported by the long-established and readily accessible CIPS Foundation and professional level specialist programmes, taught in so many locations in the UK and overseas.

In terms of the wider discipline of logistics one of the key points made by Alan Cole, Chief Executive of TDG at the opening of the 1997 Logistics Conference was: "Logistics is not a profession, nor should it seek to become one. However, logistics managers should certainly be professional"

The Institute of Logistics is meeting the industry's needs to this end with a wide range of training opportunities and courses. The courses may be practical subject bases issues and/or leading to the Institute's own Certificate and Diploma qualifications. They offer four routes to this destination: open learning, public courses, in company and multi-media options. As such both the Chartered Institute of Purchasing and Supply and the Institute of Logistics are striving to improve the quality, delivery and range of purchasing and logistics training to meet the real needs of the practitioners and their organisations in this environment of continual change and world market demands.

The need has long existed for education of similar standing, a well-structured modern syllabus, accompanied by recognised levels of accreditation of successful students. Unfortunately, most practitioners are trained by "sitting with Nellie" or by reading the manuals provided with the new computer system. Having the best tools does not help if the understanding is weak. Indeed it can be positively dangerous.

CHAPTER 2

Strategic Purchasing Management

Corporate Planning

Consider a business enterprise and ask yourself the following questions:

- What are its objectives?
- How does it operate?
- What resources are required?
- How are the resources managed?
- What influences bear upon the success or failure of the enterprise?

In so doing, you are embarking on the first steps of corporate planning. All are important questions and it is the responsibility of general management to consider these matters in terms of long-range planning. Objectives must be agreed and the provision and management of resources financial, technical and human set in motion.

The Corporate Plan

In considering the responsibilities of general management, planning objectives and controlling resources, we are considering the business strategy of the company or governing body, in other words, the corporate plan involving:

- Objectives - survival, profitability and social responsibilities
- Products and Markets
- Finance
- Material Resources
- Human Resources
- Technical Facilities
- Management and Administration

Within the corporate plan, therefore, lies the important area of purchashing resources.

What is Corporate Planning?

Corporate planning may be described as the careful systematic taking of strategic decisions. It is concerned with developing a long-term view of future developments and in designing a plan so that the organisation can achieve its chosen objectives. During the last decade many of the bigger companies in the United Kingdom recognised the need to apply a formal approach to this need. It means that companies need to prepare "scenarios" or forecasts of future developments in the environment in which they wish to operate in order to examine whether decisions taken in the present will result in a successful outcome in the future. Changes are taking place at a more rapid rate, but often the effects of decisions taken now may still be influential more than ten years later. Companies, therefore, have been developing more sophisticated techniques to analyse the risks involved in such decisions.

Consider, for example, the problem of deciding whether an oil company should invest in a new refinery, which might cost well over £100 million and which might have a life of 15 years or more. Such a company needs to know whether a market can be assured for the extra volume of its refined products and it needs to know whether they can be produced profitably. In addition, however, it is necessary to study the availability of crude oil and other supplies needed in the operation.

Corporate planning, therefore, is a process concerned with determining the long-term objectives of the organisation, with deciding what market opportunities exist and with determining a product policy to satisfy them. Any plan, however, needs to be firmly based upon a study of supply markets and a plan to ensure that the required resources can be made available at the right price to support such a product policy. In short, an essential element in the corporate plan is a strategy for purchasing. In the past, many companies have omitted this element, but problems of supply shortages and rising prices have made top management aware of the need to take into account long-term developments in supply markets.

The Need for Corporate Planning

The environments in which companies have to operate today have become increasingly dynamic and they have had to learn to live with and adapt to the changes that are taking place. Some examples of changes that have to be coped with are changes in products, in manufacturing processes, in communication techniques, in data processing techniques, as well as changes in both supply and sales markets. Companies have recognised the need to investigate these changes and to draw up plans in order to adapt to them and to survive. More sophisticated techniques have been developed to analyse the uncertainties and to assess the risks involved in the decisions that have to be made. A further impetus to the need to plan arises from the fact that companies have to invest large sums of money in new plant and equipment and they have to look carefully to see whether such schemes will offer sufficient benefits to justify the expenditure. In order to do so it may be necessary to look far ahead in the future.

The corporate plan establishes the basic objectives for the company as a whole and gives guidance to the actions of the various specialist departments, such as marketing, production and purchasing. It is also designed to co-ordinate the work of these departments to ensure that they all work together in order that the overall objectives of the company can be successfully achieved.

The Nature of Corporate Planning

One very important aspect of planning which has not yet been mentioned is the dimension of time. The consideration of this factor can lead to different perspectives and different types of plan. We are all no doubt familiar with the type of plan called a budget, which is likely to cover at most a time span of 12 months. This is essentially a short-term planning device. Plans such as this cover, therefore, only a short period of time and you may see these short-terms plans referred to as "operational" or "tactical" plans. However, many companies have recognised the need to look much further ahead (investment in new plant and equipment today may have significant implications for a long period of time into the future - often ten years or more). In recent years, especially, therefore, there has been growing support for the need to develop long-term plans for companies, covering at least five years into the future. These plans may be referred to as "strategic" or "long-range plans".

It is likewise important to develop strategic plans for the specialist functions. From the purchasing point of view, it needs to be stated here that many companies have been slow to develop such a strategic perspective of the purchasing specialism. It has to be admitted, too, that many purchasing personnel have been slow to see the need for and to develop the vision required to construct a strategic plan for purchasing.

Many companies adopt only two planning horizons - "operational" and "strategic". Some companies view the problems as being concerned with three planning horizons, namely:

- Up to one year: operational, day-to-day.
- One to two years: short-term, tactical.
- Three to ten years or more: long-term, strategic.

Having identified the time characteristics of corporate planning, it is essential to consider the basic approach to the preparation of corporate plans. It should be noted that the emphasis in this chapter will be on the longer-term, strategic type of plan. Typical studies need to be carried out:

External Factors affecting both Sales Markets and Supply Markets

- General Economic Conditions
- New Product Developments
- Key Suppliers/Competitors
- Activities and Plans
- Merger and Changes to Market
- Structure
- Government Legislation
- International Factors, eg Exchange Rates, Tariffs
- Industrial Relations

Internal Factors

- Product Development
- Production Facilities
- Process Developments
- Transport Facilities
- Industrial Relations
- Personnel Development
- Financial Resources

The objectives of these studies are to:

- develop a clear picture of existing markets and future opportunities and threats which are beginning to emerge, and
- carefully analyse the resources that the company at present possesses.

Once this work has been completed, it is possible to proceed with the development of the plan itself. Some companies employ specialist corporate planners, but others rely on departments to develop the plan.

The Contents of a Corporate Plan

The contents of a corporate plan will vary according to the nature of each company, taking into account whether the company is in manufacturing or distribution for instance. The complexity of the company may also vary depending on whether the company operates on more than one site and whether it is involved in more than one product area. Corporate plans may need to be drawn up for separate divisions or subsidiary companies.

The objective of the plan will be to set overall profit objectives and to show how these are to be achieved. In outline, this involves identifying the market opportunities that are to be pursued and showing how the resources of the company are to be utilised and developed to satisfy the target markets. In arriving at the details of the plan the following aspects will need to be considered:

Marketing
- Products to be offered - types, range, degree of flexibility
- Project volumes
- Distribution policies and methods
- Promotion strategies

Production
- Product developments
- Process developments
- Manufacturing facilities and location
- Manufacturing strategy,
  eg "make-for-stock"
  or" make-to-customer order"
  or "mixed strategies"
- Quality and reliability

Purchasing and Supply
- Make or buy strategies
- Research and development of new materials and suppliers
- Price cost analysis studies
- Inventory requirements
- Sourcing strategies

Finance
- Development of a financial plan
- Investment plans
- Financial requirements

Organisation
- Structure
- Personnel development
- Company development with regard to mergers and takeovers
- Growth strategies - horizontal and/or vertical integration or diversification into related or unrelated fields.

It is important that the plan shows a coherent competitive strategy on which the detailed plans for each function can be based. It is perhaps also important to allow a certain amount of flexibility because of the uncertainties of predicting the precise nature of future operating conditions. Risks need to be carefully assessed and contingency plans drawn up where these might be needed.

Planning has long been regarded as an essential function of management and this applies at both the highest level in the company organisation and within specialist departments of the company. Planning can be understood quite simply as deciding what to do, how to do it, when to do it and who is to do it. It involves, therefore, the setting of objectives or goals which are to be achieved and the plans or methods to be used in their attainment. If companies fail to pay sufficient attention to this function they cannot hope to have a clear sense of purpose and to be able to exercise any control over their destinies. This applies both in the public and the private sectors.

Purchasing Planning and Purchasing Strategies

This chapter has concentrated on the general aspects of corporate planning and it has stressed the need to integrate functional or departmental plans with the overall corporate plan. Purchasing aspects must be taken into account if the corporate plan is to be realistic and effective. A strategic perspective of this specialist function should, therefore, be developed. Unless the appropriate material resources are made available to the right time and the right price, no corporate plan will succeed. However, there is some basic buying information to consider and there are decisions to be made and these are given at Figure 5.

Figure 5 Basic Buying Information and Decisions

- ● Make or Buy
- ● How many suppliers do we have?
- ● What is the total value of our spend p.a.?
- ● Who are our 'top ten' suppliers by value?
- ● What are the 'top ten' products by spend?
- ● What are the critical low value items?

It has to be admitted, however, that companies and writers have been slow to appreciate the strategic role that purchasing plays. Indeed many purchasing personnel themselves have not fully appreciated this aspect; many have regarded purchasing as being only concerned with short-term, operational problems. However, the need for a strategic perspective has now been more widely recognised and it will be the purpose of this chapter to support this change of view. Several factors in recent years have given strength to the development of the strategic perspective of purchasing. Amongst these are the following:

- ● Rising prices and the need to control inflation.
- ● The need to control investment in inventory more effectively.
- ● Recognition of the importance of purchasing costs to profitability, especially in "purchasing intensive" companies where material costs as a percentage of total costs are very high.
- ● Shortages of materials.
- ● Growing scarcity of some key materials.

Although purchasing will form part of the short-term plan as represented by the annual budget, it is still important to develop the long-term view. The long-term strategic plan for purchasing provides a framework within which operational decisions can be made. Recognition of longer-term implications of today's decision should prevent the long-term supply position of the company from being put in jeopardy. It will be useful to identify the basic stages involved in the development of a strategic plan for purchasing.

Stages in the Development of a Corporate Plan for Purchasing

The first stage is to collect information and monitor factors in supply markets and the external environment of the organisation. It will be necessary to investigate, for example, what new materials are being developed, what changes in supply and demand can be expected and what price trends can be expected.

- Collect information and data concerning demand for materials and equipment within the company.
- Develop a long-term plan which establishes objectives and strategies to be adopted and which also covers short-term tactics and goals.
- Design an organisation and devise procedures and policies to implement the plan.
- Construct a manpower plan so that the required human resources are available to put the plans into operations.
- Monitor the performance of the department and of the staff to check that results are in accordance with the plans. It may become necessary to modify actions in order to get back on course to achieve the objectives of the plan.

It was mentioned earlier that "planning" is a key element in the task of the manager. In the above framework the other key functions of management can also be identified, namely, organising, staffing, and controlling. This chapter will also be concerned with these other functions, but it is the planning function which gives a sense of direction and purpose to the activities of people in the department.

Corporate and Environmental Factors

If we consider, for example, purchasing strategies, we are faced long-term with the problems of inflation, physical shortages, and energy crises. The general need, therefore, is for flexibility by alternative plans, and so continuous control and reassessment is essential as a major factor of Flexible Strategic Planning, with alternative objectives positively introduced to meet change circumstances rather than passive acceptance. A strategic long-term plan with no provision for change may lead to costly and disastrous emergency action. In-built flexibility by shorter-term progressive reassessment of the long-term plan gives meaning to the term.

Strategic Planning

The need for a considered approach to flexibility as an important factor in long-term planning is evident when we consider the two-fold influences which may affect the performance of any business: internal and external.

Internal Flexibility
This involves pressure on finance to meet unanticipated contingencies and can be referred to as the liquidity strength of the company, measured by the relationship or ratio of equity to debts and asset position current to fixed.

External Flexibility
This involves markets and research of sales and supply.

Market Strategic Flexibility

This can be answered in terms of:
- Sales spread amongst customers - the avoidance of over-dependence on a single customer or a few large areas
- Diversification of products
- Diversification of markets domestic and overseas
- Technological research into opportunity areas

Objectives and Responsibilities

It is as well to define the areas covered by what appear to be similar aims: those of objectives and those of responsibilities. Whilst they are important corporate considerations, in modern management thought they pose different approaches although they contain interacting factors. As we have already seen, these constitute aims and purposes inherent in the company processes of management and consist of planning economic development and available resources on a long-term basis.

Responsibilities

These are in the nature of social or moral considerations, for example:

- Conservation of the environment
- Avoidance of pollution
- Employment security
- Social welfare
- Philanthropic contribution to the general community

Although classed as non-economic objectives, these responsibilities can affect the strategic planning of a company. Good environmental conditions, internal and external employment security and social welfare can contribute to productivity. Philanthropy, whilst appearing to use resources otherwise available for development, often appears in the later stages of company growth, as a reflection of stability and the primary satisfaction of economic objectives.

Social Accountability

Business, essentially focused on profitability and economic viability, is giving increasing attention to its further role of social accountability. An enterprise has responsibilities directly to the customer, which demands a social awareness of the need to consider the quality of life through the product, including safety, but also responsibilities towards the many small suppliers who depend on larger organisations for their continuing existence.

Socio-Economic Factors

The question of pollution has exercised the minds of past generations and is today a matter of prime importance with governmental checks and controls. Most companies are conscious of their responsibilities in this area and have, in many cases, taken the opportunity to derive economic advantage from waste polluting materials by converting them to saleable by-products, thus avoiding environmental problems, ensuring economic returns and strengthening their position both economically and in the community.

Social Welfare

There is today an accepted awareness in modern industry of the responsibility of business enterprise to the welfare of employees the result of enlightened management, governmental control and the trades unions. The main legislative acts which have fostered good industrial relations are:

- Security of Employment: Employment Protection Act 1975
- Health and Safety: Health and Safety at Work Act 1974
- Social Security: Social Security Pensions Act 1975

Legislation is contained in the Acts covering Employment Protection (Consolidation) Act 1978 and the Employment Acts 1980 and 1982, including an important section on the individual employment rights of employees.

Business and the Community

Referred to earlier, this is the contribution of business enterprises to the community at large, mainly in terms of philanthropy by established and successful concerns in the form of charitable and artistic trusts. There is the further contribution made by the business managers themselves, in given time and energy to support company participation. Whilst in most cases the extra-mural activities spring from the company awareness of responsibility to the public environment, there is often a "trade-off" by-product of enhanced company image and increased trade.

The Effectiveness of Social Considerations

Whilst it appears at first sight that in long-term planning there are restrictive influences involved in financial outlay in matters of social accountability and philanthropy, the question of trade-offs in terms of public image and trade potential must be given full consideration. Job satisfaction, participation, profit-sharing, the question of machines and manpower, technical advancement and employment security are social matters of grave importance for employment and competitive strength.

SWOT and GAP Analyses

SWOT

SWOT is quite simply Strength, Weaknesses, Opportunities and Threats. It involves an analysis of any supply chain which will show quite clearly if any SWOT elements exist within it. A typical approach to SWOT is shown in the diagram below:

Figure 6 SWOT Analysis

Strengths	**Weaknesses**
Opportunities	**Threats**

Strategic planning involves the collection of relevant data, the identification of alternatives, the selection of the most attractive of these and the enactment of those selected. SWOT is necessary to recognise problems and opportunities. A simple technique which is also useful in this connection is called gap analysis.

Gap Analysis

Gap analysis shows graphically what the company or organisation is trying to achieve and what outcomes would be likely if its current strategy continued to operate. It shows the gap between what is desired and what is likely to happen.

Gap analysis is best undertaken at corporate level. Purchasing has a significant impact on business results and needs to be involved at the planning stage. Often the purchasing function can make significant contributions towards closing the gap. Such contributions may be an examination of supply sources, prudent make or buy decisions, value engineering and acquisition cost reduction. A typical example of gap analysis is shown below.

Figure 7 GAP Analysis

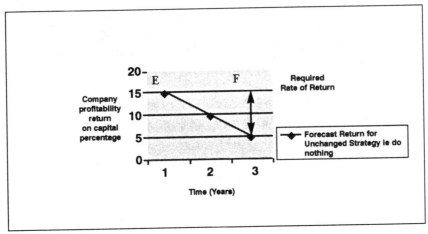

Source: M Porter (1979) **How Competitive Forces Shape Strategy, Harvard Business Review**

Functions Involved in Corporate Planning

It must not be assumed that a corporate plan emerges as the product solely of a high-level "think tank". If you consider the main area of the company audit (production, finance, technology and administration) and the external activities of marketing and purchasing involved in growth, you will readily see that these are considering functional areas of company management. Corporate planning therefore rests on functional support, in the main factual.

Corporate policies emerge as decisions to operate in those areas which are considered best for successful achievement of objectives. For example, the following alternatives may present themselves:

● Market penetration by development of the existing market, that is effort concentrated upon obtaining a larger share of the existing market at the expense of competitors.
● Limiting product utility to a particular section of the market, for example industrial or domestic.
● Diversification into new products and new markets.

Functional Contribution to Corporate Strategy

Consider the corporate audit in the light of functional activities and their particular contribution to corporate management.

Marketing

This is intimately concerned with growth and profitability. Demand regulates turnover, which must be supported by adequate and suitable administration of manufacture, logistics, technology, purchasing, manpower and finance.

Manufacture

The corporate audit will look to adequacy of production facilities and the need to expand both operationally and in the use of advanced technology and equipment to produce in economic quantities in time to satisfy the market.

Logistics

This is linked both with marketing and manufacturing operations in the movement and storage of goods at all stages to meet projected sales programmes.

Technology

This involves research and development of products functionally and visually to satisfy the need for economic production and to promote sales. Product reviews to support the company image for reliability and innovation.

Finance

Costs administration and cash management are important in promoting attractive product prices, combating inflation and conserving cash resources.

Purchasing

Effective purchasing management is vitally necessary in ensuring free flow of materials at economic prices and in suitable quantities to meet production schedules and sales programmes.

Manpower

Assessment of manpower levels to meet operational and administrative growth - recruitment and training. Management development and the need for functional managers trained to think in corporate terms.

Monitoring Performance

Master Plan and Functional Plan

The two-way provision of support data for the functional level and long-term plan of the corporate strategy becomes evident in the master and functional budgets. Appraisal of resources, their potentialities and limitations, in deciding upon objectives leads to corporate plans, estimates of financial implications and master budget, long-term with emphasis on profitability and return on investment (ROI). From the master budget stems the capital allocation of departmental budgets appropriate to support programmes functionally achievable to bring success to the corporate strategy and fulfil the company objectives. At both levels, corporate and functional, the monitoring of performance is of prime importance. Whilst many of the departmental budgets are short-term, involving the tactics of annual programmes and day-to-day decisions, the longer-term aspect of management by objectives ensures that the corporate plan is fully supported, for example:

- Personnel contributes to the manpower survey and is budgeted accordingly.
- Finance projects and monitors progressive return on investment.
- Research and development combat the possibility of shortages of supplies and demand change by seeking material substitutes and improved designs.
- Purchasing seek new supply sources, new materials, promote standardisation and rationalisation, with emphasis on cost reductions and economic materials management.
- Manufacturing is concerned with techniques and equipment to ensure production support and meet the problem of economy with flexibility.

Purchasing Needs and Corporate Strategies

The demand for goods and services to be satisfied by the purchasing department is derived from the demand in the company's market. Corporate plans must take into account marketing strategies on the output side. Production plans to support such strategies will also be drawn up; from these it is possible to determine input requirements.

We need, therefore, to develop an understanding of the implications for purchasing arising from production and marketing strategies.

Marketing Strategies and the Demand for Inputs

During the last two decades the importance of marketing has been recognised, both as a general business philosophy and as a specialist function. It embodies a recognition that the success of an organisation is dependent on satisfying a market demand for particular goods and services. It follows that a company should identify market opportunities and then develop a corporate plan based upon an appraisal of those future market needs. "Produce what you can sell", rather than "sell what you can produce". Within the marketing function, therefore, the activities of market research, advertising and promotion have been added to the selling task. Market research plays an important part in gathering intelligence about the nature of demand and the potential of particular product designs. On the basis of this information a number of different strategies can be considered, designed particularly to meet a corporate objective of growth, which many companies regard as the best way to achieve profitability in the long run.

Marketing Strategies to Achieve Growth

If growth is set as an objective, marketing plans can be drawn up to achieve this based upon four possible alternative strategies:

Market Penetration: the aim here is to increase the use of the company's existing products or service in the present markets. This increased demand may arise by increasing customers' rate of usage, attracting customers from competitors and attracting non-users.

Market Development: this strategy is concerned with marketing present products in new markets. these new markets may be opened up by expanding on either a regional, national or international basis. Alternatively, an existing product range can be sold to a new segment of the market.

Product Development: this third strategy involves the development of new or modified products designed to satisfy existing markets in which the firm operates. It may involve a broadening of the product range as well.

Diversification: this final approach covers the addition of both new products and new markets to the firms operations.

Implications for Purchasing

We can now analyse the effects of these alternative strategies on the demand for materials which are the ingredients of these products. Market penetration and market development strategies lead to an increase in sales of a company's existing product range. Therefore, there will be an increase in the volume of materials of existing specifications to meet this expansion.

Product development and diversification strategies involve the development of new and modified products and, therefore, will change the specifications of the material inputs. New and modified inputs will be required and research and development work will be needed to prepare new designs. Diversification, especially, may require the application of different technologies and purchasing may become involved in new supply markets. The supply of old ingredients will need to be phased out and new material inputs brought on stream.

So far we have considered the direct effect of marketing strategies on material requirements. We need now to look at the effect of marketing strategies upon production and further consequences arising from production plans for purchasing.

Production Strategies and Implications for Purchasing

Plans affecting the output of finished products have direct implications for the production facilities needed to produce them. An increase in output will need an increase in capacity to produce the required volumes. Thus, additional equipment, buildings and even new factories may be required. Old equipment may also need replacement during the period covered by the corporate plan. Plans for capital investment will create a demand for purchasing to buy the necessary plant and machines. The search for and installation of efficient modern equipment can make a valuable contribution to the effective implementation of the corporate plan. Changes in the level and methods of production will also affect the demand for consumable supplies needed in the conversion processes. Expansion plans may require the construction of a new factory and this leads to the problem of where this should be located.

It is essential in analysing this problem to take into account not only marketing factors and labour factors, but also an assessment of supply conditions. The location of suppliers and the cost of transporting supplies can have a significant influence on the economies of the location decision. The high costs of transporting a large volume of low-value goods or a high consumption of energy can attract factories close to the supply sources. The relative costs of transporting supplies and transporting the finished product need to be studied to find out whether the factory should be located near the market for the finished goods or near the sources of supply. The British Steel Corporation, for example, is anxious to locate basic steel-making plants on coastal sites because of the need to import iron ore.

When opening up new markets in other countries the possibility of building new factories in those countries may arise. It is essential, particularly when possible sites are in relatively undeveloped countries, to investigate the supply situation. Do such countries have potential suppliers who have the necessary skills to produce the right quality goods, at the right price, at the right time? If not, is it feasible and economic to import supplies? There is evidence to suggest that companies have ignored these factors when taking investment decisions and have been faced with unexpected supply difficulties as a result.

Corporate plans to implement marketing strategies can affect the demand for future supplies of bought-out requirements. We can now turn to the problem of devising purchasing strategies that are designed to ensure that those requirements can be satisfied. If insurmountable supply constraints are foreseen then the corporate plan, if it is going to succeed, must reflect this. However, if future supply difficulties are anticipated in advance, then solutions to overcome them can in most cases be found.

Purchasing Strategies

In order to provide the required resources to support the corporate plan, it is necessary to assess the existing supply situation and then devise strategies to ensure that these resources can be obtained. This approach is more rational than merely reacting to emergencies on an ad hoc basis. The first stage is to appraise the existing supply environment and to identify trends, threats and opportunities regarding the availability, design and prices of future supplies. Strategies need to be developed to exploit these opportunities and to find ways of overcoming threats regarding possible shortages and adverse price movements. There is a need to consider such aspects as the development of new materials, the opening up of new sources of supply and negotiating strategies in supply markets. Make or buy will be considered in depth as another important strategic decision in what might be called "resource management". The results of good buying practise by operating purchasing as a profit centre are clear and given in Figure 8.

Figure 8 Results of Good Buying Practice

- The cost of purchasing as a % of turnover reduces
- Purchases keep within budgets
- Operational, process & product cost relations
- Scrap, reworking, obsolescence costs reduce
- Better supplies co-operation & responsiveness

The Development of New Materials and Equipment

There are two reasons why buyers should be concerned with identifying and helping suppliers to develop new materials and equipment. First, innovations are an important source of cost savings and of improvements in performance. Secondly, the substitution of new materials and equipment for products bought on previous occasions can overcome anticipated shortages and adverse price movements.

The development of new designs can take a long period of time in which materials have to be investigated and tested. Purchasing personnel need to work closely with their own research and development engineers as well as the technical experts of supplying companies. Plans need to be drawn up to control the development and to introduce the changes on the basis of forecast lead times. The initiative in the development of new materials can arise either from the suppliers firm or within the buyer's firm.

The Development of Supply Capacity

Changes in supply conditions and changes in expected demand for materials may create a gap between existing capacity and the volume required. Buyers, therefore, need to take steps to increase supplies in line with the corporate plan. This may be done either by arranging for existing suppliers to expand their facilities or by developing new suppliers. Discussions should be held with suppliers regarding long-term requirements, so that suppliers can also plan ahead to meet their customers' needs and instal new plant and equipment if necessary. A programme of supplier development can also be drawn up to create new sources of supply which have the correct production and quality control facilities to supply goods of the desired quality. Suppliers should be closely involved in the corporate planning process so that both supplier and buyer can benefit from symbiotic growth. Suppliers are stakeholders in the purchaser's business and need to be viewed as such. See Figure 9 for the scope of what needs to be considered.

Figure 9 Purchasing's Need to Consider

- Single or multiple sourcing
- Supplier appraisal methods
- Supplier performance
- Finding new suppliers

Price Strategies and the Structure of Supply Markets

An audit of existing supply market structures may show that the buying company may be in an unfavourable position. Monopoly and oligopoly situations could restrict competition and thus weaken the power of the buyer as regards choice of suppliers and the negotiation of prices. Purchasing departments, especially in the larger organisations, therefore, need to develop strategies to control the flow of supplies at favourable prices. Countervailing power can be developed in the following ways:

- Develop price-cost analysis techniques to improve negotiating ability with existing suppliers.
- Allocate business to more than one supplier as a means of preserving competition.
- Encourage new suppliers to enter the market or develop foreign sources of supply to increase competition.
- Contact the Director General of Fair Trading to investigate monopolies and restrictive agreements if the public interest is considered to be in jeopardy.
- Consider the possibilities of the buyer's own company making the product.
- Investigate the possibility of takeover or merger with a supplier in order to increase control of essential supplies.
- Develop substitute materials from other suppliers to overcome shortages and resulting price rises.

It can be seen that buyers should not merely adapt to changes as they occur in the supply environment, but should take positive steps to ensure that developments are favourable to their needs and protect their interests. The pursuit of short-term price advantages may have unfavourable consequences in the long-term if the price-cutting tactics of suppliers are designed to drive competitors from the market and to build up a dominant position.

Flexible Strategies

The dynamic character of the world today means that it can be difficult to forecast future conditions and flexible strategies may be needed to cope with uncertainty. Consideration should be given to flexibility in the context of having several suppliers available and the possibility of maintaining flexibility in the choice of materials.

Single Versus Multiple Sourcing

Multiple sourcing can be seen as a response to the uncertainties of relying on the deliveries of one supplier, which can be delayed by such contingencies as strikes, transport problems and fires. A further advantage of multiple sourcing arises from maintaining contact with research and development undertaken by several suppliers. In addition, there may be tactical benefits from being able to alter the division of business between them to encourage a high performance as regards delivery and quality. Purchasing strategy, therefore, involves a policy decision regarding situations in which multiple sourcing should be adopted. Essentially this should include items which are critical in the production process and which incur high costs if the production lines are stopped. The higher unit costs which might arise as a result of splitting the business can be seen as an insurance against the higher total costs of stopped production. There is also a need to guard against buyer inertia!

Multiple Choice of Materials

It is never possible to forecast future trends with complete accuracy and, in the face of a high degree of uncertainty, a plan which allows a flexible response is preferable. A good example arises in the choice of fuels. Technological change and competition between producers, as well as other disturbances such as strikes and OPEC - controlled price rises, has made it difficult to forecast future price movements. A flexible approach, therefore, is to invest in equipment which can use more than one type of fuel. Such a strategy relegates the choice of fuel to a tactical problem of choosing the lowest cost fuel when an order has to be placed. A second example concerns the development of new materials and components. Predicting the time needed to carry out research and development projects is hazardous and plans may thus be needed to carry on using previously tried materials as an alternative. When developing the RB 211 jet, for example, Rolls Royce had to consider using fan blades made out of conventional metal material as well as the development of the new material, carbon fibre. Insurmountable obstacles meant that the new material could not be used in the end.

Plans for Stores and Stock Control

It is also important to consider the implications for stores and stock control when developing the corporate plan. Changing demand rates for materials and other goods and consequent changes in supply rates put different pressures on the stores function. Changing lead times are also relevant. It is necessary to draw up plans to provide the physical facilities for the anticipated scale of operations. Problems such as what to stock, how much to stock and where to stock need to be analysed, as well as defining the levels of service that are required. Materials handling techniques have evolved rapidly and methods need to be investigated and improved. Finally, we must not ignore the major aspect of costs, which can be as high as 25 per cent of average inventory value. Forecasts of working capital needed to finance planned inventory levels must also be prepared. Thus, the objective of planning in this area is to provide a least cost service to meet the planned levels of production.

Elements of Supplier Partnership

To compete successfully in world markets a company needs to be better than the competition and source suppliers who can both add value and reduce cost. Partnership sourcing is where a buyer and supplier develop such a close and long-term relationship that the two work together as partners in a win-win arrangement as both have a vested interest in the success of the other. The cynic will argue that in a competitive race there is only one winner but, winning per se is not the issue. Perception of winning with the success of the other in mind is the key to partnership. Building a supplier partnership takes into account the elements shown in Figure 10.

Figure 10 Building a Supplier Partnership

"Make or Buy"

For many companies, particularly in the engineering industries, "make or buy" problems are important strategic issues. This type of problem can arise as a short-term question when spare manufacturing capacity is available in times of slack demand. Technical considerations may be similar, but the financial aspects differ according to whether it is a long-term strategic issue or whether it is a short-term tactical difficulty. The former situation is of prime importance.

All too frequently in the past, companies have not taken a serious look at what should be made in the company and what should be bought from outside suppliers. Manufacturing policy has been determined by previous traditions and has not taken into account the present and future possibilities. The "make or buy" decision is not one that the purchasing function can take in isolation. It is important that both purchasing and production information is considered together, and a committee approach which allows all interested parties to express their view will be advantageous. Some important decisions may need to be resolved at board level. Nevertheless, the purchasing function should play a significant part in finding the right answer.

First, the strategic problem needs to be clearly stated. It may be concerned with the question of how existing production facilities should be used in the future or it may also be concerned with whether an investment should be made in additional plant or equipment. The tactical short-term problem, however, is concerned with how to use spare capacity, or, indeed, what to subcontract if existing capacity is fully utilised in times of an unexpected jump in demand for the finished product.

The company must first make a full appraisal of its technical capabilities with respect to proposals of what should be manufactured. This should cover existing strengths and weaknesses as regards knowledge and skills, availability of labour, materials, and finance as well as suitability of plant and equipment. If there are any deficiencies in the present picture, which mean that the company cannot produce the products in the required volumes, then a further appraisal must be made of the feasibility of acquiring the extra resources.

Some larger organisations try to close any competency deficiencies or gaps when major projects are undertaken. They set up a strategic plan (1), nominate pilot sites (2), commission a pilot framework (3), identify the gaps from a pilot report (4) and review available options (5); not unnaturally work continues (usually through a further five stages) to close the gap in competencies required. The full process is shown in Figure 11.

Figure 11 Competency Gap Analysis Process

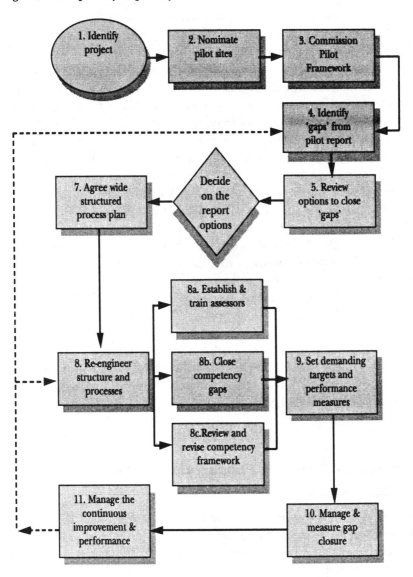

At the same time the purchasing department should make a similar assessment of the supply market to see if there are if difficulties regarding quality, delivery and price which can be solved by internal manufacture. They should also ascertain any particular advantages that external suppliers have regarding research and development expertise, long production runs and specialist equipment. The volume required by the company may be insufficient to benefit from the specialisation which suppliers can indulge in when supplying to a much wider market.

Finally, assuming that there are no major technical barriers to making the product, a comparison of the total cost of manufacture needs to be compared against the cost of acquiring the product from external suppliers. It may also be possible to compare the alternative costs and savings from a number of "make" proposals. When the issue is a strategic question, full costs of internal manufacture (capital or fixed costs as well as variable costs) should be taken into account. In the tactical situation, however, a case can be made for leaving out fixed costs for use of machinery and equipment. This approach is based on the assumption that equipment will remain idle in the short run, if the particular product in question is not made internally, but that overhead charges will, nevertheless, be incurred by the company. The financial analysis will, therefore, reveal whether it is more economic to purchase from an outside supplier or whether it should be made internally.

The purchasing function can make a valuable contribution to the decision-making process with regard to "make or buy" problems. It should also be prepared to initiate proposals to reverse previous policies if changes in supply markets indicate that the company can gain from doing so. The corporate plan should be based upon a careful analysis of what it should produce and what it should purchase from outside.

International Trade – the Implications for Purchasing Management

International factors may have a significant effect on a company either directly, in relation to the products that are bought or sold overseas, or indirectly, by influencing government actions and the activities of suppliers and customers. Purchasing management is more involved with influences affecting supplies, though changes in demand for the finished products cannot be entirely ignored.

Factors Directly Affecting Purchasing

Availability of Foreign Products: The changing pattern of world markets affects the availability of goods that can be purchased abroad. It is necessary to study changes in supply and demand and to identify new products and new markets as they develop. As a result of improvements in transport techniques, of changes in the relative competitiveness of overseas producers and of technological advances made elsewhere, the potential for sourcing overseas has increased. However, it is also important to be aware of factors which may reduce availability, for example, political changes in a country, adverse weather, exhaustion of resources, and also official or unofficial quota restrictions. Finally, it must be emphasised that buyers should be looking for possible overseas sources for not only raw materials and foodstuffs, but also manufactured goods.

Prices of Foreign Products: Factors influencing the supply of goods mentioned above will also affect the prices of such goods. Thus, reductions in supplies will lead to price rises, as will a growth in demand. The opposite trends will lead to the reverse effect. There may be time lags before adjustments in supplies can be made to adapt to changes in demand. Thus, price fluctuations can be large, particularly for foodstuffs and raw materials on the commodity markets.

Government Policies: Government measures can also have a direct effect on prices of imports through tariff policies and international trading agreements. The activities of the Bank of England, in addition, may be important with regard to exchange rates. Thus, entry into the EC affects the tariffs charged on imports into the UK. It is essential for buyers to take into account tariff and exchange rate considerations when analysing overseas opportunities and to assess the implications of changes in these factors. Devaluation, for example, may lead to a significant increase in costs if a company purchases a substantial quantity of imports from overseas.

Indirect Factors

Suppliers: A purchasing department may use suppliers located within the United Kingdom, but the latter's operations may be affected substantially by international factors if they are dependent on overseas supplies. The effects of international events cannot be insulated from their customers, therefore, and thus prices and deliveries of goods produced in the United Kingdom will also be affected. It follows, therefore, that buyers need to take international matters into account when analysing home markets in which goods have a substantial imported content.

Government Economic Policy: International factors and, particularly, balance of payments difficulties may influence government economic strategy in managing demand in the domestic economy. The implementation of government strategy via fiscal, monetary, and prices and income measures can affect home markets. If the strategy is aimed at expanding the economy at a faster rate, the growth in demand may lead to supply shortages, lengthening lead times and causing higher prices. A deflationary policy on the other hand may make supplies more easily available and prices may fall.

Difficulties of Importing Goods

The expansion of international trade has increased the opportunities of sourcing overseas, but it is also important to bear in mind difficulties which may arise when using a foreign supplier and which do not affect domestic suppliers. These problems should not be ignored and some examples are:

- Communication problems because of differences in language, distance, and time factors and may be more costly.
- Increased transport problems because of increased distance and because the United Kingdom is surrounded by water.
- Full transport costs, tariffs and exchange rate factors when comparing prices with suppliers in the United Kingdom.
- Difficulties of obtaining spares and replacements quickly.
- Difficulties in visiting suppliers.
- Complications of administrative procedures needed for imported goods to pass smoothly through customs.

Specialist knowledge and expertise is useful in handling imports and if a company is not large enough to develop this, it may be advisable to buy foreign products through distributors and agents in the United Kingdom. Larger companies have "shipping departments" which take responsibility for organising transport (unless this is arranged by the supplier) and for handling importing procedures.

The international environment is an extremely important influence and cannot be ignored in the development of a purchasing strategy. An implicit assumption of this chapter has been the need to obtain supplies for an organisation located within the United Kingdom. For some multi-national companies, however, it may be necessary to develop a purchasing strategy to provide supplies for locations in many different parts of the world. International factors have significant effects of the national economy, in which the intervention of the UK government has become a significant feature.

This chapter has covered particular purchasing strategies that can be considered in the corporate planning process. It is vital that purchasing activities should be concerned with long-term plans as well as immediate operating problems. The next chapter is concerned with purchasing policies to implement the strategy.

CHAPTER 3

Purchasing Policy

In addition to the various strategies described in the previous chapter, there are several policy issues which can influence the operations of the purchasing department. Policies regarding reciprocal trade, intra-company and purchasing ethics should be established as part of the plan for purchasing management. These allied to selecting a policy, the structure of the purchasing function, centralise or decentralise activity and interface with materials management are all relevant to effective purchasing management.

Reciprocal Trade

Reciprocity involves a two-way flow of trade between companies so that each is both a seller and a buyer. A potential reciprocal trading situation is one which can cause conflict within the company between the purchasing department and the selling department. Let us consider a hypothetical example. Company A will only buy from Company B as long as B will agree to buy goods from A. The sales department in Company B will, therefore, apply pressure on their purchasing department to buy from A. How should buyers react to such an attempt to restrict their freedom choice as regards source selection? As long as the product offered by Company A is satisfactory, competitive from a price point of view and if A is reckoned to be a reliable supplier, there is no difficulty and they can be given the contract. Buyers should, however, insist on carrying out a full market appraisal to identify the strengths and weakness's of all the possible suppliers. Any disadvantages of using Company A can then be clearly presented and weighted against the possible gains to be made by making the sales to Company B. The ruling criteria should be what is right for the company, and not what is right for purchasing or marketing in isolation. Thus, a policy decision should be made concerning the approach to be adopted in analysing reciprocal trading situations. If supplier A is chosen, even though they are not seen to be the best supplier in the market, then the reason for such a decision needs to be recorded and their performance needs to be monitored. A final point is that a decision should also be taken with regard to the provision of information from the purchasing department or the marketing department concerning the values of purchases from particular suppliers.

Intra-Company Trading

The growth of multi-product companies has increased the opportunities for internal trading between different parts of the same company. A policy decision is needed to state how such possibilities should be handled. There has been a tendency in the past for arbitrary policies to be established giving preference to internal sources and, thus, restricting the choice of the buyer. However, a preferable approach is one by which each case is examined on its merits to find where the balance of advantage lies. The cost of using an internal source should be compared with the costs of using an independent supplier. A "profit centre" approach, which regards each manufacturing division or subsidiary as a separate accounting unit, means that each must be self-supporting and should not receive subsidies from other parts. In effect, if a subsidiary buys from another part of the company at a higher price than from an external supplier, then the difference in the prices can be regarded as a subsidy. If the supplying division is not competitive, therefore, it should not be given the business (at least in the long term). Where there is no external supplier to act as a check on price, negotiations should be conducted to identify the true costs of manufacturing the product, and to set realistic transfer prices. Further difficulties regarding quality and delivery can arise in intra-company trading situations and the manufacturing division may give preference to independent suppliers. The correct policy should be to buy from the best source inside or outside the company.

Additional complications can arise in multinational companies due to the fact that supplies may cross international boundaries. Setting transfer prices will involve the consideration of exchange rates, tariff duties and tax differentials in the various countries. An overriding objective in this case may be to minimise the total tax liability of the company. Decisions may need to be taken at headquarters in such companies, as only there may all the necessary information be available.

General Comment

This chapter has provided information about the various purchasing policies that can be adopted to support a firm's corporate plan. It is important that a long-term view of activities should be prepared and that this should provide a framework within which day-to-day problems can be tackled. It is especially important for large companies to develop conscious long-term strategies in order that their monopolistic powers should be used wisely. Concentrated buying power may be able to dictate to smaller suppliers in the short term, but it is essential to estimate the long-term effects. The pursuit of low prices may bankrupt suppliers and such tactics may, therefore, alter the market structure and reduce competition. Other detrimental effects, albeit less severe, such as poor service and a high rejection rate may also arise as unwanted side-effects of the pricing policy. Purchasing, therefore, must decide whether their long-term objective on continuity of supply is more important than achievement of price objectives in the short term. The dominant buyer should seek to maintain effective or workable competition which produces fair prices in relation to cost, prompt service and a reasonable rate of innovation. The buyer must also remember the five rights of purchasing shown at Figure 12.

Figure 12 The Five Rights of Purchasing

Selecting Overall Policy

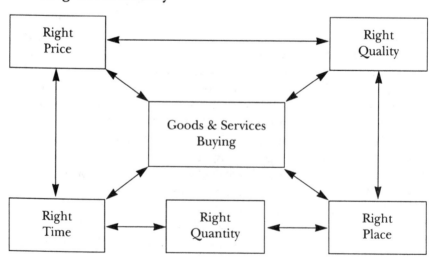

The ability of the organisation to develop and apply effective purchasing policy depends partly on the perceptions of managers at all levels. The manager charged with the development of a policy should recognise that these perceptions are affected by the existing company structure, the quality of its internal communication system, the past experience of the company and its managers, and the resources available. As has been suggested earlier, the development of a policy involves company-wide considerations. These considerations differ by industry and by company. What should be common, however, is the need to develop advantages over the competition and use them effectively.

The ability of the organisation to develop and apply effective purchasing policy will be conditioned by several factors, and there are roles for a purchasing manager which relate to the development of policy. Among these are:

- generating alternative solutions to procurement problems
- protecting the cost structure of the organisation
- minimising purchasing costs
- assuring long-range sources of supply
- maintaining good relationships with suppliers.

Each of these has a strategic as well as an operational facet. This emphasises the important point that development of a policy necessitates a co-ordinated operational response. It is of little use defining and developing a policy unless the day-to-day actions of the organisation are geared to the strategic approach. This is a deceptively simple concept, for it is not uncommon to find companies which purport to have policies where the behaviour of managers is contradictory to the stated approach.

Structure of Purchasing Organisation

An essential part of policy development and selection is to devise an organisation to carry out the activities embodied in the policy. Classical management writers have emphasised the importance of the activity of organising as a key function of management. Whilst their views have been modified in many respects this function is still important and the purchasing manager should pay close attention to the development of the organisational structure for the purchasing function. Organisation is concerned with the division of work and the delegation of authority and responsibility in such a way that the objectives of the organisation can be achieved. It also involves defining the duties of personnel and the relationships between them.

The task of developing an organisation structure has become a complex one and there is no longer a simple prescriptive model that can be applied in all situations. The business environment is now populated by a wide variety of different types of organisation. It is recommended, therefore, that an organisation structure should be tailored to the particular circumstances of the particular organisation. What is suitable for one would not necessarily be copied by another. In discussing organisational problems for purchasing management it is essential to take into account some of the important differences. Of course, the development of an organisation for the purchasing function is but part of a general problem of developing an organisation structure for the organisation as a whole. Thus, purchasing considerations will reflect the needs of this broader framework as well as internal factors.

Structure of the Purchasing Function in Simple Organisations

In this example it is necessary to concentrate upon the organisation of a centralised purchasing function within a relatively simple, single-product, single-site firm, assess the advantages of specialisation and then map out the possible range of activities that could be included. Having portrayed a typical structure diagrammatically, the place of the purchasing manager within the overall management structure of the organisation will be examined.

Benefits of a Centralised Purchasing Function

In very small firms the scope for specialisation is limited and purchasing activities would not be sufficient to occupy a person full time. Once a firm employs around a hundred or above, however, it should be possible to introduce purchasing as a specialist job. As the volume of work expands so the number of purchasing personnel will grow and the opportunities for specialisation within the function increase. Parallel with this growth, the problem of organisation assumes greater importance.

The introduction of a specialist department to handle purchasing activities means that its members see purchasing as their major responsibility and can develop expertise in conducting their work. Previously, purchasing jobs would have been done by other people for whom it would have been a major activity and for which they had no particular skills. Thus, full-time specialists can develop their abilities and use progressive purchasing techniques to obtain better value for money. The department can co-ordinate the previously fragmented purchasing pattern and can introduce a common system of procedures. Knowledge of supply markets can be built up, and an efficient record system introduced and negotiating skills can be applied. What may have started as a simple clerical function can become a sophisticated independent department.

The basic argument for the development of the centralised function rests upon the point that efficiency in controlling the flow of inputs to the firm is increased by the application of specialist expertise. The opportunities to make such improvements in efficiency can be found in different types of organisations in all sectors of the economy. Most large organisations already appreciate the advantage to be gained by effectively controlling purchasing activities, but many medium and small organisations have yet to reap the full rewards because insufficient recognition has been given to this function. The purchasing function can make a major contribution towards the achievement of corporate objectives in both the public and private sectors.

Activities in the Purchasing Function
A wide variety of arrangements can be found concerning the activities which should be included under the control of the purchasing manager. The most effective pattern is one in which the purchasing manager is given authority for all those activities which lead to the supply of goods and services to user departments. Such a range might include:

Categories of Goods Purchased: With reference to basic categories of goods purchased by an organisation we can point out that the area of authority concerning this range varies in different organisations. In manufacturing companies, the purchase of industrial materials is regarded as the major area of expenditure to be controlled, but many purchasing managers, have no control over the purchase of plant and equipment at all. In spite of this difference in delegation of authority, the arguments in favour of the application of specialist purchasing skills are relevant to all purchases. It follows that the purchasing department should be given responsibility for purchasing all bought-out goods that are required. This does not mean that other departments should be excluded from the decision-making process, but that the purchasing department should contribute its commercial expertise to this process to complement the technical skills of the other departments. A purchasing research team should also be attached to the buying area to provide information to the buyers which may include cost analysis.

Progressing or Expediting: An essential phase in the purchasing process, for the more important needs at least, is the progressing activity, to ensure that goods arrive at the desired time. The organisational problem here revolves around whether buyers should also progress the orders they have placed or whether a specialist or specialist team should be formed to carry out these duties. The division of work between buying and progressing sections allows each to develop its own particular skills for the different activities. The buyer can concentrate attention on market analysis and contract negotiation and the expeditor can build up contacts and persuasive skills to obtain deliveries from suppliers. On the other hand, others argue that having to do the progressing work disciplines the buyer in selecting reliable suppliers. On balance the first approach is preferable (if the workload is sufficient), as long as the buyers are informed about poor delivery performance.

Purchasing in Distributive Organisations: Whilst the principles of purchasing management apply equally to the wholesale and retail sections of industry, in manufacturing procedures differ. Since there are normally no production processes involved (the raw material stockholder may offer a cutting or shearing service), sales and purchasing personnel are involved in product selection and programming as a total merchandising operation. Many large organisations are headed as far as supplies are concerned by a merchandise executive or director responsible for both sales and purchasing, organised to coordinate the expertise and information available to both. In a dynamic, consumer-demand situation such as retail multi-stores or supermarket purchasing, requirement forecasting and expenditure based on product sales, subject to changing preferences, promotions and seasonal peaks and troughs, require continuous updating to data and flexible purchasing arrangements. Product knowledge, ability to interpret sales data, short and long-term, allied to continuous supply market research, are essential to successful buying for direct re-sale to the consumer.

Stores and Stock Control, Including Goods Receiving: It can be argued that there are advantages to be gained by grouping stores and stock control activities under the control of the purchasing manager. The achievement of the objective of lowest cost of supply implies that both purchasing and stock control considerations are relevant in quantity and frequency of goods required to reprovision the stores. It is easier to develop an integrated system of procedures and exchanges of information in a unified purchasing organisation than in two separate departments. Goods-receiving activities complete the purchasing cycle and transfer the purchases to user departments or, more frequently, to the stores. These, too, should be integrated into the purchasing organisation.

A Typical Structure of a Purchasing Department

It can be seen from the foregoing information that the structure of the purchasing department can be varied to give an assortment of different configurations. Figure 13 shows a typical structure for a supplies organisation in a medium to large sized company.

Figure 13 Supplies Organisation Structure

Division of Works Amongst Buying Groups

Negotiating Links

It is worth remembering that there are many links in the negotiation chain. These include bidding, bargaining and agreement, introductions, negotiation research and planning. The information flow may be complex, partnerships may be under consideration (or existing) and there is a need for continuous improvement allied to value for money. This is illustrated in Figure 14 where each link is reviewed and assessed in order to develop the full strength of the whole chain.

Figure 14 Negotiating Links

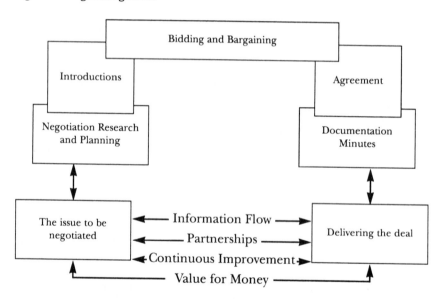

The division of work between buying groups and buyers should be made on a logical basis. In single-product, single-site organisations the major principle adopted is to divide purchasing work according to commodities. Each section and each buyer would be given responsibilities for particular groups of products. Thus Buying Group 1 might be authorised to purchase all the industrial materials, Group 2 might be responsible for industrial equipment and Group 3 might be given industrial supplies and services. Individual buyers would then be given narrower ranges within each section. However, a second principle might also be followed since more senior buyers would be responsible for high-value orders. Specialisation on a commodity or product basis allows buyers to build up expertise in a limited number of markets and they have the opportunity to get to know the nature of these products and the characteristics of the suppliers.

In more complex multi-product, multi-site companies, however, two further principles which can be adopted in the division of work may arise. Buyers may be appointed to handle purchases for a particular product line or manufacturing division. In addition, workloads can be divided up according to geographical locations.

Arrangements in the Automotive Industry

The nature of the large-volume production systems and the methods of control adopted throughout the organisation have led to the emergence of a different type of structure on the purchasing side in the automotive industry. The method of control is based upon a set of interrelated computer programmes linking market forecasts, production programmes and materials schedules (lists of products required to meet the production programme and which also take into account stocks on hand). A scheduling group is responsible for obtaining the necessary quantities at the required time from suppliers by sending out delivery schedules (usually on a monthly basis). A purchasing group has responsibility for initially arranging blanket order contracts with suppliers when the items are first introduced as part of a new or modified model programme. These contracts over the specification and price arrangements with the suppliers and provide the framework for subsequent scheduling operations. Some companies have a third group concerned with supporting research and development projects for new designs and prototypes. Finally, other purchasing groups control the acquisition of equipment and supplies following more conventional practices. Within this scheme there are variations as to whether the scheduling group is part of the supplies department or whether it is part of material control (embodying production control and inventory control) and falling under the jurisdiction of the production manager.

The Position of Purchasing Management in the Organisation

Where there is an integrated supplies organisation or, indeed, where there is a significant purchasing team, a case can be made out for the purchasing manager or director of purchasing to have a high position within the management structure. This allows the manager and his department to give full weight to commercial aspects of purchasing decisions. If the purchasing manager is subordinate to the production manager there is a danger that too much importance will be attached to the technical matters. As an independent department, the supplies department can make its full contribution towards the achievement of corporate objectives. It can be argued, therefore, that the purchasing manager should be a member of the senior management team, with a direct reporting responsibility to the general manager. The purchasing manager may also be a member of the board of directors. Thus, the management organisation might be shown at Figure 15

Figure 15 Management Organisation

The position of the purchasing manager within the organisation hierarchy is an important determinant of the impact that the department can have. A high position and high status enables an effective, progressive approach to purchasing work to be implemented. Support from the general manager helps to increase recognition for the function and to encourage good horizontal relationships with other departments. In the last analysis, however, it is successful performance that earns the respect of others in the organisation.

Structure of the Purchasing Function in Complex Organisation

The emergence of large multi-product, multi-site organisations and marketing strategies means that companies can alter product as they seek growth. They have, therefore, moved away from the relatively simple situation of operating one production site to manufacture one product line. Some have diversified into other product areas on one or more sites and others have duplicated production facilities by opening establishments in different geographical locations. Policy decisions which have brought about these transformations have also influenced the development and adoption of different organisational structures to cope with the added complexity. We have also seen the emergence of huge multinational conglomerates, in which international differences magnify the problems of geographical dispersion. One of the major organisational innovations of the twentieth century has been the introduction of the multi-divisional structure

In the simple organisation the basic breakdown of tasks was achieved by splitting work up according to the main functional activities in the multi-divisional organisation function tasks grouped around different product lines. Thus, several quasi-independent organisations are created and each has a reporting relationship to a central headquarters organisation. Each product organisation might be a separate limited company, with headquarters a holding company. In others, each division and the head office may all be part of the same legal entity. At both divisional and head office level, further divisions of work can be made on a functional basis. Thus, we have a picture at Figure 16

Figure 16 Division of Work by Product

Each division may have a management structure as above and the same functions may be present at head office level to act in a co-ordinating capacity. However, the extent of head office activities of the divisions tends to vary. Some multi-level organisations are relatively centralised and head office personnel play a detailed part in the activities of the divisions. Other decentralised arrangements, however, give more autonomous powers to the divisions. These are established as separate profit centres, with minimal interference from headquarters, and the relationship between the division and the headquarters is mainly a financial one. The division is responsible for achieving satisfactory profit figures and must apply for approval of corporate plans and investment finance. It can be argued that the more unrelated in terms of technology, materials requirements and markets the division, the more decentralised should be the method of control. There is little scope for central co-ordination as each division operates in an entirely different sphere.

The opportunities for central co-ordination are greater in situations when organisations are manufacturing the same product or offering the same service at multiple locations. Production technology, marketing problems and purchasing problems are similar and there is potential for more centralised control of operations. In this multi-level situation, therefore, more power and more activity will be located at headquarters. Indeed some of the functions can be located solely at head office.

Alternative Structures for the Purchasing Function in Complex Companies

There are three possible solutions to the problem of organising the purchasing function in complex organisations. Each will be examined in turn to establish the advantages and disadvantages inherent in each solution. The three solutions are as follows:

Complete Centralisation: one central purchasing department controls the purchasing of all supplies for various scattered units or factories.

Complete Decentralisation: each separate unit or factory has its own purchasing department and is responsible for obtaining its own requirements.

Multi-level Structure: each unit has its own purchasing department, but a central purchasing department has some powers to co-ordinate the activities of the local departments.

Advantages of Centralisation

The advantages to be gained from the establishment of one central purchasing department are as follows:

- Economies of bulk buying of items commonly used at each unit. The central department can negotiate cheaper prices on the basis of total consumption throughout the company.

- Avoidance of competitive buying by individual departments of materials in short supply.
- Opportunities for development of greater knowledge about products because buyers can specialise in a narrower range of commodities which can be handled more expertly, that is buyers place orders for the whole company for a small range of products, whereas local buyers have to handle a more general range of local requirements.
- Savings in operating costs. Fewer, but larger orders are placed and hence a reduction in administrative costs can be made.
- Development of common procedures, forms, standards and specifications.
- Simpler relationship with suppliers as a result of single, direct contact.
- Investigations of new products and materials can benefit all units in the company.
- Centralisation of stock control can reduce overall stock levels through greater flexibility and establishment of strategic reserves, that is flow of stocks between factories to meet shortages.
- Development of improved support services made possible, that is purchasing research and statistical information services.
- Enhanced importance of the supplies department and higher position of the supplies manager in management hierarchy.
- More scope for purchasing strategy and contribution to corporate plans.
- More scope for manpower planning in the function and development of training programmes.

Advantages of Decentralisation

The advantages of decentralisation can be seen as a remedy for the weaknesses of centralisation. The main advantages are as follows:

- Closer co-ordination with local organisation and buyers can build up close contacts with other departments.
- Buyer is in direct touch with the problems where they arise and can handle emergencies more easily than a distant office.
- Local buyers are better informed about local markets which may offer possibilities to a local customer which could not be offered on a national basis.

- Clear responsibility of buyers to local management.
- Local plants may need a different range of products and, thus, a local buyer may have a more specialised knowledge of these.

A Multi-Level Structure for Purchasing Management

The multi-level approach attempts to obtain the advantages of both the previous models. The division of duties between the two levels which is designed to achieve this are:

Central Office

The following tasks my be allocated to the central office:

- Determination of purchasing strategies and development of purchasing policies.
- Standardisation of procedures, specifications, codes and forms.
- Negotiation of contracts for commonly used items against which local departments can place delivery orders for supplies as required.
- Purchase of major plant and equipment.
- Importation of supplies from overseas.
- Responsibility for legal matters.
- Inter-plant stock transfers and stocking policy.
- Responsibility for training.
- Research and information service.

Local Offices

- Responsibility of placing orders for non-contract items.
- Placing delivery orders for contract items.

In this group purchasing system, the manager at the local level would be responsible to his local line management. The manager at the central office would usually act in a staff capacity. That is to say, the latter would not have executive authority, as such, over the local manager, but would act in an advisory capacity.

A number of difficulties can arise in this multi-level approach. First, there is a danger that local initiative will be stifled by having group contracts imposed by a remote head office. The relationship between the two levels may be difficult to control. The local department may resent interference and there may be a conflict of interest between local interests and head office views. The staff/line division of responsibilities does not successfully resolve the problem of the local purchasing manager who has dual responsibilities to his local management team and to the group purchasing manager, when the latter has a more senior position, but no executive authority.

In spite of these problems, however, where a large range of items is commonly used, the benefits of having a central office outweigh the difficulties. When the range of commonly-used items is small, other methods of achieving a common approach have been devised. These methods do not involve the formation of a permanent central department as such.

Sourcing Form

Whatever the form of organisation the choice of sourcing is a complex issue. Arguably there are contingencies such as the individual, markets, products and organisations; there are criteria such as economic, power, risk and social factors; the contingencies and criteria prevailing at the decision point will result in single of multiple sourcing. This is illustrated in Figure 17.

Figure 17 Factors Resulting in Sourcing Form

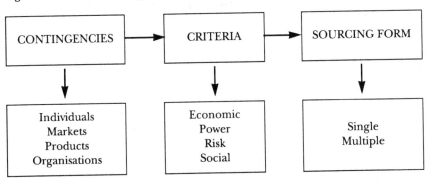

In larger organisations policies of single or multiple sourcing are often set; often where purchasing is "centralised", the sourcing form is left to the "decentralised" units.

Other Methods of Achieving Co-ordination

Several other approaches have been developed to take advantage of the purchasing power of large companies without developing a central purchasing office. These include the use of a lead buyer strategy and the use of committees of local purchasing managers.

Lead Buyer Contracting

The essential feature of this strategy is that the major user division or factory negotiates a contract, which is made available to the other parts of the company to use if they wish to do so.

Committee of Purchasing Managers

Regular meetings of purchasing managers can be held to discuss common problems and to co-ordinate activities. Tasks of negotiating bulk contracts can be allocated to individual departments.

Informal Communication

Informal communication between local departments can also lead to the formation of common policies.

These three approaches can be seen as being of a less formal kind than setting up a permanent central office. They also lack the scope of the central office for providing all the additional services indicated previously. In some cases local purchasing departments may be large enough to afford some of the specialisms we have given to head offices.

The Selection of an Appropriate Structure for Particular Circumstances

There is no single method of organising the purchasing function which is appropriate for all complex organisations. In developing a suitable structure, it is important to analyse the circumstances of the particular organisation for which it is intended. Perhaps the key question that needs to be asked is how common are the purchasing problems that have to be faced at each site. The greater the similarity of purchases the greater is the potential for centralising control. Conversely, the greater the variety, the greater the opportunity to decentralise activities. Four different situations are worth examining:

- Single product/multi-site operations
- Multi-product/multi-site operations in which products are related

- Multi-product/multi-site operations in which products are unrelated
- Very large multi-product/multi-site operations in which there is scope for multi-level structures in each division

Single Product/Multi-Site Operations

Where each factory is concerned with manufacturing the same products, the purchasing requirements are the same. Demand arises for the same products which are purchased from the same markets. There is scope for a fully centralised purchasing function to gain the maximum benefit of the purchasing power of the company and to provide common solutions to common problems. In the tertiary sector, a central purchasing department would be able to control the purchasing for individual branches of a retail or distribution network and organise central storage points from which supplies of many items could be delivered. Buying consortia for several local authorities base their arguments on such a premise.

Multi-Product/Multi-Site Operations in which Products Are Related

In organisations which have several product divisions, but whose products are related, in the sense that similar technology and similar materials are used, a multi-level purchasing system could be used. Sufficient common items and associated purchasing problems exist for a central department to make a valuable contribution, whilst local supply departments maintain close contact with local factories.

Multi-Product/Multi-Site Operations in which Products Are Unrelated

Conglomerate or diversified organisations may consist of manufacturing divisions which are entirely different in terms of technology and materials used. In such a situation, few common problems arise and there is little to be gained, therefore, from having a central department. Each divisional purchasing manager, however, should be given a high position of responsibility within the divisional management structure and should play a significant part in the planning process for the division.

Very Large Multi-Product/Multi-Site Operations

In very large organisations, individual divisions may themselves have a multi-level organisational structure. In such a situation, there may be local purchasing departments under the control of a divisional purchasing manager. On top there may be a corporate purchasing department to co-ordinate the activities of the divisions, depending on how similar their needs are.

Multi-National Supplies Structures

The multi-national character of big organisations creates additional complications. Wide variations in terms of political, economic, social and industrial conditions may exist in the countries in which operations are located. It may be necessary, therefore, to allow a local purchasing department wider latitude in determining its own supply policy and controlling its own supplies. Nevertheless, if there are opportunities to be gained from closer co-ordination, such objectives should not be ignored and the local department should be encouraged to follow group policy. The central office could be used to organise the supply of goods being imported into other countries for local factories.

Public Sector

Both in central government and local authority purchasing, the emphasis is on public accountability. This is not to underestimate the vital necessity for efficiency in purchasing, as in the private sector, and the move towards centralisation is evident in both central and local organisation.

Central Government

The procurement executive provides a central technical and procurement service for the armed services, within the framework of co-ordinated assessments of service needs and the financial constraints of budgeted allocations. To assist in the study of requirements, two advisory committees have been formed:-

- The Operational Requirements Committee (ORC)
- The Defence Equipment Policy Committee (DEPC)

The actual purchasing of equipment is made by contract, preferably on a "fixed price" basis and, as will be apparent by the very nature of the equipment, the range of contractors able to fulfil requirements is limited.

Local Government

The method of operating the purchasing of supplies is made the subject of local authority standing orders on procedures for competitive tendering and acceptance rules. The purchasing officer, whilst appearing to operate under more constraints than a colleague in the private sector, is able to combine the formality of laid-down procedures with purchasing skill. Whilst in the 1990s there were several EC Directives regulating public purchasing, initially the stimulus to efficient procurement within local authority organisations was fostered by the Local Authority (Goods and Services) Act 1970. The main points of emphasis were:

● A recommendation of the need for functional purchasing as a specialist operation.
● The advantages which could be obtained from co-ordinated purchasing by combined authorities centralised purchasing.

The UK government is currently experimenting with best value scenarios (which may replace compulsory competitive tendering) and the EC is considering modifications to procurement directives to ease perceptions of bureaucracy.

Benchmarking

One method of shaping the organisation is to benchmark from a strategic and tactical perspective.

Types of benchmarking

● Internal benchmarking is a way of identifying best practise within a group and sharing it perhaps resulting in cross-functional and/or cross-site teams.

● Competitive benchmarking is literally comparison with competitors; data collection and reliability may be a problem and there is a need to ensure similarity, for example size.

● Functional or generic benchmarking compares specific functions such as logistics; the comparison is with the best in class or best in the industry. It is easier to obtain information and often there are "clubs" which share data openly.

The Benchmarking Process

- There needs to be planning. The subject needs to be identified and data collection methods agreed, not forgetting, agreement to the plan by those involved! The need to be realistic about the scope of the process is paramount.

- The data needs analysis. Is the competition better and by how much? Why are they better? What can be learned? How can the learning be applied?

- The data gathered should be used to define the goals to establish or maintain superiority; these should then be incorporated into the overall planning process.

- The plan should be an action plan identifying clearly who will do what and establishing completion dates; similarly a monitoring process should be embodied in the plan to measure progress and ensure benchmarking becomes integral.

The Rank Xerox Experience

Rank Xerox provides an interesting example of the use of benchmarking not only to identify weaknesses and the means of improvement, but also the incorporation of benchmarking into a continuous improvement process. ("Benchmarking: A Strategic and Tactical Perspective" Cross, R and Leonard, P in *Managing Quality*, Ed. Dale, B. G. Second Edition 1994 Prentice Hall).

In 1980 when faced with increasing competition from Japanese manufacturers Rank Xerox assumed that because they were cheaper the Japanese products were of poorer quality. This belief, due largely to the culture of the organisation, led to a failure to perceive the nature of the threat to their survival and made the organisation extremely vulnerable. The decision to benchmark against their competitors revealed the truth – that the organisation was vulnerable in almost every business area. Japanese manufacturers such as Fuji were producing machines of equivalent quality and selling at a price close to Xerox's cost of sales. Xerox had nine times more suppliers, was rejecting ten times as many machines on the production line, and taking twice as long to get products to the market.

These competitive benchmarking findings brought home the reality of the business and forced senior management to acknowledge both the size of the problem and the nature of the change required to re-establish the companyís position.External competitive and non-competitive benchmarking was then used in almost every business area as the means of improving business performance with very high levels of success. Indeed to quote the *Financial Times:* "The power of benchmarking is underlined in the case of Xerox with being one of the main factors behind the company's revival in the 1980s."

Figure 18 Rank Xerox Benchmarking Process

```
PLANNING        1.  Identify benchmark outputs
                        ↓
                2.  Identify best competitor
                        ↓
                3.  Determine data collection method
                        ↓
ANALYSIS        4.  Determine current competitive gap
                        ↓
                5.  Project future performance levels
                        ↓
INTEGRATION     6.  Establish functional goals
                    Communication │ Acceptance of
                      of Data     ▼   Analysis
                7.  Develop functional action plans
                        ↓
ACTION          8.  Implement specific actions
                        ↓
                9.  Monitor results/report progress
                        ↓
                10. Recalibrate benchmarks
                        ↓
MATURITY        *Leadership position obtained

                *Processes fully integrated in our
                 practises
```

The Rank Zerox approach to benchmarking was to incorporate it into a total quality strategy which they called "Leadership Through Quality". This involved converting benchmarking into a process of continuous improvement which had five phases and ten steps.

The five phases were planning, analysis, integration, action and maturity. Within each phase there are specific steps or actions which are required. This approach is illustrated in Figure 18. Note in particular that step 10 is the recalibration of benchmarks and the restarting of the whole improvement process that is a continuous improvement process. Clearly benchmarking can determine the preferred organisation and, indeed, functional operation required to gain competitive advantage.

Materials Management

The materials management concept is based on the potential advantages to be obtained from controlling the flow of materials and goods from supplier through stores and production to despatch. The overall control would thus embrace:

- Purchasing
- Stores
- Inventory Control
- Production Planning and Control
- Physical Distribution

The functional managers would operate under the co-ordinating expertise of a materials manager or director. There has been a strengthening "lobby" for some time to give inventory control responsibility to purchasing, and materials management appears as a wider aspect of this development. Arguably both functions could be part of logistics management. Alternative structures can emerge based on functional managers responsible for:

- Purchasing: with responsibility for supplies research and acquisition.
- Inventory: stores, warehousing, movement of materials, inventory management.
- Production: control of programmes, work schedules, material quantities.
- Physical Distribution: limited either to inwards and despatch transport facilities or the wider concept of external warehousing and customer service.

- The benefits of this wider concept of materials management are reflected in:
- Higher level of departmental cooperation.
- Efficient communications.
- Improved inventory control by centralised non-duplicated records, with the possibility of data-processing support.
- Personnel development with wider experience.
- Strengthened support for purchasing.

There are no simple prescriptions to help designers prepare a plan for the organisation of the purchasing function in a complex organisation. It is necessary to examine the conditions in which each is operating. An additional determinant will be the view of senior managers as the corporate level who are the key decision makers regarding the structure of the organisation as a whole. A further feature which may require diplomatic treatment is the relationship between the parent company and newly taken-over subsidiaries. Personnel in the latter are often reluctant to alter systems and procedures and to adopt new policies. Even within old established organisations, plans to restructure an organisation can cause much conflict unless the task is carefully carried out.

This chapter has been concerned with the problem of policy and organisation with respect to the purchasing function. There are no simple solutions which have general applicability for all organisations. It is, nevertheless, extremely important to design an effective structure if purchasing activities are to make a significant contribution to the success of the company. Structural arrangements have a significant effect on the performance of individuals in the function, because it is these arrangements which circumscribe the duties to be carried out by them. It is individuals who select and implement policy.

CHAPTER 4

Quality

This chapter provides a brief overview of a lengthy aspect of logistics – that of quality. After defining quality and the costs of failure, methods of getting it right such as BS5750 (ISO9000) and total quality management are covered.

Defining Quality

The reputation attached to an organisation for the quality of its products and services is accepted as a key to its success and the future of its employees. To prosper in today's economic climate, any organisation and its suppliers must be dedicated to never-ending improvement, and more efficient ways to obtain products or services that consistently meet customers' needs must constantly be sought. The consumer is no longer required to make a choice between price and quality, and competitiveness in quality is not only central to profitability, but crucial to business survival. In today's tough and challenging business environment, the development and implementation of a comprehensive quality policy is not merely desirable – it is essential.

Quality is often used to signify "excellence" of a product or services: we talk about "Rolls-Royce quality" and "top quality". In some engineering companies, the word may be used to indicate that a piece of metal confirms to certain physical dimension characteristics, often set down in the form of a particularly "tight" specification. If we define quality in a way which is useful in its management, then we must recognise the need to include in the assessment of quality the true requirements of the "customer".

Quality is simply meeting the customer requirements, and this has been expressed in many ways by others:

- "Fitness for purpose or use" (Juran)
- "The totality of features and characteristics of a product or service that bear on its ability to satisfy stated or implied needs" (BS4778, 1978 (ISO 8402, 1986) Quality Vocabulary: Part 1. International Terms)
- "The total composite product and service characteristics of marketing, engineering, manufacture, and maintenance through which the product and service in use will meet the expectation by the customer" (Feigenbaum)

There is another word that we should define properly: "reliability". Why do you buy a Volkswagen car? "Quality and reliability" is a probable answer. The two are used synonymously, often in a totally confused way. Clearly, part of the acceptability of a product or service will depend on its ability to function satisfactorily over a period of time, and this aspect of performance is given the name "reliability". It is the ability of the product or service to continue to meet the customer requirements. Reliability ranks with quality in importance, since it is a key factor in many purchasing decisions where alternatives are being considered. Many of the general management issues which relate to achieving product or service quality are also applicable to reliability.

Quality requires that both the needs of the customer and his or her perceived needs are explored. Frequently, a choice of product or service is made upon apparently irrational grounds: identical offerings, presented in different ways, will sell in vastly different quantities, and will have different qualities ascribed to them. The detergent which sells better in a blue box than a red one, the bank account which has a higher status because of the leather cheque-book wallet, are well known. Similarly, a quality judgement is often related to the price paid without any regard to the discernible properties being purchased. The reasons for a purchase may be difficult to identify, yet their reality must not be denied.

The quality of products and services is important not only for users but also for suppliers. For manufacturers, quality deficiencies result in additional costs for inspection, testing, scrap, re-work, and the handling of complaints and warranty claims. In the service industries, errors, checking, enquiries and complaints account for losses in efficiency and productivity. Repeat sales and future market share will also be affected, with significant effects on profitability and survival. Quality must, therefore, be taken into account throughout all the areas of marketing, design, purchasing, production or operations, and logistics. It must be controlled in all these functions, and their activities co-ordinated to achieve a balanced corporate quality performance. Quality performance will not just happen; effective leadership and teamwork is the only sure recipe for success. Real understanding and commitment by senior management, together with explicit quality policies, lead to an improvement throughout the entire organisation, which in turn generates a momentum for the improvement of products, services and performance.

Achieving quality relies upon consideration of both the external environment and the internal resources: the identification of the customer's requirements must be matched by the ability to produce a product or generate a service which will be recognised as satisfying the needs. In the event of a conflict between these two determinants, the intended market segment may have to be changed, or the internal resources may have to be re-examined. The customer's perception of quality changes with time and any organisation's attitude to quality must change with this perception. The skills and attitudes of the producer are also subject to change, and failure to monitor such changes will inevitably lead to dissatisfied customers. Quality, like all other corporate matters, must be reviewed continually in the light of current circumstances.

A traditional approach to many transformation processes is to depend on "production" to make the product and "quality control" to inspect it and divert that output which does not meet the requirements. This is a strategy of detection and is wasteful because it allows time and materials to be invested in products which are not always saleable. This post-operation/production inspection is expensive, unreliable and uneconomical.

It is much more effective to avoid waste by not producing unsaleable output in the first place, to adopt a strategy of prevention. The prevention strategy sounds sensible and obvious to most people. It is often captured in slogans such as "Quality right first time". This type of campaigning is, however, not enough on its own. What is required is an understanding of the elements of a systematic control system which is designed for the prevention of products or services which do not conform to requirements. Management must be dedicated to the on-going improvement of quality, not simply a one-step improvement to an acceptable plateau. A quality policy then requires top management to:

- establish an "organisation" for quality;
- identify the customer's needs and perception of needs;
- assess the ability of the organisation to meet these needs;
- ensure that supplied materials and services reliably meet the required standards of performance and efficiency;
- concentrate on the prevention rather than detection philosophy;
- educate and train for quality improvement;
- review the quality management systems to maintain progress.

The quality policy must be publicised and understood at all levels of the organisation.

Design and Conformance

We have defined quality as the degree of satisfaction of customer needs. So the quality of a motor car, or washing machine, or a banking service is the extent to which it meets the requirements of the customer. Before any discussion on quality can take place, therefore, it is necessary to be clear about the purpose of the product, in other words what those customer's requirements are. The customer may be internal or external to the organisation and his or her satisfaction must be the first and most important ingredient in any plan for success.

The quality of any product or service has two distinct but interrelated aspects: quality of design and, quality of conformance to design

Quality of Design

This is a measure of how well the product or service is designed to meet customer requirements. If the quality of design is low, the product or service will not satisfy the requirements. The most important feature of the design, with regard to the achievement of the required product quality, is the specification. This describes and defines the product or service and should be a comprehensive statement of all aspects of it which must be present to meet customer requirements.

The stipulation of the correct specification is vital in the purchase of materials and services for use in the transformation process. All too frequently, the terms "as previously supplied" or "as agreed with your representative" are to be found on purchase orders for suppliers. The importance of obtaining quality inputs cannot be over-emphasised and this cannot be achieved without adequate specifications.

A specification may be expressed in terms of the maximum amount of tolerable variation on a measurement, the degree of finish on a surface, the smoothness of movement of a mechanical device, a particular chemical property, the number of times the phone rings before it must be answered, and so on. There is a variety of ways in which specifications may be stated and ingenuity must be constrained in order to control the number of forms of specifications present in any organisation.

Quality of Conformance to Design

This is the extent to which the product or service achieves the quality of design. What the customer actually receives should conform to the design, and direct production or operating costs are tied firmly to the level of conformance achieved. Quality cannot be inspected into a product or service; the customer satisfaction must be designed into the whole system. The conformance check then makes sure that things go according to plan. A high level of final product inspection or checking of work is often indicative of attempts to inspect-in quality, an activity which will achieve mostly spiralling costs and increasing viability.

The area of conformance to design is largely concerned with the performance of the process, which transforms a set of inputs, including actions, methods and operations, into desired outputs products, information, services, etc. In each area or function of an organisation there will be many processes taking place, and the output from one is often the input to another. Clearly it is essential to have an effective system to manage each process. The recording and analysis of data play a significant role in this aspect of quality.

The Costs of Quality

Manufacturing a product or generating a service which meets customer requirements must be managed in a cost-efficient manner, so that the long-term effect of quality costs on the business is a desirable one. These costs are a true measure of the quality effort. A competitive product based on a balance between quality and cost factors is the principal goal. This objective is best accomplished with the aid of competent analysis of the costs quality. The analysis of quality costs is a significant management tool which provides:

- a method of assessing the overall effectiveness of the management of quality;
- a means of determining problem areas and action priorities.

The costs of quality are no different from any other costs in that, like the cost of maintenance, design, sales, production/operations management, information and other activities, they can be budgeted, measured and analysed.

Having specified the quality of design, the task is to achieve a service or product which matches it. This comprises activities which will incur costs that may be separated into the categories of failure costs, appraisal costs and prevention costs. Failure costs can be further split into those resulting from internal and external failure.

Internal Failure Costs

These costs occur when products fail to reach designed quality standards and are detected before transfer to the consumer takes place. Internal failure includes:

- Scrap defective product which cannot be repaired, used or sold.
- Re-work or rectification the correction of detective output or errors to meet the required specifications.
- Re-inspection the re-examination of output which has been rectified.
- Downgrading product which is usable but does not meet specifications and may be sold as "second quality" at a low price.
- Waste the activities associated with doing unnecessary work or holding stocks as the result of errors, poor organisation, the wrong materials, etc.
- Failure analysis the activities required to establish the causes of internal product failure.

External Failure Costs

These costs occur when products or services fail to reach design quality standards and are not detected until after transfer to the consumer. External failure includes:

- Repair and servicing, either of returned products or those in the field.
- Warranty claims: failed products which are replaced under guarantee.
- Complaints: all work associated with servicing of customer's complaints.
- Returns: the handling and investigation of rejected products and services, including any transport costs.
- Liability: the result of product liability litigation and other claims, which may include change of contract.
- Loss of goodwill: the impact on reputation and image which impinges directly on future prospects for sales.

External and internal failures produce the costs of getting it wrong.

Appraisal Costs

These costs are associated with the evaluation of purchased materials, processes, intermediates, products and services, to assure conformance with the specifications. Appraisal includes:

- Verification of incoming material, process set-up, first-offs, running processes, intermediates, final products and services, and includes product/service performance appraisal against agreed specifications.
- Appraisal activities.
- Vendor rating: the assessment and approval of suppliers of all products and services.

Appraisal activities result in the costs of checking it is right.

Prevention Costs

These are associated with the design, implementation and maintenance of the quality system, including quality audits to check that the quality system is functioning satisfactorily. The calibration and maintenance of any equipment used in prevention costs are planned and are incurred prior to production. Prevention includes:

- Product/service requirements: the determination of quality requirement and the setting of corresponding specification for incoming materials, processes, intermediates, finished products and services.
- Quality planning: the creation of quality, reliability, production/operation supervision, verification and other special plans (eg trials) required to achieve the quality objective.
- Quality assurance: creation and maintenance of the overall quality system.
- Appraisal equipment: the design, development and/or purchase of equipment for use in appraisal.
- Training: the development, preparation and maintenance of quality training programmes for operators, supervisors and managers.
- Miscellaneous: clerical, travel, supply, shipping, communications and other general management activities associated with quality.

Resources devoted to prevention give rise to the costs of making it right first time. Total direct quality costs, and their division between the categories of prevention, appraisal, internal failure and external failure, vary considerably from industry to industry and from plant to plant. The work of Juran has suggested that total quality costs in manufacturing average ten per cent of sales turnover. Another writer on quality, Freigenbaum, has introduced the idea that in the average organisation there exists a "hidden plant", amounting to approximately one-tenth of productive capacity. This is devoted to producing scrap, re-work, correcting errors, replacing defective goods/services and so on. Thus, a direct link exists between quality and productivity, and there is no better way to improve productivity than to convert this hidden plant to truly productive use. A systematic approach to the control of quality provides an important way to accomplish effective control. One such approach may be to use British Standard 5750.

British Standard 5750

The BS5750 series are the national standards which promulgate, for use by UK suppliers and purchasers, the ISO 9000 series international standards for quality systems. They tell suppliers and manufacturers what is required of a quality-orientated system. They do not set out extra special requirements which only a very few organisations can, or need, comply with, but are practical standards for quality systems which can be used by all UK industry.

The principles of BS5750 (ISO9000) are applicable whether you employ ten people or 10,000. They identify the basic disciplines and specify the procedures and criteria to ensure that products or services meet the customer's requirements. The benefits of applying BS5750 are real: it may save money because procedures may be more soundly based and more efficient; it may ensure satisfied customers because you may have built in quality at every stage; it may reduce waste and time-consuming re-working of designs and procedures.

Constituent Parts

- Part 0: Section 0.1/ISO 9000 is a guide to the selection use use of the appropriate part of the BS5750/ISO 9000 series.
- Part 0: Section 0.2/ISO 9004 is a guide to overall quality management and the quality system elements within the BS5750/ISO 9000 series.
- Part 1/ISO 9001 relates to quality specifications for design/development, production, installation and servicing when the requirements of goods or services are specified by the customer in terms of how they must perform and which are then provided by the supplier.
- Part 1/ISO 9002 sets out requirements where a firm is manufacturing goods or offering a service to a published specification or to the customer's specification.
- Part 3/ISO 9003 specifies the quality system to be used in final inspection and test procedures.

Purpose

BS5750 (ISO9000) sets out how you can establish, document and maintain an effective quality system which will demonstrate to customers that organisations are committed to quality and are able to supply their quality needs. It is an internationally accepted standard and is simply common sense set down on paper in an organisation way. It has been broken down into sections to enable manufacturers to implement it easily and efficiently.

Using BS5750 (ISO9000) may bring real economies in its wake: economies in production because systems are controlled from start to finish; economies in resources and in time spent on re-planning or modifying designs. There is a complete record of every stage of production, invaluable for product or process improvement and in relation to any product liability claim.

Who Uses BS5750 (ISO9000)?

Suppliers can use BS5750 (ISO9000) when setting up their own quality systems; customers may specify that the quality of goods and services they are purchasing shall be controlled by a management system complying with BS5750 (ISO9000); and customers or third parties may use it as a basis for assessing a supplier's quality management system and thus ability to produce satisfactory goods and services. In fact, it is already used in this last way by all major public sector purchasing organisations and accredited third party certification bodies.

The direct benefits to firms who have been assessed in relation to BS5750 (ISO9000) and who appear in the Department of Trade and Industry's Register of Quality Assessed United Kingdom companies are apparently considerable: reduced inspection costs, improved quality and better use of scarce resources. Exporting firms who have been assessed may find that assessment helps them to obtain reciprocal recognition of certificates where needed by overseas authorities.

Comments

A slavish adherence to sources being BS5750 (ISO9000) approved can deny to the buyer organisations having the integrity and ability to deliver reliability. Bluntly it can deny access to "quality" companies, it can reduce choice and eliminate flexibility. A cynic might argue that it allows "ordinary" companies to masquerade as "quality". Perhaps there is a more obvious need to ensure integration of the organisation and total commitment to quality. One method is total quality management.

Total Quality Management (TQM)

Competitiveness is often measured by three things: quality, price and delivery. It is often a misconception that quality costs extra money in terms of inputs. The theory behind a TQM system is that, as quality improves, costs actually fall through lower failure and appraisal costs and less waste. TQM involves much more than assuring product or service quality; it is a system of dealing with quality at every stage of the production process, both internally and externally. TQM is truly a system requiring the commitment of senior managers, effective leadership and teamwork. The processes are shown at Figure 19.

Figure 19 Key Processes for TQM

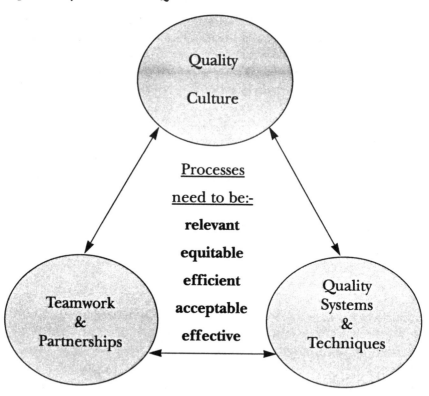

The TQM system requires that every single part of the organisation is integrated and must be able to work together. The main elements of the system are:

Teamwork: this is central to many parts of the TQM system where workers have to feel they are part of an organisation. In addition, teams of workers will often be brought together into problem-solving groups, quality circles and quality improvement teams.

Commitment: to be successful, TQM needs to be truly organisation-wide, and therefore commitment is required at the top from the chief executive as well as from the workforce. Middle management have an important role to play in not only grasping the concepts themselves but also explaining them to the people for whom they are responsible.

Communication: poor communication can result in organisational problems, information being lost and gaps occurring in the system. A good flow of accurate information, instructions and feedback is vital in maintaining the cohesion needed by the system.

Organisation: a cohesive system needs to be an organised one, with clear channels of responsibility and clearly-defined reporting procedures. Quality-related errors can be quickly rectified if an efficient organisational structure is in place.

Control and Monitoring: the TQM system will not remove the need to monitor processes and sample outputs, neither will it simply control itself. Many organisations use after-the-fact control, causing managers to take a reactive rather than proactive position. The TQM system needs a more anticipative style of control.

Planning: processes need to be planned carefully if they are to be efficient. This usually requires recording activities, stages and decisions in a form which is communicable to all. A clearly-defined process reduces the scope for error, and provides the basis of an analysis into possible improvements that might be made.

Inventory Systems: it is in the storage of raw materials, components or the finished product that quality can diminish. The keeping of stocks is also physically expensive and can lead to cash-flow problems. An inventory control system is therefore required to keep stocks to a minimum, whilst ensuring that supplies never dry up. One such system is the "Just-in-Time" system.

A breakdown in any part of the TQM system can lead to organisational gaps where wastage may occur or quality be overlooked. Errors have a habit of becoming multiplied, and failure to meet the requirements of one part of the organisation creates problems elsewhere. The correction of errors is time-consuming and costly. TQM can provide a company with a competitive edge, which will be important given the increases in competition resulting from the Single European Market. This means that managers must plan strategically both externally and internally, and that internal strategic planning has to involve everyone in the workplace. TQM is an approach aimed at improving the effectiveness and flexibility of business as a whole through the elimination of wasted effort as well as physical waste (that is improving the effectiveness of work so that results are achieved in less time and at less cost).

The buying process is very relevant to TQM. If quality is priceless then the TQM diamond at Figure 20 is appropriate!

Figure 20 The TQM Diamond

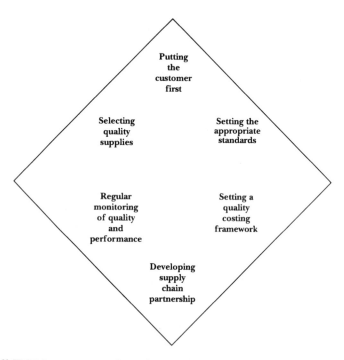

Overall TQM appears to be a better integrative process. A reminder of the benefits:

● Focuses individual's roles on customers and constant improvement.
● Develops teamwork and commitment and innovation as vehicles for employee ownership of improvement process.

- Identifies and eliminates waste of resources and costs.
- Provides a basis for management development and training focused on company values and the shift from policing to enable style.

Generally TQM may increase profits and market share the positive way, by delighting the customer and doing it right first time!

Food for Thought

"Investors in people" is a process of ensuring that all employers are educated and trained to meet the business objectives; a clear business objective is quality.

CHAPTER 5

Definitions and Concepts of Logistics

The Role of Logistics in Profitable Companies

With major changes occurring in industry, the perception of logistics in executive offices has failed to evolve in concert, principally due to continual changes in logistics terminology. Nevertheless, business executives are increasingly questioning the logistics potential for contributing to overall profitability. These questions are typified by the following comment from a chief executive of a leading company:

> I now know what logistics can do to save money. Tell me what it can do to improve my profits, to increase my share of the market, to improve my cash flow, to open new territories, to introduce new products, and to get the stockholders and board of directors off my back.

Notice that the chief executive asks if logistics can do anything important for profitability, and if so, what? Logistics must make this profitability contribution if it is to expand its role in the company.

Expenditure on purchasing goods and services in a company may account for between 30-75 per cent of total costs. Expenditure on storing and distributing materials may absorb a further 10-20 per cent of total costs.

Using some very different benchmarks, stock as a proportion of total funds employed can account for anything between 30 per cent and 50 per cent. Total distribution costs expressed as a percentage of sales range from 9 per cent (Industrial Manufacturing) to 34 percentage (Wholesale Consumer Goods).

The effective sourcing of material (embracing raw materials, components, assemblies and finished goods), and the subsequent management of that material through a production or value-adding process and on to the end customer is critical to the end customer, and is therefore critical to the success of most businesses. Moreover, these activities have a major impact on some of the main strategic problems facing many businesses today. Such problems will often include:

- How to reduce costs and best add value to products and services.
- How to sustain the highest quality standards.
- How to improve customer service.
- How to adapt to ever increasing environmental pressures.

Logistics management is a powerful means of resolving these problems. Understanding and management of the logistics supply chain is critical to any company's drive to improve productivity and profitability.

What is Logistics?

The underlying philosophy of logistics management is straightforward and can be defined in several ways:

- Logistics is the process which seeks to provide for the management and co-ordination of all activities within the supply chain from sourcing and acquisition, through production where appropriate, and through distribution channels to the customer. The goal of logistics is the creation of competitive advantage through the simultaneous achievement of high customer service levels, optimum investment and value for money.
- Logistics is the detailed organisation and implementation of a plan or operation.
- It is a term that was originally used in the military sphere to describe the organising and moving of troops and equipment. It is now applied to any detailed planning process in an organisation which entails the distribution or redistribution of resources.

Logistics concepts invoke a strategic view of thinking which seeks to account for all links in the flow of materials and related information in a flexible but integrated manner so that they perform in unison to achieve an overall optimum result for the business. Such a view is shown in Figure 21.

Figure 21 A View of Logistics

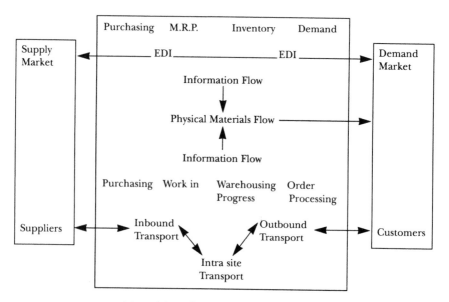

Adapted from C D Wareham (1991) *Competitive Logistics* CIPS Easton

Logistics is not simply a vogue word for holistic supply chain management, which evolved as an ideal rather than a management function, or materials management which is often narrower in scope. Logistics does indeed embrace these management philosophies; and does so without difficulty. Just as marketing grew in the 1960s to encompass sales, retailing, advertising, customer relations, product design, market research and in so doing encouraged an overview which then revolutionised the approach to serving the customer, so logistics has evolved to encourage a similar integration of materials-related functions. Moreover, what is perhaps more important, the logistics approach recognises the importance of those functions both individually and collectively and the need to manage then in totality.

Logistics management co-ordinates and integrates all of the materials-based functions inherent in planning and forecasting, coursing, manufacturing or servicing and processing a product, and its distribution:

- The aim is to enable businesses to keep ahead of market changes where quality, price, response time and service are crucial factors.
- The goal is to link the market place and its distribution channels to the procurement and manufacturing operations in such a way that competitive advantage can be achieved and maintained.
- The benefits accrue in cost reduction, sales generation, much improved service levels, and increased profitability.

The Logistics Mix

The business functions which fall within the scope of logistics management are included in what is commonly known as the logistics mix:

Planning and Marketing Strategy: the major influences of design and marketing on materials requirements and distribution requirements.

Purchasing: source research and selection, negotiation, building supplier partnership programmes.

Production Planning: plant capacity, location and layout, scheduling, manufacturing resource planning, and the control and support of work in progress.

Storage and Materials Handling: the handling and storage of goods, utilisation and packaging.

Inventory Management: control over inventories, sustaining minimum practical stock levels, minimising holding costs, wastage and obsolescence.

Warehouses and Stores: location, capacity, mix and operation.

Transport: mode decisions, scheduling, routing and operation.

Customer Service: demand forecasting, service levels, order processing, parts/service support, and aftermarket operations.

Technical Support: the provision and management of the systems needed to support these activities.

Not all of the elements in this mix will necessarily coincide with all business interests. The logistics concept, however, actively concentrates on those elements which do. Again, as examples, for the retailer or FMCG (Fast Moving Consumer Goods) distribution, sourcing and distribution are likely to be the key elements. For the manufacturer, purchasing and production planning are naturally more dominant.

Rarely will all of these elements be of equal importance to a business, but depending on its characteristics a number may be identified as having a major impact on the bottom-line, as well as having a critical inter-relationship which requires skilful management to secure the most profitable results.

Market Strategy and Product Design: in combination determine the nature, volume and timing of demand to be met by the purchasing operation. Additionally marketing and engineering functions can greatly influence the extent to which the product to be procured or manufactured is "logistically friendly".

Materials Management: embraces all aspects of materials flow from determination of requirements and capacity planning through purchasing, source search and selection, and scheduling - the latter including the planning and control of production processes, applicable most commonly when manufacturing is central to the business. Tools employed to achieve effective planning and execution may include Manufacturing Resource Planning (MRPII), Just-in-Time (JIT, the elimination of waste) and Optimised Production Technology (OPT), as appropriate to the individual needs of the business.

Inventory Management: (often seen as part of material management in manufacturing enterprises) determination of stocking policy to ensure continuity of suppliers with minimum investment costs, including the effective control and execution of that policy.

Storage and Materials Handling: covers the safe, secure and disciplined handling of materials as initial receipts, as parts awaiting processing, as work in progress during manufacture, and subsequently as finished product. It embraces packaging design, unitisation and the full range of simple to sophisticated aids to storage.

Distribution: includes warehousing and both inbound and outbound transportation, all strongly influenced by demands for higher levels of customer service, JIT requirements and the evolution of contract distribution. With an estimated 500,000 vehicles dedicated to freight movement in the UK alone, distribution is under increasing pressure for greater control on environmental grounds.

The Scope of Logistics

The basic nature of business is that it procures or buys something, whether goods or information, changes its form in some way which adds value, and then sells a product or service on to someone else. In manufacturing industries in particular, this sequence may occur a number of times:

Inbound Logistics		Core Business		OutboundLogistics
Raw materials	-	process or refine	-	supply others
Refined materials	-	manufacture	-	components/assemblies
Components	-	assembled	-	finished product
Finished goods	-	distribute	-	customer

At a similar, albeit oversimplified level, within a manufacturing or processing organisation we can identify three basic operations:

- Change of form - production or process
- Change of ownership - marketing or internal transfer
- Change of time and place - logistics

But these three operations are not clear cut and do not stand alone. Taking over-packaging as an example of a process, it does not strictly change either the form of the product or its time and place, but rather its outward appearance. Packaging must, of course, be designed with a change of ownership in mind, for example unitisation to suit an industrial customer's needs, or display packaging for marketing. It must also be designed for movement, for example protection against damage, ease of handling or for security in transit. However, which requirement takes priority not only has a major influence on the costs of the packaging but also distribution costs. There are, therefore, some apparently discrete activities which can be influenced by a number of individual functions or management areas. The logistics concept aims to capture and to analyse such activities.

Logistics, an Integrative Process?

The organisational emphasis of traditional business is normally on vertical line management within individual functions. Such a framework actively promotes sub-optimisation as many of the trade-off opportunities outlined above are not visible. It is essential to highlight the pattern of materials and information flows and their interdependence. An example of the strategic process of planning integration is shown in Figure 22.

Figure 22 Logistics Planning Process

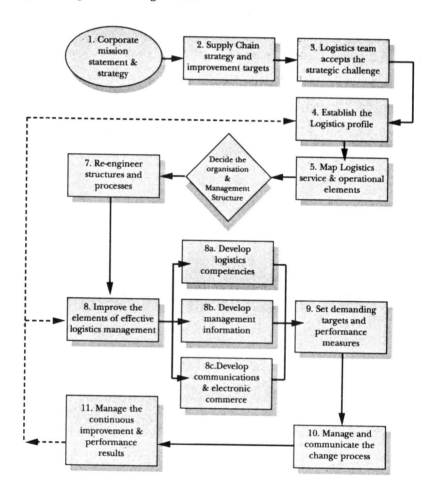

Each of these planning functions are discussed throughout this text with an emphasis on the need for integration as part of the logistics process. The key steps in the planning and integration process highlighted by Figure 22 are:

1. The organisation sets up a corporate strategic plan and mission statement.
2. The supply chain/logistics element of the corporate plan. Identify the broad logistics strategy and improvement targets.
3. The logistics management team accepts the challenge of developing and managing the process.
4. Logistics strategic management team identify the full supply chain/logistics base profile and mission statement.
5. Mapping process, SWOT analysis, strategic review: where   are we now? Where are we going? How do we get there?
6. Start the organisational and structural review and change plan.
7. Re-engineer each element of the logistics map and the supply chain process.
8. Identify the best practice gaps, overcome the obstacles, improve the elements of effective management and processes.
    (a) Identify the best practice standards, develop personal competencies to bridge the gap.
    (b) Develop and improve on relevant management information.
    (c) Develop state of the art communications within the supply chain.
9. Set demanding targets for each mapping element within the total logistics service profile and plan.
10. Manage the project individual and group elements within the team plan.
11. Manage the performance outputs and the process of continuous improvement at every level. Feedback to process 8 and re-work as required. Feedback to process 4 and re-work as required.

The role of logistics in today's and tomorrow's profitable companies will change as the value of products changes, and also as the value that buyers or customers ascribe to product changes. This statement represents a new concept for many logistics managers, who were trained in transportation, warehousing, and other such functions to conduct their activities based on lease-cost or other hard measure priorities. Modern logistics managers must find innovative ways to help their companies improve profits, increase market share, improve cash flow, open new territories and introduce new products. However, logistics neither creates demand nor product. Logistics is the organisation that responds to demands, and creates a bridge between that demand and those who supply it. A professional and integrative approach is clearly needed!

CHAPTER 6

Managing the Logistics Function

The logistics manager is concerned not only with managing the flow of materials and resources, he or she is also concerned with managing the human resources through which control of materials is achieved. In this chapter we will investigate the problems associated with staffing the positions or roles that have been defined in the structure. We shall consider aspects of recruitment and training and the preparation of job descriptions and operating manuals.

In addition to these elements of the staffing problem we shall also focus attention on a closely related managerial requirement. This concerns techniques of directing and motivating staff to achieve departmental and corporate objectives and to provide opportunities for members of the logistics function to satisfy their own individual goals at the same time. This topic is a controversial one and, in the social environment of today, traditional views have come under severe attack. We shall consider these opposing views in the context of logistics management.

Staffing the Logistics Department

Audit
In an established organisation structure, a periodic audit of company resources must essentially include a survey of personnel in terms of adequacy of numbers and skills to meet the needs of changing programmes, particularly in a period of growth. A responsibility rests, therefore, with the departmental manager to determine the effect of corporate plans on the department and in conjunction with the personnel department to arrange participation in the training and development programme and for recruitment where necessary.

The logistics department audit will need to relate workload to current staff and assess future needs. A programme of training and experience should be obtained through job rotation (particularly an advantage to the specialist in developing product knowledge), visits to suppliers to obtain first-hand experience of industrial processes, and formal education courses for professional training. Job evaluation for recruitment and grading requires a description of the job, and a job specification describing the personal skills and attitudes required by the duties and responsibilities (matching person to job is important in recruitment and training).

Job Description

One of the classical principles of organisation is to carefully define the duties and responsibilities of each position in the organisation structure. Job descriptions specify what the holder of the position should do and they are a major determinant of the behaviour of the holder. They provide a broad statement of the purpose, scope, duties and responsibilities of particular jobs and allocate job titles. The need for such descriptions increases with the size of organisation, but even in smaller organisations it is important that the occupants of job positions know what is expected of them. They act also as a guide for recruiting staff and for the assessment of training needs.

For organisations who have not yet developed job descriptions, the following steps should be taken. The first task is to prepare an analysis of existing jobs by a series of interviews both with job holders and other staff. Job analysis is concerned with establishing why a job exists, its objectives and how they are to be achieved. It is also necessary to establish its relationships with other jobs in the department, what supervision is given and received and what qualities are needed by the job holder. On the basis of the information which is collected, job descriptions can be compiled. The following list includes the headings which could be included in a plan for the preparation of job descriptions.

● Job title
● Title of immediate supervisor
● Brief summary of the job
● Detailed description of duties
● Specific reports or information to be provided
● Decisions and recommendations made by the holder

- Responsibility for work of others
- Responsibility for accuracy of work and effect of errors
- Education and experience required

In many organisations, job descriptions form the basis for job-grading schemes, which in turn are related to salary and wage structures. The ultimate objective is to prepare a rational salary scheme which gives similar pay to jobs of a similar grade throughout the company. In order to do this, it is necessary to compare the content of jobs in different departments. Various methods have been developed to evaluate jobs, such as ranking, points rating and factor comparison, with respect to such features as duties, supervision given and received, the nature of decisions taken, and the qualifications needed by the occupant. Such exercises are likely to be carried out by personnel departments, with the possible assistance of organisation and methods (O & M) specialists.

Staff Appraisal

The staff appraisal meeting between manager and supervisor and between supervisor and individual staff member, gives an opportunity for:

- setting objectives and targets jointly in key areas of the individual's duties and responsibilities;
- the supervisor or staff member to participate in choice and setting of targets, promoting job interest and confidence in planning and in handling of problems;
- supplying the manager with facts on individual performances in support of personal judgements;
- the setting of key objectives and the discussion and counselling involved at this stage and at the end of the period under review involves leadership and motivation, benefiting management and staff in a common purpose.

Examples of objectives agreed might be:

- a specified percentage of on time deliveries to customers;
- a specified percentage saving against standard costs within a given period;
- a reduction in administrative costs per £100 of expenditure on transport;
- a warehouse stock reduction through improved supplier relationships and supplier development.

Operating Manuals

Many organisations have found it useful to prepare logistics manuals as a guide to company personnel. These act as a guide, firstly, for the logistics department itself, secondly, for employees in other departments and, thirdly, for suppliers. Manuals describe the procedures to be adopted to achieve particular purposes and the rules for making particular decisions. They will usually contain information about job responsibilities and reporting relationships, inform people about the service provided by the department and service as a guide to departmental policies regarding such issues as business ethics. The objective of such a manual is to provide a clear statement of how things are to be done and it is a useful help to newcomers. Also, it can help to resolve disputes. The drawback with this approach, however, is that it might lead to a stifling of initiative and a reluctance to tackle new problems which do not seem to be covered by the manual. Thus it is possible to argue that an operating manual is a more useful device in relatively static conditions, but less appropriate in a rapidly changing environment in which old methods and procedures may quickly become ineffective.

Qualities of Logistics Personnel

Discussion of organisational aspects of logistics work has indicated the wide variety of jobs that exist within the function. The desired qualities of job occupants need to be tailored to the needs of particular positions. In other words, it is not possible to prepare a simple blueprint of the ideal person for logistics work. Skill and personality profiles should vary according to the nature and complexity of the job. In spite of these reservations, however, we can make some general comments about the characteristics apparent in a member of the logistics function.

It has often been said that the logistician is a "jack of all trades, master of none". In the sense that an effective logistician needs a sound general business knowledge this is true. He or she needs a thorough understanding of the commercial and economic background to logistics work and must develop a detailed picture of the particular markets in which the company is operating and be able to make a careful analysis of the abilities of suppliers within them. He or she must also develop sufficient product knowledge to gain an appreciation of the alternative possibilities, and the commercial implications.

Technical Expertise

The extent to which detailed technical knowledge is required is a controversial issue and policies differ from organisation to organisation. One the one hand, it has been argued that the main contribution of the logistician is that of providing and analysing commercial information and of playing a leading role in distribution. Supporters of this view suggest that logisticians should not attempt to become "pseudo-technologists" and take on the roles of designers and engineers. On the other hand, there is the belief that logisticians can only make a full analysis of the commercial aspects of a logistics problem if they have got a detailed knowledge of the technical features. Other departments may gain a greater respect for the logistician and may cooperate more closely with a person who demonstrates an understanding of the technical problems. Thus, some organisations do see technical training as an essential quality for some posts in the logistics department. It is not possible to make a judgement in this debate which would be valid for all situations. The degree of technical knowledge required can be expected to vary.

The expert logistician will have a sound understanding of advanced techniques and should be able to apply a creative approach to logistics problems. In applying such techniques, competence in accounting and financial areas is also important. Increasingly it is becoming more and more important to develop skills in mathematics and statistics for the purpose of undertaking analytical work. Finally in this list of required skills and knowledge we can refer to the addition of managerial skills as logisticians move into more senior positions involving supervisory and planning work. We can now consider personality traits that are appropriate to logistics work.

Personal Qualities

It is apparent that one of the most important characteristics which is necessary in a professional logistician is integrity. Communication skills play an important part in relationships. These involve the ability to perceive and understand points of view and information presented by other people, as well as being able to communicate in a concise and easily comprehensive manner. Logisticians must be able to work closely with other people, both inside and outside the organisation and at times patience and diplomacy may be necessary when working under pressure. In situations which may threaten to stop an assembly line from operating because of logistics shortages, logisticians have to be able to cope under pressure.

Recruiting Personnel for Logistics Function

In developing a personnel policy in the logistics function it is important to plan for internal as well as external recruitment. Individual members of staff should be encouraged to develop their abilities by providing them with training facilities and an appropriate work programme with a view to future advancement to positions that will become available as a result of expansion and/or the retirement or promotion of existing incumbents. Records of existing members of staff should be kept and reviewed for training and recruitment purposes. Records showing educational qualifications, specialised technical skills, appointments within the organisation and career experience with other firms, training received and a summary of appraisals and personal particulars should be maintained. Internal promotion can improve morale and act as a spur to better performance.

Careful planning should precede interviewing work, to decide what questions should be asked and how assessments are to be made. Many organisations like to use intelligence tests and aptitude tests as additional devices. It is important to get the applicants to talk and to provide an opportunity for them to ask questions. Two possible schemes for interviewing can be outlined.

The Seven Point Plan

The National Institute of Industrial Psychology (now defunct) has suggested a scheme for selection interviews, which covers the following features which are still valid:

- Physical characteristics
- Attainments with regard to education, training and previous experience

- General intelligence
- Special aptitudes
- Interests
- Disposition: personal characteristics with regard to manner, and ability to get on with people
- Circumstances: domestic situation

The Five-Fold Grading Scheme

An alternative scheme places more emphasis on the dynamics of personality and motivation. It also involves the use of a five-point scale for each of the five headings.

- First impression and physical characteristics. This covers appearance, speech, manner and personal method of dealing with others.
- Qualifications and expectations. This includes details of education, training and previous experience, but also expectations for the future.
- Brains and abilities. Much will have been learnt from qualifications, but the results of tests can also be included.
- Motivation. This is concerned with finding out the type of work the applicant likes and the "interest pattern" of the candidate.
- Adjustment. This covers distinct qualities such as integrity, reliability, acceptability to others and behaviour under stress or difficulties.

If, after considering the internal potential, it is decided to recruit externally, the logistics manager will, in most cases, call in the personnel manager to assist. External recruitment is expensive. Adverts should be placed in the papers or journals which are likely to be read by the type of person that is required. Especially in times of high unemployment, this is a competitive process and the advertisement must be carefully prepared to attract the right person by giving a clear account of the nature of the post and future prospects, as well as giving a specification of the required quality. If applicants are asked to fill in a standard application form, the task of comparison is easier. A short-list of candidates for interview can be compiled from this initial screening.

Recruitment is a costly process and it is important, therefore, to fully utilise the abilities of staff once they have been recruited, otherwise they will leave. Further development of their skills is another objective and we can now, therefore, study training and education of staff as a further aspect of personnel policy in the logistics function.

Training and Education

Successful training and development policies will enable the organisation to attract and retain able people. In today's rapidly changing world, with developments in knowledge and techniques, it is also important that staff at all levels in the organisation are provided with facilities to keep up to date. In the last analysis, better trained staff will give a better performance. No longer can organisations rest content that employees have received sufficient education and training before entry into the organisation. Many organisations have developed a training department to help in this area and to assist departmental managers in devising the right policy.

During the last two decades or more there has been a rapid expansion of facilities to provide education and training. The government, through the 1964 Industrial Training Act, gave active encouragement towards this and, through the state education system, has provided various courses at colleges of technology, polytechnics and universities. Under the Act, Industrial Training Boards collect levies from organisations, which are then used to pay the costs of training and which can be claimed back by organisations as grants towards approved forms of training courses including correspondence courses. The major problem today is to diagnose training needs and to select the appropriate course from the wide variety that are available. Various training agencies have superseded or complemented training boards; the concept however, remains the same!

A number of steps are important in developing and supervising training. The first task involves identifying the training needs of individuals. An assessment of individual strengths and weaknesses in relation to existing and possible future jobs is a starting point. The emergence of new knowledge, new techniques and new legislation must also be monitored. Having analysed the training needs, a programme of how these can be met must be drawn up. The training programme, once in operation, must be evaluated in terms of the benefit accruing to the individual and the organisation. In discussing the various types of education and training that can be given, it will be useful to distinguish between in-house or internal training and external training, although some schemes combine aspects of both.

Internal Training

As regards internal training, we can first consider commercial, undergraduate or graduate apprentices. Such programmes are run mainly for employees upon entry into the organisation and are concurrent with attendance on external courses. The training in the organisation may commence with an induction course to introduce the newcomer to the structure and activities of the company as a whole. This will be followed by special work assignments under the supervision of senior staff to provide experience in the different types of work involved in the function. Commercial apprentices may be on sandwich degree courses. In addition, they may be involved in specialised courses such as those offered by the appropriate professional body.

Other internal training courses can be devised for members of the logistics function. The emphasis of these courses, usually intensive and of short duration, would be placed on specific aspects relevant to the particular needs of the organisation. These courses, frequently of a participative kind involving case studies and role-playing exercises, can be used to develop knowledge and skills, but also to influence attitudes and encourage cooperation. Courses can be organised and run by the organisation personnel or by consultants and can be tailored to the particular needs of the organisation.

External Courses

External courses can take several forms. First, there are part-time or fulltime courses provided by the state education service. These cover NVQs, HNC, HND, and undergraduate and postgraduate degree courses in business studies as well as the specific courses by professional bodies. They provide a general education in commercial aspects of business and a more specific education in logistics management and the techniques used in this field. Several European universities now offer masters degrees covering logistics/logistics management. In addition, courses in technical subjects may also be considered. Correspondence courses provide another route by which the student can gain these qualifications.

The importance of providing the right training in order to operate an effective logistics department is crucial. Attention must be given to the qualifications of employees upon entry, but these abilities must be supplemented and built upon by further programmes tailored to their needs and the needs of the company. The human resources of the organisation and of the logistics department should be regarded as valuable assets which need to be carefully cultivated. The maximum benefit can only be gained from providing the right environment in which the knowledge and skills of personnel can be properly applied. Often the benefits of training courses are lost because those attending are not permitted to practice what they have learnt.

Managing the Logistics Department

When considering the managerial function of directing or guiding and supervising the work of subordinates, we move into one of the most controversial topics in business. The relationship between managers and their subordinates is at the heart of what has been called industrial relations. Whilst attention in the media, especially newspapers and television, tends to concentrate on industrial relations on the shop floor, relations in "white collar" work are just as significant. During the post-Second-World-War period, ideas concerning how managers should direct their staff have undergone many changes. In addition, social changes have taken place so that attitudes affecting the expectations of employees towards their jobs have been transformed. In particular, different views concerning the nature of authority in organisations have emerged and the importance of employee interests has received increased attention.

We shall consider the development of ideas with regard to the supervision and motivation of the work force in the following areas:

- the classical and neo-classical management tradition;
- the human relations tradition, and
- more recent ideas concerned with participation.

The Classical and Neo-Classical Management Tradition

The school of writers and ideas that can be labelled in this manner has been and still is extremely influential. Indeed, the framework of ideas upon which this chapter has been based has been drawn from this tradition. Many of the ideas concerning the functions of management, with regard to planning, organising, staffing and controlling, remain as key thoughts in organising an employer in general or a logistics department in particular. However, the major weakness in these traditional ideas lie in the area of manager/worker relations and the somewhat naive ideas of earlier writers concerning motivation and leadership.

The cornerstone of this tradition with regard to industrial relations lies in the view of authority and the prerogatives that this appeared to confer upon managers. Authority within the structure of organisations in the private sector was seen to be derived from the shareholders and this delegation of authority gave the board of directors and the executive managers authority to issue instructions and direct activities designed to enhance the interests of the shareholders. In turn, they were held responsible for the achievement or failure to achieve the objectives of the shareholder. In return for the material rewards of the wage or salary agreement, employees were expected to accept without question instructions that were given to them. The pursuit of efficiency and the pursuit of profit was conducted with little attention to other interests of employees. In the public sector, managerial authority was seen to be derived from either parliament or the local council and ultimately from the electors. Strict adherence to this hierarchical view of authority has led to what might be called an "authoritarian" or "dictatorial" style of management. However, this view of an arbitrary style of management has come under fierce criticism for a number of reasons.

First, the view of authority itself has been challenged, particularly by the trade unions. The essence of this opposition is that insufficient attention is given to the rights of employees and these need to be protected, particularly through collective bargaining processes. Other ways of extending the powers of the employees, such as representation on boards of companies, works councils and an extension of collective bargaining have been put forward. Government legislation has already been passed to protect the rights of employees and it is possible that other measures to increase industrial democracy will emerge in the near future, particularly in view of existing legislation.

Secondly, the authoritarian style of management has been attacked on the grounds of expediency. It is argued that it is based on a misconception of human nature and that it does not contribute to maximum effectiveness. Indeed, this view classifies authoritarian or dictatorial rule as being inefficient and warns that undesirable results will emerge, such as strikes, poor performance and a high turnover of staff.

The Human Relations Tradition

The foundations of the human relations tradition are generally accepted to rest upon the Hawthorne Studies, which were conducted in the United States during the 1930s. The essential finding of these studies, conducted by Elton Mayo, is that individual performance can be affected by the attitudes formed by informal work groups in which the employees are located. It was discovered that the morale and attitudes of such groups could be either favourably or unfavourably disposed towards the achievement of corporate objectives and the acceptance of managerial instruction. Furthermore, it was suggested that workers were concerned with obtaining not only monetary rewards, but also satisfaction of social needs from belonging to the group. The implication for management of this point of view is that attention must be given to techniques of supervision. Instead of relying on coercive methods, using only financial incentives and punishments, supervisors are recommended, by this school of thought, to develop ways of influencing group attitudes and gaining the support of employees for organisational objectives. The emphasis is placed, therefore, on the social skills of supervisors, designed to remove any antagonism in informal groups towards the formal requirements of the organisation. Importance was attached to communicating a sense of purpose and developing teamwork.

However, difficulties attached to this view have become apparent; it tends to underestimate the importance of material rewards and it ignores some of the factors which can influence group attitudes. In particular, it ignores the influence of external forces, such as trade unions. Nevertheless, the development of this tradition was a useful counter balance to the instrumental view of employees adopted previously.

Participative Approaches

New ideas have emerged during the last ten years or so which have their origin in both the findings of the human relations school and in the more general opposition to authoritarian rule in society as a whole. These ideas are also based upon a different conception of the basis characteristics of human nature. The thrust of these views is to allow individual employees greater scope to exercise their basic talents and sense of responsibility. Instead of giving a rigid prescription of what job holders should do, it is advocated that more discretion should be allowed so that they can use their initiative in solving problems. This extension of responsibility has been called "job enrichment" and to it others have added "job enlargement". The notion, underlying this second term, is that jobs should not be divided up into too narrow a task, which might lead to boredom and monotony. Furthermore, the roles allocated to employees should include participation in the setting of objectives and the making of decisions which affect them. The essential features for management in this school of thought is that managers should adopt a consultative style and encourage a joint problem-solving approach.

Psychologists agree that this participative approach allows individuals the opportunity to develop the full potential of their abilities and satisfies their wishes to exercise more control over their work. It is argued that this desire for autonomy is increasing in advanced industrial societies. On the basis of this analysis, managers, in designing organisations, should establish a less rigid structure which creates an environment in which abilities can be developed. Too much reliance on prescriptive and coercive techniques will not utilise the full potential of employees. Rewards should be closely related to the achievement of objectives, but employees should be given freedom to select the means of achieving them. They should also be allowed to participate in the setting of the objectives in the first place.

The right of the manager to manage following these later ideas is justified less in terms of managerial prerogative and more in terms of expertise. Acceptance of managerial authority by subordinates may also be based on the competence of the managers. Concern for people as well as concern for results is important in motivating people according to this third school of thought.

The drawback with these later ideas concerns the problem of whether all people want, or feel happy with, the participative approach. Some people prefer to be given detailed instructions of what to do and experience stress if they are left to decide for themselves. In situations which are straightforward and unchanging, there is evidence to suggest that firm decisions taken by the managers are more effective.

Implications for Logistics Management

In the dynamic and rapidly changing environment that exists today, there are no simple prescriptions to guide the logistics manager in directing the work of the department. It is necessary to develop a sensitive perception of the needs of both the organisation and of subordinate staff. Attitudes need to be based on an analysis of the situation which exists and situations vary from organisation to organisation. In some organisations, in which unions play an important part, a different approach is required from others in which employees are accustomed to a more authoritarian style. However, it is possible to argue that the task of the logistician is one which can be done more effectively by people who are permitted to exercise initiative. Very often, within their particular commodity range, they are the ones with the most expertise. There is scope, therefore, for encouraging a participative approach, at least in the higher levels of the logistics department. It is important that the logistics manager maintains an awareness of new developments and, in particular, an awareness of new legislation. Many people have suggested that social technology lags behind advances in other forms of technology. Nevertheless, it is of fundamental importance to develop a personnel policy and a managerial style that effectively utilises the talents of members of staff and that satisfies both organisational and individual objectives. In achieving this ideal managers need to develop a sensitive awareness of the factors influencing performance. It is important to provide the appropriate training support to increase the value of these human resources.

Management and Implementation of Change

In order to achieve objectives within an organisation, changes are likely to become necessary from time to time. These changes are achieved through staff. The outcome will depend upon the effectiveness with which this process is managed.

Strategic Change

- Internal and/or external factors are likely to signal the need for change.
- External factors might include legal changes, socio economic, technological, and so on.
- Internally, it might be a change of objectives or mission, new men with different ideas, etc.

Managing strategic change is concerned with a change in the "culture of the organisation". One can identify two main stages in the process of change: unfreezing or breaking down previously held beliefs and assumptions; reformation of new sets of beliefs.

Recipe for Change

The recipe is a set of beliefs and assumptions which form part of the culture of an organisation, and have been called paradigms, recipes and interpretative schemes.

Unfreezing Process

We can identify from the above, a number of ways of unfreezing the existing recipe:

- signal - downturn in performance;
- challenge and exposure of the existing recipe;
- reconfiguration of newer structures;
- intervention of an outsider, that is someone with little commitment to the existing recipe.

Other Methods

We can implement change by:

- altering formal control mechanisms;
- structural changes;

- symbols of change, for example the new image given by Harvey Jones, a flamboyant character, wearing bright ties and not in the traditional ICI mould;
- organisational structures, because they communicate "readily understood" visions of the organisation's mission or role.

Political Nature Of Change

Management of change has political implications. If change is to be successful, you will need to "manage and manipulate" the political power structure.

Logistics and Change

Increasingly, proactive organisations are recognising that logistics, far from being just another operational variable, is uniquely placed within the organisation to manage the inter-relationship of all the factors which affect the flow of both information and goods necessary to fill orders. This flow begins when the customer decides to place an order and ends when the order is fulfilled and monies collected.

Organisations which believe that the single output of any organisation is customer service understand the strategic significance of logistics in this process. They know that, to succeed in today's environment, they must adopt a disciplined and systematic approach to the market, create carefully considered priorities, allocate resources in the strictest possible manner and make often difficult trade-off decisions.

It is not yet common for the logistics manager to be involved with the initial phases of an organisation's strategic planning. However, the size of the corporate profit slice which logistics affects is sufficiently large to suggest that the logistics manager should be a key figure at the strategy formulation stage.

In describing strategic planning as the process of formulating plans which ensures the long-term profitability of an organisation, we referred earlier to actions taken in anticipation of customer needs. The logistics manager is the only person in the organisation charged solely with managing all flows of information and materials in the conception to consumption chain, and their interactions. It is this unique position that provides the logistics manager with an appreciation of the organisation's capacity to respond to expectations.

Strategic planning forces management to reconcile two almost contradictory tasks: long-term (visionary) planning with short-term responsiveness to customers. To achieve this seemingly impossible balance we must focus on the "strategic" side of planning and not consider strategy to be just another word for "long-term". Strategic planning covers three steps as far as logistics is concerned:

● vision statements (what we stand for) ;
● aims (directions we want to go in) ;
● objectives (specific quantified targets).

The chief executive is in the best position to understand the expectations of "stakeholders" (shareholders and employees) and the organisation's long-term goals. Accordingly, he or she must be the one to articulate the vision statement. The difference between aims and objectives is the difference between quantitative and qualitative analysis. Aims are the qualitative statements, the expression of desires and goals. Objectives are quantitative and therefore must be measurable. It is not enough to set an objective as "increasing sales" because there is no way to determine if the objective has been met. Increasing sales may be the aim, but increasing sales by three per cent within six months is the objective. This gives a finishing point and a specific target. Once the aims and objectives are established, operational plans can follow.

Proper procedures for implementation, control and evaluation are needed to translate plans from mere words on paper to actions on the ground. This is where effectiveness of the logistics manager will determine the success or failure of the whole planning effort. The creation of a strategic plan does not provide a guarantee of success, rather it provides a frame of reference against which changes in the environment external to the organisation can be evaluated. In this way the organisation can respond to both anticipated and unexpected changes in the external environment in a planned manner. It is this ability to evolve and adapt that distinguishes the strategically-oriented organisation from its endangered counterpart.

The strategic planning process points the way forward for organisations which aim to be progressive and proactive in the years ahead. Logistics, and the role of the logistics manager, are being recognised by strategically oriented organisations as key ingredients in successfully meeting the challenges of these increasingly turbulent times. Logistics managers must adopt a strategic approach if they are to be equal to the challenges that await them in the future.

CHAPTER 7

Operating Environments

Understanding logistics in operating environments is important to understanding the total concept. To be able to do this we need to examine a new method and compare it to problems of existing methods. In order to illustrate this, a specific example of logistics support in the aircraft industry needs to be considered; the principles, however, are the same for any capital equipment project.

Integrated Logistic Support (ILS)

Integrated logistic support is a structured and co-ordinated approach to support planning that will produce the most technically efficient and cost-effective support solution. ILS is an American concept that was introduced by the US government in an attempt to combat their spiralling support costs and to give a structured approach to support planning so as to let it influence the design process. The concept was developed and became Mil.Std.1388. This standard now provides a frame work which can be tailored to suit individual projects and user requirements dependant upon budgets, time scales and project size. We shall not mention "1388" again but bear in mind that all the concepts are based on this Mil.Std.

The reason for adopting ILS is that the customer will make it a contractual requirement of the project with the aim of meeting the same objectives.

Integrated Logistic Support - Main Objectives

So, what is wrong with present systems and why do we need ILS? Past problems can be grouped together to give three main objectives.

These are: reduce support costs, past project support costs have now risen to an unacceptable level; ensure support influences design, so that the product is designed to be as supportable as possible at the first attempt; ensure the timely development and acquisition of resources – all the required resources are to be in the right place at the right time. So, let us look at the first of these objectives.

Reducing Support Costs

The "support cost" is the cost, incurred by the customer, through owning and operating a product such as an aircraft. It includes repairable components, technical publications, aerospace ground equipment (AGE), petrol oils and lubricants (POL), contractor site representatives, and biggest of all, the customer's labour costs.

Previous Support Costs

As products have become more complex so the support costs have risen. The effects of these high support costs seriously jeopardise the chances of being awarded export contracts.

Potential Export Contract Support Costs

An example of the effects of high support costs on a quote for an export contract would be useful. As an example, assume the product is an aircraft. If we allow £20 million per aircraft then the support costs, at present rates, come to around £11m for each aircraft. To keep costs within the customer's budget the present support rates mean that the customer is going to be limited to eight aircraft. A fleet of eight aircraft means no better then six aircraft being available on the line, and having only six aircraft means sortie patterns of three pair or one diamond four.

The effectiveness of all this in air defence terms, in relation to the total cost, is probably not a viable defence option compared to other national budget demands. In any national budget squeeze an early cancellation of the aircraft sale is likely, and the loss of important export revenue to the manufacturer.

Potential Export Aircraft Support Costs

To emphasise how support costs dictate the number of aircraft a customer can purchase let us have a look at support costs. The effect is that high support costs can affect the actual numbers of aircraft that the customer can purchase. Bear in mind that these support percentages are expressed as a proportion of the cost of an aircraft. At 100 per cent support costs the customer gets six aircraft for £120m and £120m worth of support. At 50 per cent support costs the customer gets eight aircraft for £160m and £80m worth of support. If we reduce the cost of support to 33 per cent of the aircraft costs then we could supply nine aircraft.

But the bottom line, and this is where we should be aiming, is that if we managed to reduce the cost of support to 20 per cent of the cost of that aircraft then we could supply the customer with 10 aircraft – a more realistic figure with which to form a defence policy. Manufacturers do not lose orders through poor product performance – they lose orders because prospective customers cannot afford to keep the product in service.

Costs Initial and Recurring

Having established the effect the support cost can have on a project, and that it must be kept to a minimum, let us look at what support costs are made up of. Support costs fall into one of two categories:

Initial costs: those borne at the time of the initial purchase such as test equipment, training, spares and publications.

Recurring costs: those costs that are continued throughout the life cycle of the project. The major cost drivers in recurring costs are usually the upkeep of documentation, the cost incurred by the need to keep training manpower, but invariably the major cost driver is labour in the form of maintenance and repair.

It is, easy to see that the more we can improve the reliability of the product, the less would be the requirement for maintenance and repair, thus the lower the recurring costs. The main reason for keeping recurring costs to a minimum is that they are subject to inflation and as such can considerably influence the support costs throughout the life cycle.

How Support Can Influence Design

As well as trying our best to plan the support requirements it would help if the product was designed to be as supportable as possible in the first place. Let us look at an example of how costs escalate because of a poor supportability design and failure to rectify it. In this particular example, a small alteration is needed to make the fitment of an item easier by changing the size of a securing bolt.

If, during the design stage a possible alteration is identified that could make the product more supportable it would take £10 to alter the drawing and no more than that would have been required. Had the project been in the development phase, a modification (Mod) kit would have been introduced and the drawings altered, which would have taken £100. During the production phase the stores quantity would have been altered, the Mod kit purchased, and the drawings altered and the cost would have been nearer £1000. If the product had been in service and the same bolt size changed to improve the products supportability, by the time you take into account the modification kits, stores catalogues, stores changes, product downtime, retrospective fitting and labour, the cost of the change is nearer £10,000.

The costs quoted are fictitious but the effect is not. If we can influence the design, savings of more than a factor of x1000 can be made in certain areas and we shall end up with a design that has been influenced by support, not support that is influenced by design.

The Final Objective – to Ensure the Timely Development and Acquisition of Support Resources

The date the product (again an aircraft) will enter service is called the in service date – ISD. Three months before this occurs all the agreed support requirements, facilities and equipment are to be in service and ready for use. This date is called the logistic support date – LSD. To achieve the requirements for LSD there is a large amount of work to be carried out. Try and imagine the planning that is required to ensure that everything is ready to go:

- All the necessary training has been carried out so that both aircrew and engineers are competent.
- The National Publications database is compiled and up to date, and that publications are printed and are available, as required.
- All support equipment has been identified, developed and is in the place at the correct levels ready for use.

And so on for all the support requirements for the aircraft or any other significant product. It is the job of ILS to ensure that the agreed support package is ready, in all respects, for LSD.

Three Main Objectives

So there are three main objectives we need to concentrate on. To re-cap they are:

- to reduce support costs;
- to ensure that support influences design;
- timely development and acquistion of resources.

As well as our three main objectives there are always mistakes that have been made on previous projects that under no circumstances can be allowed to happen again.

Past Problems

In the past the various support disciplines have often been left to their own devices in producing support plans for their particular area. These are just a few examples of what went wrong in a fictitious aircraft programme.

The initial intention, stated in-service repair, would be from day one (ISD). So, all the planning for the provisioning of spares necessary to support this date was carried out only to find that the ISD had slipped three years. This may look like a "God send" in that it provided a lot more time; unfortunately it also allowed numerous modifications to be introduced which resulted in the support disciplines planning for targets that had long since changed.

The technical publications departments of the various partner companies were working together to compile a joint set of publications. Unfortunately, these partner companies were not interested in Batch 1 aircraft, as their respective airforces were not going to receive aircraft until Batch 2. Therefore the three partner companies were working to widely differing logistics support dates. You can imagine from this the confusion that reigned. It is a prime objective of integrated logistics support to ensure that the lessons have been learnt and that we do not allow these same mistakes to occur again.

Unco-ordinated Logistic Support

There has been very little use of automatic data processing systems and when they have been used they have been for individual needs rather than as a co-ordinated attempt to construct a common support database. So you can picture this unstructured and uncoordinated approach to support planning with some disciplines "talking" to each other – and others not at all. This, along with an unstructured approach to support project management, has contributed much to the problems encountered.

Co-ordinated Logistic Support

What we need is to bring everyone together and pool all their efforts into one co-ordinated and planned structure. That structure is "integrated logistic support". This focal point is the means of achieving the objectives of ILS which is "logistic support analysis". We shall look at LSA in more detail later but first let us see how the structure of ILS management will help us achieve our objectives. For consistency the example is an aircraft; the principles remain the same for any major product.

ILS Management Structure

Integrated logistic support management is divided into three groups:

- Aircraft support group
- Supplier control group
- Programmes and budgets group

The ILS manager can be responsible to two directorates: to the support director and also to the project director. Although it may look unusual for a manager to be responsible to two different directorates, if we are to accomplish the objectives then the ILS manager needs to be on equal standing with the technical managers on the project.

This is normally a condition of the contract placed upon the manufacturer to ensure that ILS and the support directorate has equal standing alongside the technical areas.

Aircraft Support Group

The aircraft support group's main task is to ensure that progress towards the "total support of the aircraft" is kept in view at all times and that the support disciplines work towards this concept. To this end we undertake various tasks:

- Ensure that the costs of support are reduced and that only the most technically efficient and cost-effective approaches are adopted.
- Review the maintenance policies produced by LSA.
- Monitor the reliability and maintainability targets and help propose ways that we can recover from any shortfalls.
- Carry out lifecycle costing between comparable procedures and policies.
- Introduce ILS procedures into aircrew synthetic training aids (ASTA) and groundcrew training aids.
- Ensure that interfaces are established between disciplines using ADP systems.
- Act as interface for queries, particularly from the customer but also from any section in the company involved in the support process.

Supplier Control Group

The supplier control group acts as the ILS/LSA interface with the suppliers of aircraft equipments and, in due course, the suppliers of test equipment for these equipments. Its duties include:

- Control of vendor assessments relative to ILS.
- Control of vendor supplied support information.
- Production of line item networks against each equipment vendor – their primary objective is to identify items of equipment that will become phased support candidates.
- Planning and controlling the introduction into service of Phased Support Items.

Programmes and Budgets Group

Finally, we have the programmes and budgets group. They plan, monitor and report progress on ILS matters both to management and, on behalf of the management, to the customer. They also issue the work directives to the ILS disciplines and manage the ILS budgets. To achieve this they are split into three areas:

- Programming and reporting
- Budgets and directives
- Meeting and briefings

Let us look at how the work packages for the integrated logistic support disciplines are issued and how they link in with the programmes that are used to monitor the overall ILS progress.

SOW and Work Packages

Initially, a "statement of work" (SOW) is issued from the customer detailing work packages that need to be undertaken for the project to be completed. The SOW consists of various work packages, all required to ensure that the required tasks are fully completed, on time. These packages are then discussed with the relevant disciplines and their contents and time scales agreed. Finally, the work package is issued as a formal directive.

As tasks are completed and the project progresses there will be a need to update the directives and issue new ones as targets and requirements change. Once the directives have been issued we need to monitor their progress and ensure that they are completed by the required dates.

Integrating the Support Elements

We have outlined the main objectives and some of the shortfalls of previous projects. We have also shown you an organisation that can be set up to implement ILS and manage the support activities. Now we will discuss the system that will integrate, discipline and structure support planning activities. This system is called: logistic support analysis.

The aim of this part is to give you a working level view of logistic support analysis. It will not be an explanation on how each discipline should carry out logistic support analysis in a particular area or a guide on which computer systems you may need to employ. It will be an overview of how LSA works; how the information is generated, what happens to it once it has been compiled and how each of the disciplines fits into the process.

Logistic Support Analysis

Logistic support analysis is used to:

● add discipline to the ILS task;
● integrate the support disciplines, and
● provide a structured process to achieve optimum upportability.

```
┌─────────────────────────────────────────────┐
│                                               │
│        LOGISTIC SUPPORT ANALYSIS              │
│                                               │
│     is the means of achieving the objectives of │
│                                               │
│      INTEGRATED LOGISTIC SUPPORT              │
│                                               │
└─────────────────────────────────────────────┘
```

Systems Breakdown Structure

So, what do we carry out analysis upon. Let us look at for example the aircraft system breakdown structure. The aircraft is divided into systems. These are divided again into sub-systems, sub-sub-systems and then, through the LRIs (line replaceable items), down to module level. If you imagine a matrix over the whole aircraft then every item on the aircraft will be identifiable.

Candidate Item Identification

For any part of this breakdown structure to become a candidate for the LSA process it must be classified as either a maintenance significant item or a functionally significant item. That is, it must be potentially repairable or that it causes a maintenance task to be carried out: an inspection, a removal or replacement, a functional test, etc. We have identified candidates for LSA but how do we keep track of each them?

Logistic Control Number

We can assign each candidate an individual logistic control number (LCN). The LCN is made up of up to 10 digits depending on what level of the system you are looking at. Firstly, a letter identifies the aircraft. The next two digits represent the appropriate system. Following that the sub-system and then the sub-sub-system. The next two digits represent the individual LRIs in the sub-sub-system.

Following that, we identify the modules within that LRI and, finally, the last is the sub-module, which is normally a character.

Logistic Control Number and System Breakdown Code

If we look at a typical system, for example the crew escape and safety system, we can see just how a system breakdown code and numbering conventions work. At the top we have the system, numbered in this example 95. Below that we have the sub-system, designated the "ejection seat and survival kit". As it is the first sub-system in the "crew escape and safety system" it is designated 951. The first sub-sub-system is the "ejection seat" (single seat and twin seat rear) and is therefore numbered 9511. The fourth LRI is identified by its LCN which 951104 and in our example this corresponds to the "parachute".

So, you can see how each LRI has its own individual Logistic Control Number and how that number is generated. Below this level, modules within the LRI would have the same LRI LCN but they would have two further identifying digits. Finally, a sub-module would have the full LCN for the module but it would normally have a character rather than a digit at the end. This system breakdown structure and numbering system gives traceability we can easily identify where an LSA candidate belongs within the aircraft.

So, we have our list of candidates and they have all been numerically identified, but how does this logistic support analysis work? The easiest, and only, way to imagine LSA is to forget whatever you have heard and to think of the most logical way in which you would analyse an item of equipment in order to identify what its support requirements will be.

Support Requirement Identification

First of all we take an item of equipment and tabulate all the basic information that is available for it. This information will come from the items' spec., the information supplied by the manufacturer of the item the use study. The next step is to analyse this information. We need to identify maintenance tasks because it is only through knowing how we will maintain the aircraft that we will know what support requirements will be needed.

To identify a maintenance task for an item we must anticipate how the item will fail. To this end we carry out a failure modes, effects and criticality analysis (FMECA) on the item and predict how it will fail and how critical that failure will be. It cannot be stressed enough how important the role of FMECA is in any support requirement identification process. If we do not know what the potential failure modes of a particular item will be then we cannot identify maintenance tasks.

If the mathematical part of the analysis is incorrect then the reminder of our support analysis, and that of the provisioning activity that is based on "mean time between failures" and "mean time between maintenance actions" will be incorrect. Provisioning is in essence calculating the quantity and type of spares required. The result of an FMECA allows identification of essential maintenance tasks to prevent failures occurring.

Even if no preventative tasks are identified the fact that a failure mode exists means that at some point the item will fail and have to be replaced by a serviceable item. This action is called "corrective maintenance" because its sole task is to restore the system to a serviceable state. Having identified the maintenance tasks that are applicable to the item through analysing the failure modes effects the next logical step we take in identifying support requirements is to group all the tasks identified together so that we can then look at each one in more detail.

Sequential Tasks

We can now take each task and carry out an in-depth analysis on it. Each step of the task is itemised so that a sequential description is documented. Obviously, as we go through this procedure then we may identify the need for support requirements. For example if we are going to change a transfer isolate valve when it fails we would need tools to remove it and these would be identified. If the valve needed to be functioned after it had been fitted then it would not be unreasonable to identify a training requirement if the function involved new test equipment. And so on. So, we now have a list of tasks, described in full sequentially, and a list of proposed support requirements.

In-Depth Analysis

Now the remaining support disciplines can become involved and analyse the support requirement, as applicable to their own areas. For example, support equipment can look at the requirements for tools for work on the removal of the valve and training can analyse the need for new courses to train tradesmen in the use of new test equipment to function the valve. Facilities will look at the requirements for providing the buildings and support to carry out the work. And so on. So, to re-cap:

- We have itemised the maintenance requirements for the equipment under consideration.
- We can highlight potential failure modes. From these we can identify the corrective tasks and the preventive tasks after carrying out the maintenance analysis. We then list the tasks that are applicable to that item together.
- And lastly we can analyse each task in full and identify the support requirements needed. The remaining support disciplines can now carry out their in depth analysis on their own particular areas and in doing so the complete support package for the valve will be generated. Part of this support package will be the level of repair required. Given industry's general inability to effectively manage repair, this area of analysis is particularly important.

Level of Repair Analysis (LORA)

From the end of the support requirement identification, a basic supportability trade-off is carried out that will identify whether it is more economical to repair the item in service or to just discard it when if fails. Should we identify the fact that the item will be discarded when it fails then the LSA process will be stopped here; there is obviously no need to carry out further in depth analysis to identify support requirements when as soon as the item goes unserviceable it is thrown away!

Assuming the item is repairable we can carry out a more in-depth level of repair analysis. If an item is identified as being more economical to repair then, as industry would provide all the support facilities, the LSA process will be stopped here. Normally it would be most unusual to find industry cheaper for a repair option over the lifecycle of an aircraft because the customer has extensive repair and overhaul facilities. But should this be the case then the most economical support option will be implemented.

LORA determines the most cost effective maintenance policy for each item in the system over the whole lifecycle of the aircraft. Each combination of support options is examined for each item, both as an individual and as part of the overall system. In the absence of any overriding customer policy constraints the option showing the least lifecycle costs is chosen.

Undesirable Features

At times such as this we can provide the justification through LSA to the design engineers that an alternative approach on their behalf is needed. If we can highlight the undesirable areas and point out the savings that can be made if we alter them, we have the ability to influence the design process. This is a main objective in integrated logistic support.

Early Design Influence

The need for early design influence by support is therefore clear. The major support decisions are made as the item is designed due to the inherent designing-in of support requirements. In doing so they are committing the majority of our costs at an early stage. Unfortunately, although these costs are committed at an early stage they are not actually paid out until the items go into service and it is at this time everybody starts complaining about the costs of support. That is why we must influence design to reflect our supportability requirements.

Whether the design has been changed or we have come up with an alternative approach or data is updated we shall have to re-enter the data and re-analyse our analysis. At least with an LSA system we are able to change our minds and view the consequences over the whole of the support disciplines quickly and with a relative amount of ease. This process of refining data, known as iteration (a good LSA buzzword!) enables us to achieve the optimum support solution.

Logistic Support Analysis

To recap on the objectives of LSA.

- We can add discipline to the requirements of the integrated logistic support tasks by providing a process that is common to all disciplines.

- We can integrate the support disciplines.
- We can produce a structured process using the analysis steps that will ensure that all decisions are recorded and that an audit path exists for each decision.

This has been a very basic and broad overview of the LSA process. Large areas of information have been discussed in a very short period and much of this has been stated in a very simplistic manner to ensure that you have had an insight into all the different areas of LSA. LSA is new method of carrying out what has gone on for many years but it is here to make us more efficient and the product we sell more supportable. Integrated logistic support is a structured, co-ordinated and disciplined approach that will:

- harmonise all aspects of support or a product;
- optimise support levels to customer's policies at minimum costs;
- ensure that the product is fully supported to the required level at logistic supply date;
- produce a more reliable and maintainable product;
- ensure that the support costs are a much smaller proportion of the total costs and that recurring costs are as smaller a percentage of initial costs as possible;
- lower the product lifecycle support costs.

The adoption of ILS, working within its structure, and cooperation between the respective functions will lead to greater customer satisfaction.

Logistics Information Systems

It would not be prudent to recommend a specific information system or database primarily because each business entity has its own needs. To effectively manage a concept such as ILS, each business needs to establish its information needs; a method of establishing such needs is to carry out an information strategy planning project.

The purpose of the information strategy planning (ISP) project is to examine the information needs of the business and to develop a plan to ensure that the logistics function is effectively served with information systems that match the business and its needs and provide clear business benefits. It uses a business-driven approaches. It is fundamental that the ISP is driven by the business and this will be achieved by the following approach:

- Development of a partnership between the information technology (IT) function and business management who will direct and steer the process.
- Development of a clear understanding (by the IT community) of the business, its needs and priorities as identified by the businessmen.
- Identification of the business systems and supporting equipment infrastructure required by the business.
- Development of an approved investment plan for the provision of the system identified, together with the respective costs and benefits.

Methodology: Workshops and Questionnaires

It is important to allow everyone within the logistics chain to discuss what they do, how they do it and ideas for improvement. Following the workshop, questionnaires covering objectives and strategies and communication need to be completed by the same group of people. This is the key to prioritisations.

Detailed Analysis of Results

This will involve:

- Identification of all the systems required by the business. This will be achieved by detailed analysis of the results from the workshop and questionnaires using formal systems analysis techniques for structuring information.
- Identification of the coverage of current systems against the business systems required.
- Deficiencies between the business systems required and those already in place will be highlighted and taken forward into detailed plans for the enhancement or replacement of existing systems.
- Equipment infrastructure required to support the findings will be identified and plans developed for its implementation.

It should be noted that the purpose will not be to replace the existing infrastructure and systems across the board. While in some areas this may be necessary, it is envisaged that the plans resultant from the ISP will enhance much of what is already in place.

The foregoing is a brief summery of what is required. We need now to look at the methodology most suitable for the workshop. The purpose of a workshop is to gain a collective understanding of the linkages between the business plan and the business information needs in the area(s) which the workshop is examining. Not surprisingly, these linkages are expressed using the same terminology of business plans and strategy, mission statement, objectives, but it should not be thought that they are redefining these elements.

Mission Statement

The business plan contains a mission statement briefly defining the overall purpose and direction of the organisation. This statement will not be changed as a result of the ISP analysis. A mission statement might be: "To provide the customer with a total quality service and secure continuing and expanding profitable business to year 2000 and beyond". There may be lower-level mission statements to give a particular group of business activities focus. For human logistics the mission statement could be identified as: "To provide a quality pro-active logistics service to enhance and support the programme aims to the customer". However, a local mission statement is optional.

Objectives

The business objectives are defined as the broad long-term results that the organisation wishes to achieve. Topically, objectives relate to the financial, market, customer service, quality, products and services and people aspects of the organisation. They are likely to be represented in the form of a hierarchy. For example, for logistics a key objective is: "To secure a measured improvement in the quality of logistics services provided to the customer". This has supporting objectives: "Comply with the customers' support requirement both in terms of quality and timeliness in the supply of spares." "Work towards a marked improvement in the clearance of repairs". Typically, 10 to 20 key objectives would be identified at each workshop.

Strategies

The strategies will define existing or planned initiatives deploying the organisation's resources, to achieve one or more objectives. Strategies are the "means" by which objectives are achieved.

The more specific the strategy, the more useful it is to the formulation of the IT plans. For example, the strategy "To improve clearance of repairs" is rather vague. The strategy "To improve clearance of repairs by wider product inspection and more selective testing" is stronger, pointing to specific information needs and activities and indicating where IT could provide support.

For example, in relation to the logistics objective above "Expand the content of hands on training through extending the time operatives spend on the actual product", or "Examine the speciality training standards and make adjustments where appropriate".

There should always be at least one strategy supporting an objective and, in many cases, more than one.

Performance Measure

Progress in the achievement of objectives and the implementation of strategies is monitored by performance measures. For example, for the logistics objective above: "Number of Customer Warranty Claims", or "Products delivered against products found faulty on delivery"

It is possible for an objective or strategy to have many performance measures and a performance measure to support many objectives and strategies. It is a characteristic of a mature business strategy plan that a high proportion of objectives and strategies have performance measures. It is envisaged that in the region of 20 performance measures will be identified at each workshop.

Critical Success Factors

A critical success factor is a key area where things "must go right" for the organisation to achieve its objectives and goals and implement its strategies. Examples of typical critical success factors are: "Must clear repairs within one month for all customers". By definition, the number of critical success factors is small. It is envisaged that in the region of ten CSFs will be identified at each workshop. Their main use in the ISP process is to understand the overall priorities of the organisation.

Critical Assumptions

Associated with every business plan are critical assumptions. It is essential that they are made explicit and fully understood. Critical assumptions will usually relate to the organisation's structure, competitor activity, technologies market and economic conditions and legislation. For example, from logistics: "It is highly probable that the customer will move more and more towards incentive contracts to minimise defects found on product delivery".

Business Activities

The high-level activities (functions) performed by the organisation will be identified. The activities will implement the strategies identified, support the operations of the business and generate the information need requirements. It is anticipated that, initially, 50 to 80 activities will be identified.

Example activities associated with logistics are repairs/spares management, employee administration, manpower planning and monitoring, logistics strategy and policy management, recruitment management, employee development, employee relations management, health and welfare management. These can be divided into sub-activities. It is anticipated that 30 to 50 business activities will be documented at each workshop.

Information Needs

Information needs are unstructured statements defining the data required to support the organisation. Information needs relate to a range of strategy planning objects including:

- Objectives
- Strategies
- Critical success factors
- Performance measures
- Business activities

This is why it is so vital to identify these and gain an understanding of how they relate together. Information needs will be categorised by the type of need they satisfy, that is whether they satisfy strategic, planning and analysis, monitoring or transaction requirements. Examples of information needs for the logistics area are:

- "Number of repairs received in any given period".
- "Number of new spares orders received in any given period".

- "Number of vacancies to be filled, broken down by position and skill".

It is anticipated that approximately 100 to 150 information needs will be documented at each workshop.

Issues and Problems

These will include:

- Current systems support for the business strategy.
- Major planning concerns and issues raised by management.
- Areas of business plan which are incomplete or are lacking in detail.
- Conflicts between departments within the business, including incompatible strategies.
- Major areas of uncertainty and risk regarding the business plan.
- Differences in perceived priorities (from the objectives and strategies priority questionnaire).

Each workshop will be run by members of an ISP core team, with a further ISP team member documenting the results. These will be issued to all workshop attendees immediately following completion of the session. The ISP team members will ensure continuity between workshops and more than one workshop may well be needed in order that the results from each workshop are progressively built upon.

End Product

An information system that will meet the needs of the business and not the desires of a salesman!

Logistics and Other Organisational Functions

The principal inter-relationships between logistics and other organisational functions are:

- The relationship between the marketing function (or non-commercial equivalent) and the physical distribution sub-function of logistics.
- The relationship between the manufacturing function and the physical procurement and materials management sub-functions of logistics.

However, for the organisation to be properly served by an effective logistics system then rather similar co-ordination problems have to be solved in both inter-relationships.

Logistics is concerned with activities from throughout the enterprise. These activities interact for purposes which are to the enterprise's benefit. Materials flows affect all parts of an organisation and its relations to other organisations. The major difficulty is that the traditional functional orientation of managers puts organisational activities into departmental boxes – production, marketing, purchasing – which tends to limit an overall appreciation of the management issues which affect the entire organisation. Logistics can only be efficiently and effectively conducted if it is seen by managers as being concerned with the totality of related functions within the organisational systems:

- Production
- Marketing
- Purchasing
- Finance
- Personnel
- Information processing

Also, logistics can only be efficiently and effectively conducted if it is seen by managers as being concerned with the total sub-functions within the logistics system:

- Materials handling
- Transport
- Warehousing
- Inventory control
- Unitisation
- Packaging
- Information processing

The twin objectives of logistics are: to minimise logistics costs and to optimise customer service levels (and ideally to do both simultaneously). These objectives are achieved by trade-offs between these sub-functions and functions so as to minimise total logistics costs and/or optimise total logistics service levels.

To take the first objective, costs may be deliberately incurred in one function or sub-function in order that the performance across several functions or sub-functions may be optimised. To put it more simply, total logistics costs can be minimised by balancing individual logistics costs. For example, the more depots a company owns, the less its transport costs but the more its investment and running costs. Examples of possible trade-offs between elements of logistics sub-funtions are:

- Choice between more sophisticated and expensive packaging against reductions in other handling and warehousing costs.
- Choice between improved efficiency in prediction of demand for inventory against the holdings of inventory levels sufficient to cope with uncertainties of demand.
- Choice between the firm's own road freight transport (own account) against bought-in (hire and reward) road freight transport. (Own account is more expensive per mile travelled but much more flexible so it might reduce overall logistics costs).

Trade-offs between logistics sub-functions are:

- Choice between improved warehousing facilities and reduced materials handling costs and improved flexibility in modal choice.
- Choice between improved cost control procedures in warehousing and reduced difficulties and costs in total logistics planning.
- Choice between improved information processing facilities and reduced costs and improved service levels elsewhere through greater organisational intelligence.

Trade offs between organisational functions are:

- Choice between more selective and distribution cost-conscious marketing initiatives and a rationalised physical distribution effort.
- Choice between improved materials planning and control and rationalised requirement for warehousing space and materials handling.
- Choice between improved order processing facilities and rationalised manufacturing planning procedures.
- Choice between research and development investment in producing products which can easily be distributed and reduced logistics costs.

Trade-offs between the organisation and its sources and customers are:

- Choice between promoting improved materials handling facilities on the part of customers and improved possibilities for unitisation and palliation.
- Willingness of suppliers to make deliveries within a time window convenient for the organisation and reduced costs for delivery.
- Willingness of suppliers to deliver just-in-time and reduced organisational requirements for inventory holding and control.

Total logistics management must to be built around the search for cost and service trade-offs to improve efficiency. There is a clear need for the development of information systems sophisticated enough to support the demands of comprehending the detail of costs trade-offs; cost versus service level trade-offs and trade-offs within varieties of service. Equally as important is having the skilled personnel to conduct logistics management.

Logistics Action Planning

The example of aircraft logistics clearly shows the need for planning. Indeed planning is almost a generic activity throughout the discipline (and this text!). At Figure 23 is an action planning table for "inbound" logistics activities.

Figure 23 Inbound Logistics Planning

Customer Requirements Forecasting	Supplies Forecasting	Purchasing	Suppliers Vendors
Better customer sales/demand forecasts	Improve forecasting methods	More effective buying methods	Improve supplier relations
Quicker information flow	Better computer systems	Better purchasing research	More reliable suppliers
Improve customer informaton data	Use of EPOS (electronic point of sale	Adopt better buying methods/techniques	More competitive suppliers
Develop customer partnering	Quicker flow of information	Apply VFM (value for money) criteria in buying	Set up supplier benchmarking
Clearer specifications	Better market trend and status data	Better qualified buyers	Develop supplier partnering
Better requirements planning	More regular updates of forecasts	Better Logistics management methods	Use TQM (Total Quality Management) suppliers

In many ways the action plan reflects the messages in earlier parts of this text; it should not be viewed as "utopian" since without it effective logistics will be extremely difficult. At Figure 24 is the corresponding action planning table for "outbound" logistics activity.

Figure 24 Outbound Logistics Planning

Stores Management	Distribution to customers	Customer service
Lower stockholding costs	Better distribution service	Match/Exceed customer expectations
Better use of stores space	Quicker distribution service	Improve existing service
Lower stores operating costs	Lower distribution costs	Deliver better service
Better use of capital equipment	Improved distribution planning	Deliver faster service
Higher stores service levels	Right first time	Get everyone's commitmwnt to better service
Agree performance and levels & targets	Minimum of paperwork/ admin. costs	Continuously improve service

Again all of these are essential for an effective logistics service.

Other Examples of Logistics Operating Environments

Symbol Technologies Limited (Wokingham UK) and ICL have assisted the major high street supermarket Waitrose to introduce self-scanning to its stores to enable customer checkout time to be reduced. Called Quick Check, the system began at Waitrose's Abingdon store. It does away with the tedious task of unloading and reloading goods at the checkout and allows shoppers to keep a running tally of their spend as they tour the store.

The system is based around Symbol Technologies' Portable Shopping System (PSS). The hand-held terminal allows customers to scan the bar codes of items they select, totalling their bills as they fill their trolleys. The customer then returns the PSS terminal to a special dispenser, where a bar-coded bill is automatically printed for taking to a dedicated express checkout. Quick Check is also installed in four other stores (Reading, Ruislip, Wokingham and Finchley) and roll-out to a further 16 branches is expected.

Securicor Omega Express has invested £3 million in a project which will radically enhance its existing proof of delivery service, via the implementation of 3,500 hand-held terminals to all its drivers.

The largest company within Securicor Distribution, Omega Express is the UK's leading business-to-business parcels carrier, handling over two million parcels every week. Omega Express' Nextday service operates from a national network of 98 branches, employs 8,500 staff and runs a fleet of 4,000 vehicles.

Central to the customer's decision to use Omega Express to despatch its consignments is the company's reliability, customer service and its ability to provide prompt and precise information regarding the whereabouts of all its consignments. Customers access this information, either through Omega Express' Signline customer service centres or automatically via their own IT systems. Symbol Technologies portable data terminals (PDT3100) and ring scanners (RSI) are speeding up the availability and accuracy of this information.

This Omega Express initiative is in direct response to customer demand. To select the ideal technology, its Keighley branch was chosen to pilot the project. Omega Express' operations begin early in the morning and continue throughout the day and night. During the night, parcels are received from the 3,000 square miles covered by the Keighley branch. Drivers arriving at the branch at 5.00am now use the hand-held PDT3100s which Omega Express call Express Trackers to scan bar codes on parcels loading up for delivery that day. The Express Tracker has a scanning head, a screen and key pad: the data scanned comprises details of the number of parcels, service type and date and time. These are then loaded into the delivery vehicles. Before leaving the branch, the driver downloads the data captured on his handset, which automatically transfers to the main system, confirming departure of consignments from the branch for delivery that day.

At the destination the driver again uses the Express Tracker to scan the bar code. Name of recipient, time and all vital information is captured, plus any special information, which the driver keys in on the integral key pad. On returning to the branch, the driver replaces the Express Tracker in the handset and all data stored during the day downloads, updating the main system.

Parcels in the system move in a "hub and spoke" operation. Having been collected at the branch during the day they are couriered to the main terminal servicing that branch, in this case Leeds, for onward destination. For this function, operators use ring scanners (Symbol Technologies' RSI). The operator slips the compact ring scanner onto the forefinger and scans parcel bar codes by quite literally "pointing" to them. This hands-free scanner is connected to the PDT3100 which the operator wears at the waist. Bar code data is automatically recorded and relayed to the main system, plotting the passage of the parcel through the network.

More information on these two further examples of logistics operating environments is available from Symbol Technologies of Wokingham UK (++44 7000 796265 or fax ++44 7000 329796); Symbol have an impressive array of supply chain solutions. In the next chapter we will look at the "nitty-gritty" of provisioning and inventory control.

CHAPTER 8

Provisioning and Inventory Control

Provisioning

A necessary pre-requisite to deciding upon provisioning and stock replenishment policies, it to codify and classify stock. Some 20 per cent of stock items account for 80 per cent of the value of stock held. Therefore if you strictly control stocks of these items, you are controlling the greater part of stock values. Classification enables these items and the remaining 80 per cent of stock to be easily identified. This is sometimes known as Pareto analysis and is illustrated in Figure 25.

Figure 25 Pareto Analysis

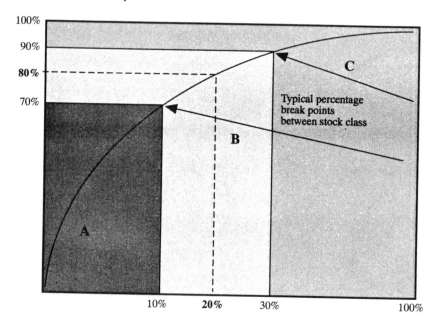

A system of reduction and the standardisation of stock items will reduce the number of individual items carried in stock, and enable stock control to be more effective. First consider what the term provisioning means, so that you have a clear definition in your mind. It is the determination of when to order and how much to order so that stockholding may be kept in line with management policy.

The responsibility for provisioning will fall on different departments, depending on the size of organisation and the class of stock. In small organisations provisioning will be carried out by the storekeeper who will raise requisitions against minimum or re-order levels, any items not stocked being requisitioned by the user's department. As size increases so the responsibility moves to stock control, production control or planning departments, until you find separate provisioning sections in the largest organisations.

It is impossible to generalise where the provisioning function will fall in the overall structure. However, in one class of stock it will certainly be the responsibility of the stock controller, this being those items shown on a general stock list. A general stock list shows those items which will be held in stock for common use and not for specific contracts. Based on a policy of this nature, the responsibility for provisioning must be with the stores manager, through his stock control and provisioning staff.

General Stock Items

The two main points relating to provisioning are when to order and how much to order. The factors affecting the need for stock are shown in Figure 26.

Figure 26 Factors affecting stock needs

Ordering should take place when stocks fall to re-order levels or when an additional forward load has been advised.

There are many links in the stores chain which should be reviewed and assessed in order to develop the full strength of the chain which is shown in Figure 27.

Figure 27 Stores Links in the Chain

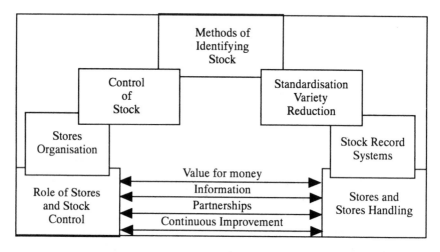

Ordering Quantities

There are five main considerations to remember when arriving at an order quantity and these are the basis of any formulae.

The Accuracy of Forecasts

This will be of prime importance and every effort should be made to check as the period of a forecast passes, to compare actual usage with the estimated usage. Where differences occur some action is required to adjust forecasts in order to increase the accuracy of these. An important point to keep in mind is that as the period of the forecast increases, so does the probability of error, a point which is obvious but often forgotten. Where long-term contracts are placed, close attention must. be given to the rate of call-off as alterations are not always easy to arrange, particularly in the short term. Therefore if the rate is insufficient it may well be two or three months before an increased rate can be obtained, longer if further production equipment is necessary.

Storage Space

It is essential that all items provisioned have suitable storage facilities on receipt, bearing in mind that any overflow may have to be housed by an outside warehouse for which rent will be payable. The main point to bear in mind that any such extra facilities should be known in advance from careful consideration of the intake, and not be discovered when goods are left outside because there is no room in the storehouse.

Cost of Storage

The cost of holding stock can be represented in Figure 28.

Figure 28 Cost of Holding Stock

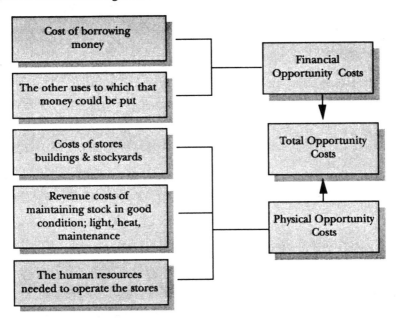

The cost of storage is calculated over a year and averaged to give a nominal value as a percentage of value of each item. It does not necessarily represent the true cost of stocking a particular item.

Cost of Ordering

The cost of ordering is calculated over a year and averaged to give a nominal value of ordering each item; the cost encompasses enquiry, proposal, evaluation and order placement.

Acquisition Cost

The acquisition cost is the cost of storage plus the cost of ordering and if you consider this statement you will appreciate that there is a balance between frequent ordering and high stockholding. The following examples show this and the relevance of the value of the item.

Commodity X

Purchase Price	- 10p each
Rate of Use	- 4 per week
Cost of Storage	- 5 per cent
Cost of Placing Orders	- £1 each

	Ordering every week	*Ordering 1 year's stock*
Purchase price	£20.80	£20.80
Cost of Storage	NIL	£ 3.12
Cost of Ordering	£52.00	£ 1.00
Total	£72.80	£24.92
= Price Each	35p	12p

Commodity Y

Purchase Price-	- £20
Rate of Use-	- 4 per week
Cost of Storage-	- 15 per cent
Cost of Placing Orders	- £1 each

	Ordering every week	*Ordering 1 year's stock*
Purchase price	£4160.00	£4160.00
Cost of Storage	NIL	£624.00
Cost of Ordering	£52.00	£1.00
Total	£4212.00	£4785.00
= Price Each	£20.25	£23.00

These examples demonstrate that the higher the unit purchase price becomes, the lower is the relevance of the ordering cost. They also demonstrate that there is a relationship between the cost of storage and the cost of ordering.

Items Not Contained in the General Stock List

There are still two questions which provide the key: how much to buy and when. Consider these two problems separately.

- What quantity should be bought? This must be governed by the programme laid down for production of the finished items, usually a function of top management. What are the factors affecting this?
- When should the purchase be made? Again this must be governed by the laid down programme, but there is room here for local initiative to decide when to purchase, ensuring that the material arrives by the required date.

Responsibility for Provisioning

In considering items not on the general stock list the responsibility for provisioning cannot rest with the stores manager. The opening paragraphs of this chapter provide some ideas as to where this responsibility may fall.

Methods of Provisioning

The provisioning department, or user if the item required is not a production material, raises a purchase requisition for the requirement. This requisition may take several forms. It will, however contain the following information:

- Code No: where these are used.
- Quantity: in standard unit of issue or accounting.
- Description: where this is not supported by a code number it must contain all the information necessary for purchase. It may be dispensed with when code numbers are in use and the description inserted at a later date.
- Standard price: where these are in use, again this may be inserted at a later date.
- Suggest suppliers: this may be left blank or completed for special items to assist the purchasing department.
- Job or contact number: showing which works order the material is for.
- Date required.
- Delivery address: this will be within the organisation and indicates where the goods should be routed after inspection.
- An authorised signature.

There may be other information required, depending on the needs of a particular organisation.

The completed requisition is then sent to the stores manager so that he or she can check that this item is not held in stores. He or she may also keep a record of recurring items with the object of putting them on general stock or offer an alternative. After this check it is passed to the purchasing department for action.

The provisioning department makes out planning sheets for each assembly or sub-assembly giving details of material requirements. These will show the quantity of an item per unit, which has to be extended for a total requirement. In many instances parts lists are used for this purpose. These provisioning sheets are sent to stock control, who action those items which are held in stores and forward the remaining items to the purchasing department for action. It may well be that you will find a situation where stores provisioning section do not pass on the planning sheets, but forward purchase requisition for action. There is a great disadvantage to this system where one item is used in more than one sub-assembly, as all the requirements will not appear on one sheet.

The provisioning department issues a complete list of parts, or bill of materials, to stores who action this in the same manner as a planning sheet. This gets around the problem of parts appearing in different sub-assemblies.

A computer issues a purchase requisition for those items not on general stock and a stores requisition for items on general stock. This is a very fast operation and has the advantage of being able to present the information in the most useful manner, for example presenting items in part number, supplier or unit order.

An important point to keep in mind is the fact that although the responsibility for provisioning does not rest with stores, all the items may require storage prior to use and therefore all purchase requisition activities may be carried out by this department. There are several classes of goods which will be provisioned direct from the user department to purchasing, stores being advised of their future receipt by a copy of the purchase order. The following are typical:

- Plant and machinery
- Office equipment and furniture
- Special items for the maintenance department
- Vehicles

A great deal of the information on which provisioning is based relies on forecasting. Because of this it is desirable to consider some aspects of the foregoing techniques used. An outline of the main foregoing techniques is given below. However, bear in mind that they are relevant to many aspects of management and not only to stores and inventory control.

Graphs: you will find many examples of graphs used to illustrate situations where there are two variables. It is of course possible to present the historical data graphically and then project the future trend by draughting. This is useful to predict future trends in a general manner but not satisfactory for detail forecast. As an example, the forecasting of next year's financial needs could not be arrived at by this method, but the trend of future capital requirements in the succeeding years could be.

Exponential Smoothing: this is a technique where a weighting factor is incorporated in the average demand. The weighting factor is known as alpha, written with a value between 0 and 1. The basic equation arrived at is:

New Average Demand = D + (1 -) Old Average Demand

D = the actual demand for the most recent period

The use of this equation gives emphasis to the latest actual demand figures.

Forecast Error: extending the principle above the following equation is used:-

New Average Forecast Error = $\dfrac{\text{Current Error} + (1 -)}{\text{Old Average Forecast Error}}$

This forecast error is important when using statistical methods for determining future requirements, because it will influence the setting of minimum stock levels. The higher the forecast error, the higher the minimum stock will be for safety reasons.

Cyclical Provisioning

There is one method of ascertaining when to order which has not yet been covered, namely cyclical provisioning. Where items of a similar nature are in constant use. There is likely to be a constant flow of purchase requisitions resulting, in many instances, in uneconomic purchasing. This can be overcome by provisioning the whole group of items at the same time at regular intervals such as one week, one month, every six months or possibly once a year. The following classes of items, which can often be purchased from one source to advantage, are typical examples of those suitable for this type of exercise:

- Small tools: drills, tool bits, soldering iron bits.
- Fastenings: nuts, bolts, screws and washers.
- Toilet items: soap, towels, toilet paper, disinfectant.

Although provisioning of this nature is performed regularly, there must be protection against stock running out. To do this minimum levels are set and urgent action taken if stocks fall to this level, there must also be a maximum to prevent overstocking.

The Provisioning of Matching Items

Varying the principle of cyclical provisioning, there is one aspect that is often neglected: an appreciation of the need for a mating part, for example, the provisioning of a bolt without a matching nut or washer. Although this is not an easy problem to solve, attention can be given to lessen the likelihood of a stock imbalance, marking stock records to bring matching items to the notice of the provisioning clerk. This will also lessen the danger of an item being deleted from the general stock list without actioning the mating item. There is one danger in this approach that you may recognise, namely that a mating part may be used for several different parts. Going back to the example of a nut and bolt, the nut will almost certainly be used on several bolts of varying length.

Other Examples of Demand

A wholesaler holds stocks of products for retailers. Stock is held to satisfy the wholesaler's customers, the retailers. The demand for the products arises from outside the organisation. Therefore the wholesaler has no control on this independent demand. However, the successful wholesaler forecasts the needs and demands. This is demonstrated at Figure 29.

Figure 29 Solutions to Independent Demand

• Independent Demand

When requirements arise in a way unconnected with the organisational activity

Some solutions

Each item can be viewed singly

Forecast patterns can be studied

EOQ (Economic Order Quality) decisions can be used

Traditional stock control processes

A manufacturing company assembles components into a finished product; stocks are held to meet planned production quantities. These are items held against a dependent demand. The finished stocks offered for sale are however, demand independent. This is demonstrated at Figure 30.

The use of computers can greatly facilitate the provisioning activity, particularly where mathematical formulae are used. This is an operation which is carried out at great speed. A computer also has a good memory and can rapidly assemble and compare data, a useful asset when provisioning mating parts.

Figure 30 Solutions to Dependent Demand

• Dependent Demand
When demand is related to some predicted activity such as production or planned maintenance

---

Some solutions

Stock items are not considered singly

Items are stocked to meet assembly plans and quantities

MRP (Material Resource Planning) a dependent demand inventory control. They are demanded by their application

---

Automatic Replenishment

This is an adaptation of the old "two bin" method of provisioning, when the storekeeper had two bins for an item. When both were full, it represented maximum stock, when one was empty this represented re-order level.

Today under automatic replenishment methods, figures representing these levels are indicated on the stock record, and when the are reached the correct action is automatically set in operation. In practice this would be built into the computer programme, and the computer will print out either a recommendation for action, or a purchase order if it is a routine item; appropriate purchasing information is also programmed.

The Use of Computers

The use of advanced electronic equipment is becoming widespread in many fields. The use of computers is leading, and is particularly prevalent in, the accounting function coupled with management statistics. Gradually the use of computers is extending into many activities – airline bookings, railway timetables and stock control are typical examples that make use of a special quality possessed by this equipment. That special quality is memory, from which the machine can draw information and make decisions. Any decisions made will only be as accurate as the information and instructions given to the machine but they will maintain this accuracy when repeated. Remember, a computer can make decisions!

Information is an integral element of business management in general and the logistics process in particular. Systems support all key processes: finance, marketing, production, planning, design and all support services. Depending on the size and capacity of systems the links and outputs vary widely. Within logistics and supply chain management there is a vast range of systems available to operational and strategic managers. In a recent supply chain software survey the key findings for logistics users were:

- Over the next two to three years, users anticipate strong growth in the use of technology to manage the supply chain.
- The highest growth areas are forecasting software and warehouse management systems.
- The total integration of the supply chain processes and EDI are the two key issues face by supply chain managers looking to maximise effectiveness through new technology.

"As companies are becoming more and more reliant on new technology to improve efficiency and maintain a competitive edge, so the focus on integration becomes increasingly important in the race to deliver a 'seamless' supply chain." (LinkIT – Supply Chain Software, 1997). Further developments within the integration process are also being driven by worldwide Electronic Commerce systems and the internet and its many derivatives.

The CIPS and the Institute of Logistics are actively involved in reviewing and reporting on the latest systems for practitioners. Other associations with key interests in computer applicatons are the Computing Services and Software Association (CSSA) and the Electronic Commerce Association (ECA). The major shop-window and workshop forum for the industry has been the annual Softworld NEC exhibition.

Case Studies of Computer Solutions

The Problem: Marston's the Brewers needed a comprehensive warehouse management system for their bottled beers, wines and spirits warehouse in Burton on Trent. In achieving the objectives for the new warehouse, all physical aspects of the operation had to be managed, with decisions made minute by minute, based on what was actually happening on the warehouse floor. The Logistics Business warehouse management system was chosen. The software is configured from core modules and is designed to be adapted to the precise operational requirements of each user. At Marston's a paper-based version of the system manages all aspects of the operation. In designing the solution particular attention was paid to ensuring the system meets current and anticipated future storage and warehouse throughput requirements of the warehouse.

The software operates on a PC Novell network, linked to Marston's host mainframe computer system. Fastest moving items are picked from a forward picking face which is a dynamically managed addition of Radio Data Terminals. The system may also be integrated by the Logistics Business with other logistics operational software. For example, a proof of delivery system or vehicle scheduling and routing software.

The Success: productivity has improved. Operators are directed to put-away and picking locations. The operating disciplines of a computerised warehouse management system have improved stock accuracy and allow a true perpetual inventory to be maintained.

The Problem: Europe's leading manufacturer and distributor of door, window frames and cubicles, Crosby, supplies directly to buildersí merchants and construction sites. Deliveries are large, involving a full trailer travelling two or three days on the road to satisfy orders. An independent review of Crosby's logistics recommended the creation of stockless depots with more flexible delivery capacity. Optrak3, the vehicle scheduling software supplied by The Logistics Business was the choice. Goods are trunked overnight on vehicles with draw bar trailers to the stockless depots. Onward delivery is by smaller vehicles with demountable bodies.

The key to operating with Crosby's stockless depots is planning the scheduling and routing of vehicles with Optrak3. Crosby had a manual pigeon hole system which was too slow and limiting for the new approach. Optrak3 is a state of the art vehicle scheduling package designed for use with Microsoft Windows. The package is easy to use, with modules for both daily operational or strategic planning purposes.

The Success: more efficient load planning has helped to reduce distribution costs. The scheduling process is reduced to a short period each afternoon. Customer service has improved. Optrak automatically takes account of delivery time windows, vehicle access restrictions, vehicle and drivers' hours regulations.

The Problem: Quaker Oats wanted to be able to control and monitor the despatch of haulier loads and receipt of supplier deliveries at one of their major production sites in London. They needed a system to book time slots on vehicle docks for deliveries and finished good collections. The system was also required to provide information on supplier and haulier conformance. The Logistics Business were able to supply Dock Manager, their yard management software to meet these requirements. This is a networked PC-based package which provides booking clerk, dock management and gate functions. It can give a real-time overview of what vehicles are on-site and on-dock as well as providing key management information.

The system was initially installed to handle the haulier loads only. It allows the cheapest haulier for a given route to be selected from a database containing standard rates, contact names and telephone numbers. A booking time can then be agreed and reserved on a dock. A terminal in the dock office is used to book the vehicles on and off the dock and to record the number and type of pallets received and despatched. As the security gates were not initially available Quaker made use of a parameter which allows vehicles to be booked directly onto the docks. Once the gate was operational changing the parameter allowed vehicles to be booked on and off-site as well as on and off the dock.

The Success: vehicle movements on site are efficiently managed, avoiding congestion. Haulier-billing is now just a matter of printing the appropriate report. Detailed reports on the performance of hauliers can be produced allowing poor performing hauliers to be identified. Vehicle turn-around times are monitored.

More information about The Logistics Business Systems and Software can be obtained through the company's Birmingham UK Office (++44 121 333 6303 or fax ++44 121 333 6407).

The Objectives of an Inventory Control System

Whatever decisions have been made on stockholding it is essential that there is enough capital to back up policy. Because this capital will be tied up in stores, management will want this money to provide the maximum return or use. Consider the following points which can affect efficiency.

Efficient Control by Stores

- There is no need to stock large quantities of goods which are available at short notice. It may be possible to avoid any stockholding if stocks are under review constantly.
- Stores can ensure that any supplies received are directed to the location required and not routed for use on another project. You should note, however, that stores cannot ensure that an item is used for a particular job and that stores should forward items as directed by a responsible authority in the user department.
- Any materials which are lost because of their perishable or fragile nature or through theft, represent capital which has been expended to no purpose.
- A close watch on the rate of turnover can ensure that the minimum of working capital is required to finance stockholding.

How Controls are Exercised

- The basis of control is the setting of standards in stock levels, receipts, issues and rates of turnover. These standards are set in relation to a known programme. By regularly reviewing actual performance against the present standards, the success of the laid-down programme can be assessed. The system for setting standards must be flexible to allow for correction after each check.
- Various classes of items should be treated separately showing any variations that indicate that the inventory is out of balance. For example, the value of sheet steel held in sock has increased by 20 per cent, but the value of paint used for finishing it has dropped 10 per cent. This is worth investigation.
- Often, when studying the standards for various classes of goods, it will be found that certain of them account for the bulk of the money held in stock. These should be given special attention to ensure that they have a regular rate of turnover. This does not mean that other classes should be neglected.

There is one important point to be remembered: constant checks should produce some action when a departure from the plan is found. Remember, the ability of the organisation to control such activities can be a measurement of the success of the original budget or plan. For this reason the budget must be flexible.

Why Do Controls Have to Exist?

Stock values have to be ascertained for the purposes of budgetary control, financial accounting and confirmation that items are priced correctly when issued. This is done from stock records or a physical check of stock, more probably from a combination of the two. You must remember that those materials which have not been charged out, but which have been physically issued, should be included in the evaluation. Typical examples are materials which have been sent to a site and free-issue materials sent to suppliers. These are sometimes missed. When a stock valuation has been arrived at for the various classes of stock, possibly covering different storehouses, the inventory control account is checked to see if the balances agree. However, discrepancies arise, even in the best of organisations, for any of the following reasons:

- Goods received notes and issue notes have been incorrectly priced and consequently entered at an incorrect value on stores or accounts records.
- Prices for issues have been made against standard costs.
- Prices for issues have been approximated to the nearest selected monetary unit, for example two decimal places. This often occurs where item are purchased at a price per 100 or 1,000 and the price of each unit does not coincide with a unit of money.
- Through an incorrect posting on a stock record (which will cause two errors), for example, through a posting not being entered on any stock record or through incorrect reading of code numbers.
- When variations found during stock checks are not entered on records.
- Incorrect arithmetic causing the balances to be entered wrongly.
- Errors made during any copying of the reports.

When you consider the above points, discrepancies are bound to occur. If this is so, why bother to check them? You should think about this before going on. When discrepancies occur the inventory control account has to be adjusted. This is done by a stock valuation adjustment entry, and a debit or credit note made to the balance. This entry has, of course, to be verified and agreed by the accounts department who will usually keep a separate subsidiary account for these entries.

Strategic Planning

What the previous sections reinforce is the need for a strategic planning process. This is shown in Figure 31. The key steps in the stores and inventory planning process derived from Figure 31 are shown below.

- The organisation sets up a corporate strategic plan and mission statement.
- The supply chain stores and inventory management element of the corporate plan identify the broad logistics strategy and improvement targets.
- The stores and inventory management management team accepts the challenge of developing and managing the project and process.
- Stores and inventory management strategic management team

Figure 31 Stores and Inventory Management Strategic Planning Process

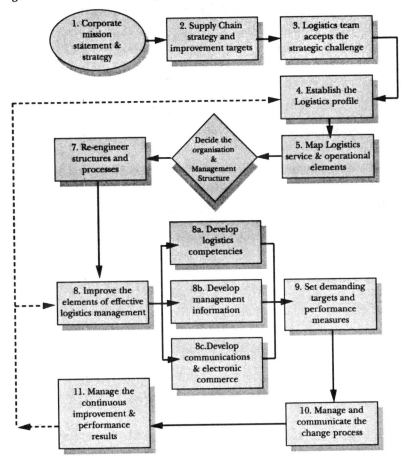

identify the full supply chain base profile and mission statement.

- Mapping process, SWOT analysis, strategic review: Where are we now? Where are we going? How do we get there?
- Start the organisational and structural review and change plan.
- Re-engineer each element of the stores and inventory management map within the supply chain process.
- Identify the best practice gaps, overcome the obstacles, improve the elements of effective stores and inventory management and processes by

identifying best practice standards, develop personal competencies to bridge the gap;

developing and improve on relevant management information; developing state of the art communications within the supply chain.

- Set demanding targets for each mapping element within the total stores and inventory management service profile and plan.
- Manage the project: individual and group element within the team plan.
- Manage the performance outputs and the process of continuous improvement at every level.

Feedback to process 8 and re-work as required.

Feedback to process 4 and re-work as required.

The Physical Aspect of Inventory Control

Since we are considering the physical aspect of inventory control it will be useful to restate the main purpose of this aspect, which is to provide user departments with materials as and when they are required whilst making the most economic use of working capital and minimising storage costs. The first problem to be considered when engaging in inventory control is deciding what items should be stocked. The following are some of the factors affecting this choice:-

- Delivery: rate of usage
- Delivery : uncertainty
- Bulk purchasing
- Bulk manufacturing
- Insurance
- Work in progress
- Finished units

The following are some of the factors influencing the extent of stockholding:

- Operational needs
- Lead times
- Capital
- Cost of storage
- Insurance

There are two means available by which the consequent inventory levels can be maintained.

Regulating Input

Input can be regulated by advice to purchasing who can then contract outside suppliers to increase or decrease supplies. If supplies are obtained through internal sources similar action can be taken by liaison with the production control department. Time is an important aspect of this control for the measures regulating output are seldom instantaneous. This means that control levels must make allowances for changes in input to have effect.

Regulating Issue

This is not an easy exercise to carry out because the main function of stores is to provide a service: issues must be made to the requirements of the users. Regulating input usually takes time to have effect and the same is true of issues, although some regulation of daily issues is desirable. Some control of issue can be made by consultation with production control and any issues against schedules should be reviewed.

Methods of Inventory Control

A stock record database and system is advisable. Typically such as system is shown in Figure 32.

Visual

Here the level of stock is controlled by physically separating stock so that a remainder may be isolated. This can be done by partitioning a bin, tying a quantity of stock with tape or keeping a separate bin. When a storekeeper has to break into this separated stock he or she knows that a new order must be placed.

Visual methods aid the control of stock by quantity and, as you will realise, are limited in use. They can be employed successfully only on items for which demand is regular or for which supplies are available at short notice. With predictable items for which there is regular demand and easy supply, it is possible to carry on without any stock records other than the bin card. This requires periodic checks to ensure that supplies are satisfactory.

Control of Inventory by Quantity

When controlling inventory it is essential that every item receives attention. Records are therefore essential. To run a stores function

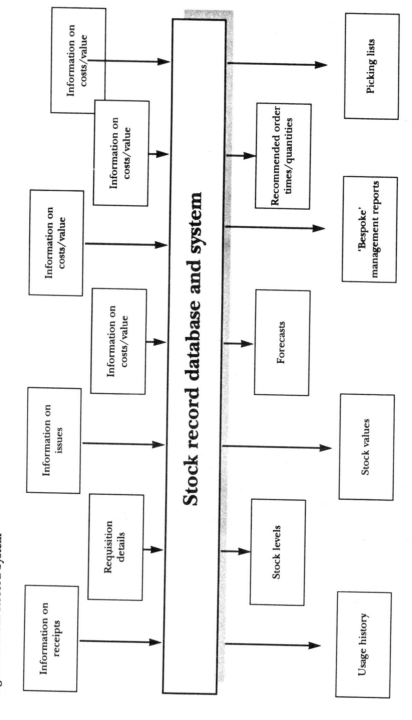

Figure 32 Stock Record System

efficiently detailed information on past history and present policy is necessary. Records provide this information and should give a case history for every item which can be used to forecast future trends. The following factors have a marked effect on quantity control:

The Unit of Issue: this may be in terms of quantity, weight or numbers and is the smallest unit that is issued. Once this unit has been set for each item, all documents must be made out using that unit. The only exception to this may be the purchasing requisition which must be understandable to suppliers. If any alterations are necessary it is up to the individual firm to decide whether they should be done by the purchasing department or before sending the purchase requisition.

Probable Requirements: of necessity this must be an estimate and to be effective needs close liaison with other departments. Future trends have to be adjusted against requirements ascertained from past records.

Lead Times and Availability: as with probable requirements past knowledge must be supplemented by close liaison with the purchasing department.

Quantity Prices and Discounts: savings of this nature must be compared with storage costs to arrive at a true saving.

Cost of Ordering: since the necessary paperwork and labour are expensive the frequency of ordering must be considered, particularly on item of low value.

Rate of Issue: it is necessary to consider what batches or economic loads will have to be made.

High Value Items: attention must be given to items of high value.

Frequency of Deliveries: two factors affect this aspect of supply: the size and nature of the item and the distance the goods have to travel. As you will realise, frequent deliveries over long distances are not very practical and are to be avoided as much as possible.

Seasonal Fluctuations: these occur for several reasons which are related to changes in demand, supply or labour available. These fluctuations occur on a regular basis and cannot always be explained by obvious phenomena such as the Christmas period or the harvesting period for crops. It is necessary to review historical data to keep in touch with these fluctuations.

Stock Allocations: when calculating stock quantities, allowances must be made for any stock allocated for particular uses. Such decisions are reflected in Figure 33.

Figure 33 Comparison of Stockholding Decisions for Various Stock Control Processes

Stockholding Decision	Stock Control Process	
	Order level system (Perpetual)	Order interval system (Periodic)
Order quantity	Fixed	Variable
Re-order level	Fixed	Variable
Re-order interval	Variable	Fixed
Buffer stock	Low	High

Standard Ordering Quantities: you should not confuse this with the unit of issue, although the two may be identical. A standard ordering quantity is one which is set by usual trade conditions. A typical example is the sale of wood screws, bolts and other small items which are sold in multiples of 100 or a gross.

Obsolescence: constant checks must be made to minimise the risk of overstocking items which may become obsolescent.

Control of Inventory by Value

When an inventory policy is formulated, attention must be given to the amount of finance available for use in storing materials. It is vital that the capital allowed for this purpose is not exceeded. The first step is to set a limit against which the main stock account can be compared. This monitors the overall performance. Where the stock value is shown to be excessive, action must be taken to lower the total value, the problem being to know which class of material has caused the error. This can be overcome by splitting the financial limit between the classes of materials and/or storehouses and running separate accounts for each.

It is most important that a commitment record is kept, showing the value of outstanding orders. This can be compared with the average level of issues to forecast future stock values. Action can then be taken to ensure that the financial limit is not exceeded by deferring future deliveries. Accurate value control requires regular information, in detail, of the following: current balance, committed costs, and current rate of issue, all these figures being in monetary terms. Control by value is exercised on groups of items in monetary terms. Any detail required must be obtained from the stock records.

Minimum Stock Level

This level is most important because it indicates the amount of stock which is essential for the continued running of the organisation for the period of the lead time for new supplies. As an insurance it normally will include a margin of safety to allow for extended lead times which may occur due to unforeseen circumstances. For example, it may be the case that the rate of use of an item is 1,000 per month with a lead time of two months. The minimum stock level would be 2,000 plus 750 safety margin, making a total of 2,750. You will realise that the setting of these levels demands careful consideration and will have a marked effect on the smooth running of the organisation.

The Maximum Stock Level

This level is set to limit the quantity held in stock to a figure that is within the financial limits laid down as a policy. Consideration must be given to items which are likely to become obsolete and maximum levels may well be lowered to avoid excessive redundancy.

The Re-Order Level

This level is set at a quantity which normally should bring in further supplies before stock falls below the minimum level. Occasionally the re-order level is incorporated in the minimum level particularly where the items have a steady supply and demand.

There may be a further level set between the re-order and minimum levels known as the hastening level. This indicates that supplies are approaching the minimum and that action should be taken to check that further supplies have been ordered and will be supplied in time. Stock control by quantity then becomes a matter of checking stock records whenever a posting is made, comparing balances with stock levels and taking action accordingly.

Stock Balance at Minimum Level: ensure that further supplies are ordered and progress outstanding quantity.

Stock Balance at Re-Order Level: take action to provide further supplies.

Stock Balance at Hastening Level: ensure that further supplies are ordered and progress outstanding quantity.

Stock Balance at Maximum Level: check for any outstanding orders and advise purchasing to delay deliveries.

To make stock control by quantity effective there must be a regular review of stock levels, adjusting those which are ineffective. This does not mean that levels should not be altered between reviews, should this prove necessary. It is also essential that personnel operating these records are trained adequately and made aware of the importance of accuracy in posting and acting on stock levels when balances are made.

Economic Order (or Batch) Quantity

Purchasing in large quantities can give lower prices but leads to higher levels of inventory. Long production runs spread set-up costs and increase efficiencies. However, they can result in stock levels that are too high. Meanwhile, other finished stocks are unavailable, while they await their turn to be produced. A balance needs to be stuck. Economic order (or batch) quantity theory (EOQ or EBQ) tells us that when total stock holding costs are the same as total stock ordering (or set-up) costs, this balance is achieved.

$$EQD = \sqrt{\frac{2\,F\,D}{H}}$$

where F is fixed ordering or set up cost independent of batch size, D is constant demand rate per period, and H is holding cost per item per period. This theory has shortcomings. It may be difficult to arrive at ordering or set-up costs. The formula assumes linearity. Fortunately, the overall result is not affected too much by errors in arriving at these figures. A 10 per cent error in, say, the set-up costs only changes the EOQ by 5 per cent.

A word about set-up costs. EOQ theory tends to institutionalise these costs. The greater the set-up cost, the greater the economic batch. So we must strive to reduce these costs. Assumptions must be challenged. Methods study techniques simplify and speed up changeovers. Spare change parts can allow cleaning to be carried out within the cycle time. "Just-in-time" thinking looks at all ways to eliminate or reduce these costs.

On a positive note however, EOQ can and does work. For example an engineering company purchased castings in batches of 25. After carrying out EOQ analysis it found that the economic order quantity was 40. The purchasing department, armed with this information, negotiated a better price. The new price was fed back into the EOQ equation and a new EOQ of 48 was indicated. The buyer then renegotiated a second price improvement.

Cost of Inventory Investment

There are three costs involved.

● Cost of carrying inventory.
● Cost of ordering.
● The inventory records show allocated stock. What are the costs of these items?

Cost of Carrying Inventories

These comprise stores operating costs (labour costs, rent, rates, etc), loss of interest on capital, deterioration and obsolescence, insurance and cost of inventory control.

Ordering Costs.

These comprise the cost of placing the order (typing, stationery), progress costs and receipt and inspection costs.

Cost of Running Out of Stock.

This comprises of the cost of production down time, cost of arranging special orders and delivery and the loss of goodwill through lost customers.

Inventory Control and Accounting Methods

Inventory Control Accounts

These accounts are necessary:

- to provide figures for the final accounts;
- to provide the information necessary to run a costing system for materials;
- to provide a means of operating inventory control within the financial limits laid down by the management policy;
- to give detailed figures for the various classes of goods and for different storehouses or stockyards.

The Main Inventory Account

This account should be kept by the finance department and shows the total value of stock currently held, this figure being used, after adjustment, for balance sheet purposes. To maintain this figure all receipts are debited to the account and all issues are credited. You may be confused over the use of the terms debit and credit when talking about receipts and issues in the main stock account. To understand this clearly you must remember that items in stock, although an asset on the balance sheet, are a liability in the stores account. Another point that you should be clear about is the method of entry. Receipts are added to the existing balance and issues are subtracted.

For example:

DATE	RECEIPTS	ISSUES	GOODS RECEIPT OR REQUISITION NO	BALANCE (STOCK IN HAND)
1.1.70	£100		0020	£100
3.1.70	£250		0021	£350
4.1.70		£150	3412	£200
5.1.70		£70	3413	£130
5.1.70	£300		0022	£430

Subsidiary Accounts

The main inventory account gives only a general picture of the financial situation and therefore has to be supported by more detailed accounts kept by the stores organisation. These subsidiary accounts are separated into classifications in the same way as the inventory, giving a means of controlling specific areas of expenditure. An alternative method of control can be obtained by separating the subsidiary accounts according to storehouses. In large concerns this may well be done in addition to classification accounts. There are therefore, three methods of separating subsidiary accounts:

● by classification of inventory, using code numbers where these exist;
● by storehouse, where several are in use;
● by both of the above methods.

Remember that the main inventory account is run separately from the subsidiary accounts, thereby giving a means of checking both, as the stock values shown in subsidiary records should equal the total value in the main account. Why are these checks necessary?

Inventory Records

To support the subsidiary accounts which are kept in monetary terms, detailed records showing physical inventory quantities are necessary. The inventory records provide these details and are kept in three forms.

- Showing quantity only.
- Showing quantity and unit price.
- Showing quantity, unit price and values of all entries, that is receipts, issues and balance.

Which system is used depends entirely on the particular requirements of an organisation and the following points should be considered when deciding.

- The simpler the system the less risk of errors.
- Where a minimum of information is used, reference has to be made to other documents to extend physical balances in monetary terms.
- When prices are shown on the inventory record this can be used as a price list and special attention can be given to expensive items when provisioning.
- Where a full record is made checks can be readily performed on all major transactions, avoiding the necessity of checking entries that represent minor values.

Coding of Accounts

All subsidiary accounts will bear a code number to identify the class of material and user department or storehouse, which enables immediate identification to be made on any particular class or location of expense.

For example:

Material Code	002	=	Steel
Material Code	003	=	Brass
Material Code	004	=	Copper
Storehouse Code	100	=	Storehouse No A
Storehouse Code	101	=	Storehouse No B
Storehouse Code	102	=	Storehouse No C
Account Code	100/002	=	Value of Steel in Storehouse A
Account Code	101/002	=	Value of Steel in Storehouse B

The whole purpose of having detailed accounts is, therefore, to provide information from which control can be exercised and to be able to provide the earliest possible warning of excess expenditure.

The Integration of Accounts and Material Codes

It is possible to combine the account number with material codes. This is particularly useful where computers are used and can print an analysis of a particular class of goods.

Pricing Issues

It is most important for the successful running of an organisation that material costs are accurately computed, for the following reasons:

- To ensure that all material expense is recovered during the course of a period, usually twelve months.
- To ensure that jobs that are costed for the purpose of quotation to customers and do not bear unrealistic material costs that make them either below a reasonable profit margin or, high enough to be uncompetitive, when selling the finished products.

Before considering pricing methods you must be quite clear on one point: the purchase price is the net cost incurred to obtain the material delivered to the required location. Starting with the basic price quoted, adjustments have to be made for the following factors:

Discounts

These are allowances made by suppliers to members of a particular trade, or given because large quantities are ordered. The trade discounts may vary according to quantity. Discounts are usually quoted as a percentage which has to be deducted from the price list.

Transport

Where the cost of transport is not included in the supplier's price it must be added on to the supplier's met price; this may have to include movement within the organisation.

Packaging

Care must be taken to ensure that where a supplier's price does not include packaging, an addition to the price must be made. No allowance need be made for returnable packaging, unless the full cost is not refunded, but accurate records and quick return of packaging is essential.

Insurance

Where "ex works" prices are quoted and goods are insured in transit at a separate charge, an addition to the basic price must be made.

Duties and Taxes

When duties or taxes are payable on goods, these must be included in the total purchase price. Particular care must be taken on import duties and other levels which may be refundable under certain conditions.

Methods and Pricing Issues

Cost Price

Issues are made using the actual purchase price, in one of two ways:

- First-in-first-out, referred to as FIFO. As the name implies each consignment is priced out at the purchase price of that quantity, the price changing when issues are made from a batch having a different purchase price.
- Last-in-first-out, referred to as LIFO. This works in the same way as FIFO but uses the purchase price of the latest consignment as a base. It is rather awkward to work and is very seldom used.

The advantages are as follows:

- Very simple to operate as no calculations are necessary, with the exception of balance totals.
- Balances are related to fact therefore no difficulty will be found in reconciliation of accounts.
- It is very simple to find the total value of goods in stock, by the addition of balances.

The disadvantages are as follows:

- Where prices change frequently, it requires a great deal of clerical effort to keep stock records and price issues.
- The comparison of job costing is difficult when prices vary on different issues.

- When prices rise or fall there is an equal over-valuation or under-validation of stock. This may be particularly undesirable when stocks are over-valued as it becomes necessary to "write off" the excess value.

Standard Price

Issues are made at a fixed price irrespective of actual purchase price or quantity. This standard price is determined by analysis of market prices, future requirements and must be set for a specific period, usually six or twelve months. When consignments are received the difference between the purchase price and standard price is credited or debited to a "variance account". The balance of this account at the end of the financial period is reflected in the profit and loss account as an overhead.

The advantages are as follows :

- This is an easy method for pricing issues.
- The possibility of error due to changing prices is reduced.
- Issues and receipts are priced at a constant rate and it is not necessary to extend financial balances. When such a balance is required it can be readily obtained my multiplying the physical balance by the standard cost.
- There is less clerical effort in posting entries on stock records.
- Job comparison, in terms of material use and manufacturing efficiency, is easier.

The disadvantages are as follows:

- When material prices rise or fall there is an equivalent under or over-validation of stocks.
- Unless the standard price is set with a close degree of accuracy, there will be a danger of losing the profit necessary for the successful running of the business. It is possible that material costs are being over-recovered, but this may well make the organisation unprofitable due to quotations being uncompetitive.
- Very careful recording must be carried out to ascertain why differences between standard and actual costs occur, so that future standards may become more accurate.

Average Price

An issue price is arrived at by dividing the total purchase price by the total quantity in stock, giving an average price for each item. When a further delivery is received the total purchase price and quantity must be added to the existing stock balance and value (at average cost), and a new average calculated. This exercise must of course be repeated for every new receipt.

The advantages are as follows:

● Each item bears an equal proportion of the total purchase price.
● Pricing issues are easier.
● Easy to operate when machine accounting is used.
● Stock balances when calculated into monetary terms are at cost.
● Large or frequent price changes are levelled out.

The disadvantages are as follows:

● Calculations are necessary after every receipt.
● Goods returned to stores may be difficult to price.
● The difficulty in comparison of job costs due to varying material costs.
● The balancing of accounts becomes more difficult.

Market Price (or Replacement Price)

All issues are charged at the current market price at the time of issue. The advantages are as follows:

● It provides a good basis for quotations to customers, because the material content is priced at current rates.
● Variations in material costs, with the resulting profit or loss, are shown up in the stores accounts rather than the works account.

The disadvantages are as follows:

● A great deal of work is necessary to maintain a record of current prices.
● Stocks are likely to be over or under valued.

Selling Price

Issues are priced out at a rate which includes a profit margin, calculated to recover stores costs. The advantages are as follows:

- Stores units become self-supporting because the stores costs are recovered directly from issues and not through overheads.
- Profits or losses that occur tend to be standard throughout the organisation, and this often results in discrepancies being noticed more frequently. This is very often the case where different divisions of a large organisation are critical of the prices charged on stock transfers.
- The balancing of individual storehouse accounts is made easier.

The disadvantages are as follows:

- Due to profit being included in stock values, the true value of the stock held requires detailed examination of stock records to arrive at the correct figure.
- For balance sheet or tax purposes the cost price is necessary, and this requires calculation.

General Comments

The choice of pricing method is dependent on the nature of the business and the class of material, many organisations using several systems. The following are typical examples of use:

Cost Price

Used for short-run jobs that are typical in jobbing shops. Commonly used for pricing main equipment, machines or high-value items and bought-out items which require no processing before despatch to a customer.

Standard Price

Used where there are large-scale issues regularly made as in the mass production industries or large supply organisations such as county council stores or the armed services.

Market Price

Used mainly for raw materials where prices fluctuate, particularly in merchantile organisations dealing in such commodities.

Average Price

This is a variation on cost price and selection of this would be a matter of choice in a particular situation.

Selling Price

Used by supply organisations primarily, to simplify the recovery of stores costs.

When selecting which system to use, one fact must be kept in mind. Inventory values for balance sheet and tax purposes are required to be at cost or market price, whichever is the lower. This requirement is necessary to eliminate any possible inflation of figures, giving an unrealistic appraisal of inventory in the balance sheet.

Price Analysis

This is still the most important value-added function of purchasing specialists. An example from the USA serves to demonstrate the point. The Federal Acquisition Institute and the Air Force Institute of Technology have partnered on a pricing curriculum built around five desk /references: "price analysis", "cost analysis", "government negotiation techniques", "quantitative techniques for contract pricing", and "advance issues in contract pricing". The Federal Acquisition Regulation (FAR) will soon reference these desk/references in lieu of the Armed Services Pricing Manual. However, some interesting questions arise regarding the relevance of these desk/references in the new era of competitive commercial acquisition. The basic question is: why analyse prices in such acquisitions rather than relying on commercial competitive market forces to guarantee a good price?

First, price analysis is performed whenever you compare the price of offer A to the price of offer B. Comparing competitive offers with one another is the first comparison base in price analysis. If price is always a factor in sources selection, then, by definition, price analysis is always performed.

Second, "price analysis" is a function that begins well before receipt of offers. Price analysis begins with the purchase request and the independent government cost estimate therein, in terms of questioning that estimate as a potential base for price comparison. Another step in price analysis in collecting pricing information during market research. Another step is selecting price-related factor forward, also done prior to soliciting. Another step is applying price-related factors to determine evaluated prices for use in the source selection. In short, price analysis is an integral part of the process of soliciting and evaluating offers.

Third, price analysis is a necessary enabler in persuading suppliers to submit better prices. Time and time again, the Armed Forces Comptroller General has defended buyers from charges of "auctioning" for talking price in competitive discussions; on the contrary, the Comptroller General has supported buyers for making an issue for price in competitive discussions even when price was the only subject discussed, and for good reason. There are documented savings of nearly half a billion dollars over a three-year period by negotiating price based on market research. Price analysis is vital to detecting both unrealistic and unreasonable initial offers, and equipping buyers with the facts necessary to convince suppliers that their pricing is deficient.

Fourth, private sector buyers question every price and so should government buyers. A primary reason that industry employs buyers is to negotiate price. Corporate managers regard pricing as one of the most important value-added functions of industry buyers. In fact, many large firms have such little faith in the competition these days that they are largely abandoning "cut throat price" competition in favour of single sourcing and/or limited sourcing with heavy emphasis on cost analysis as the basis for price negotiations.

Fifth, buyers cannot afford to ignore available price comparison information. If buyers have information on historical and current market prices but fail to use that information, will their defence be that : "I received two offers, so I ignored the fact that the offered prices were five times higher (or lower) than the price paid last month"? This is not a hypothetical consideration. The USA government once awarded a contract to a buy-in price millions of dollars below other offered prices. Contract administration was a nightmare. The true cost of the deliverable (including the government's overhead for contract administration) was far higher than the government would have incurred had the buyer rejected the buy-in price as unrealistic. And, to add insult to injury, the contractor, who lost money on the contract, went to the Congress for extraordinary relief, claiming that the contracting officer knew that its price was unrealistically low and therefore should never have awarded at that price. The Congress paid off that contractor. Hence, buyers cannot afford to ignore information in hand which suggests that a price is unrealistic or unreasonable.

Finally, if the assumption is that downsizing has reduced buying staffs to the point that they have no time for price analysis, that we have to be penny wise and pound foolish, then the time has come to challenge downsizing as having passed the point of diminishing returns in terms of the taxpayer's interests.

Inventory in the Final Accounts

It is necessary at least once a year to arrive at a figure, which represents the value of inventory in hand, for entry in the profit and loss account, this figure being subsequently entered in the final balance sheet. The accuracy of inventory valuation is important for the following reasons:

- For taxation purposes the figure is required to be at cost or market price, whichever is the lower.
- Where inventory has appreciated, (that is increased in value) care must be taken when adding a provision to the cost value. In many instances this is considered unwise, due to the possibility that the situation may change and the value fall. In addition, appreciating inventory is in effect claiming profit which will not be obtained until a sale is made.
- Under or over-valuation of inventory does not show the true percentage of working capital that is employed for stockholding purposes.

Calculation of Net Value

Starting with the balance figure shown in the main inventory account the following adjustments are necessary:

Price Adjustment: depending on the method of pricing issues, with the exception of the cost price method, there will be a difference between the inventory stock account figure and the actual cost, this difference being shown in the variance account. If the cost price method is used it is necessary to calculate the difference between the cost or market price. Using the figures obtained above, a decision can be made on what provision should be made for price adjustment. This figure will usually cover the variance that has occurred during the past year and the anticipated variance for the coming year.

In nearly every case this provision will result in a deduction form the inventory account figure, as it is inadvisable to appreciate inventory values. Should the inventory value appreciate, no provision adjustment to the main inventory account figure is necessary.

Obsolescence: this is the period when the future use of an item is limited, but there is still a demand for it. When the item is no longer required it becomes obsolete. A typical example is the spares holding for machinery in present use, which is due to be replaced in one year's time, or the phasing out of certain piece parts. Although every effort must be made to keep the level of inventory down on obsolescent items, until they finally become obsolete, some stocks must be kept to maintain the necessary service to users.

It will be possible to ascertain from the previous years' records the value of obsolete items that occurred, which can be related to the present year's situation, making due allowance for any known changes in requirements. This information can then be used to arrive at a figure, usually expressed as a percentage of the total inventory figure for the year, which can be deducted from the main inventory balance. Obsolescence is not confined to any one class of inventory, but the most difficult to make allowance for is that caused by a design change or production programme amendment and the provision for this requires careful consideration.

Deterioration: this can be considered in the same manner as obsolescence and is dealt with in the same way. "Shelf life" is one of the factors affecting the setting of levels, but however carefully these are controlled some deterioration is often inevitable.

Inventory Appreciation: where value has increased with the passage of time, it may be necessary to add provision to the main inventory account figure, although this must be done with extreme care.

Uninvoiced Goods: where goods have been received and entered on the inventory accounts, but no invoices have been received, those items must be shown in detail in the final accounts. If these goods are not shown as a separate item, the main inventory account figure will show an asset that has not yet been debited to the purchase ledger. The value of inventory for balance sheet purposes, put in a simple form, is the following:

- Main inventory account balance
- Plus or minus price adjustment provision
- Minus obsolescence provision
- Minus deterioration provision

You may well find that the last two are grouped together as one provision for obsolescence and deterioration, known under another name, such as wastage. This provision is often used to cover another aspect of loss that occurs, namely pilfering. This is a point to consider with great care, particularly when any discussion takes place, because it has personal implications. It is, however, a significant factor in some organisations, particularly large retail stores which have to make fairly large provision for it. Remember this question of pilfering is a very sensitive subject and you should choose your words carefully when it arises.

Identification and Coding of Materials

The Importance of Identification

The wide variety of materials and components moving in and around an enterprise is constantly being referred to, for one purpose or another, by one of the following departments:

- Design and development
- Process planning
- Production control
- Material control
- Production
- Stores and inventory control
- Invoice section
- Cost accounting

In some cases other departments may be involved, but it should be fairly clear that if every department uses a different language in describing or identifying and item considerable confusion will occur.

This kind of confusion can lead to a number of inefficiencies in a company and result in financial losses and unnecessarily high costs. It is vital, therefore, that a common means of identifying material supplies is devised and implemented firmly throughout the company. The factors that need to be taken into consideration are shown in Figure 34.

Methods of Identification

We normally refer to or identify most things by a name or description, and in some cases this method is quite satisfactory. Provided that all interested parties use the same name or description, and provided that it is clearly understood how records should be maintained for the items in question, no confusion need arise.

Example: 3" x $^1/_2$" Bolts and Nuts may also be called
3" x $^1/_2$" Nuts and Bolts, or
$^1/_2$" x 3" Bolts and Nuts, or
$^1/_2$" x 3" Nuts and Bolts, or
3" x $^1/_2$" Hex, Rd, Hex. Bolts and Nuts, etc. or
3" x $^1/_2$" Pins and Nuts, etc. or
3" x $^1/_2$" Screws and Nuts, etc.

This is a relatively simple example of differences in terminology, which can result in the same item being referred to by a score of different names, so that several stock cards are in being filed under the different descriptions. This in turn may result in several batches of the same items being ordered or manufactured, so duplicating requirements many times.

Multiply this simple problem by the thousands of items in the inventory and you can see the difficulties which may result from "identification by description". Furthermore, the administrative operations of classification, filing or analysis, are complicated by the many items which, though different in themselves, have very similar descriptions. Another problem is that clerical activities become unnecessarily prolonged where there is a continual need to reproduce long descriptive titles.

Stores/stock location basis

Publication of a classified stock list

Assists buyers and suppliers in using a common code

Accuracy of identification, selection, picking of stock

Stores Coding System

Generic alpha-numeric systems:
Military systems, NATO
Medical systems, NSV
Bar code systems, EAN systems

Better recording, analysis and reporting

Simplicity of common language

Assists standardisation and variety reduction

Links with I.T. systems, bar codes, E.P.O.S and E.D.I processes

Figure 34 Stores Coding Considerations

Only where there are relatively few items involved, where the descriptions are short and cannot be misused or confused, where the point of reference for filing purposes is quite clear, is "identification by description" likely to be satisfactory. In other cases an alternative method must be devised, and the usual approach is to use alphabetical numerical or alpha-numerical coding.

It is clear that some form of coding will be essential in firms where a wide variety of materials is in use. This need would be even greater where sophisticated forms of classification, analysis, or data processing were to be used. Coding could simply involve allocating a number to each item as it arises, but this method makes the identification of items from their codes more and more difficult as the number of items involved increases. This difficulty is reduced by grouping like items together and devise coding system to indicate the groups into which items are classified, as well as identifying the individual items within each group.

The first stage, therefore, in any coding exercise is classification. This involves grouping items into types or classes. It will be necessary to identify and specify each item and then categorise it within the group or sub-group to which it belongs. Having classified all the items into groups, we can devise a coding system which will be much more helpful in readily identifying items from their codes and which will provide a better basis for analysis of information. The complete sequence of operations therefore would be:

- Identify: what the items is, what it does
- Specify: its description, dimensions, tolerances, etc.
- Classify: to its correct group and sub-group
- Code: by allocating group, sub-group and item designations.

Benefits of a Coding System of Identification

Having decided that, in the majority of cases, coding is likely to provide the most effective method of identification, we can study this technique in more detail. In the first place, we should consider the major benefits which may accrue from the use of the technique, so that our subsequent planning of the system will achieve the most advantageous results. The application of a coding system may achieve the following benefits:

- It will identify each item accurately
- It will become a common means of reference by all functions throughout the organisation

- It will obviate the need for the repeated use of descriptive titles
- It will assist in the simplification or rationalisation and subsequent standardisation of materials
- It provides a better means of recording and analysis
- It provides a better means of physically controlling stocks
- It will help to prevent unnecessary duplication of stocks
- It will provide a better basis for instruction and training or personnel throughout the company
- It may be used as a stock location reference.

It therefore, eliminates many of the problems that may occur when "identification by description" is in use.

Methods of Coding

Before deciding which method of coding is to be used, it is important that we consider the main purposes being served and the principal functions that are going to be affected. Frequently, there will be a conflict of interests between the management functions that will use or be affected by the coding system; it is essential that the method we ultimately decide upon gives the greatest overall benefit to the company. The main purposes and the principal functions interested may be:

- Better identification of the physical materials in the factory: this will be of the greatest interest to the stores, inspection and production functions.
- Easier reference for recording and analysis purposes: this will obviously be of concern to the administrative and clerical functions.
- Better means of identifying and classifying for charging the value to jobs: this will be an objective of the accounting functions.
- An aid to all activities of materials management and control: this will be of significant importance to top management.
- An aid to applying mechanical or electronic methods of recording and control: this will be the aim of data processing personnel.

Some systems of coding will be more suitable than others in achieving one or other of the above purposes. We must decide which of the objectives is the most important, in the particular company with which we are concerned. The method of coding must be tailor-made or that company.

When we have decided the main objectives of our coding system and have obtained agreement from all the functions affected, we must then determine the basis on which materials shall classified and coded. Methods available include the following.

Identification by the Nature of the Material: this is the method most commonly used because of its flexibility. Materials are classified into groups and sub-groups by virtue of what they are, for example:

Main Group	Sub Group	Item
Steel	Bar	$1/2$" Rd Mild
Steel	Strip	4" x $1/4$" 18/23 Carbon
Fixings & Fastenings	Bolts & Nuts	3" x $1/2$" Hex Rd Hex
Fixings & Fastenings	Rivets	1" x $1/4$" Pop rivet
Oils & Greases	Lubricant	20/50 Engine oil
Oils & Greases	Coolant	Transformer oil

From the examples above it can be seen that, however wide the variety of materials in use, classification by the nature of the item is flexible enough to cope. This factor is extremely important if we wish ultimately to use a digital significance coding, such as the Brisch system.

Identification by End Use of the Material : this is the method of classification which works back from a finished product and all materials are ultimately coded according to the finished product, of which they form a part, for example:

Model	Main Assembly	Item
Escort	Engine	Cylinder Block
Escort	Engine	Cylinder Head
Escort	Steering	Steering Arm
Escort	Steering	Column
Escort	Transmission	Universal Joint
Escort	Transmission	Drive Shaft

It can be seen from the above examples that this system of classification is less flexible because materials are used on more than one finished product. Provision must also be made for items common to the range of products, such as oil seals, bearings, etc, and a coding system will be required for such "common" items. Consumable items and spares will also require separate coding systems.

There are other bases for the classification of materials which may be used in rather special circumstances, such as:

● Identification by sources of supply
● Identification by customer
● Identification by the location of the item
● Identification by the handling characteristics of the item.

These methods are very limited in their application and are usually inflexible once they have been implemented.

The next consideration in devising our coding system is to determine the whole range of information that the system must be designed to cover, so that every item is individually recognisable from its code number. We may want the code to indicate the following items of information:

● Main group classification
● Sub-group classification
● Item within sub-group
● Sizes or shape of item

- Colour of item
- Chemical composition of item
- Differences in use of item
- Unit of quantity (eg sets, dozens, rolls, gallons)
- Variations from standard
- Accounting significance

Many systems go no further than coding by group and sub-group and then merely allocating a number to each item within each sub-group; but where there are many items within sub-groups, quick identification becomes virtually impossible.

Finally, we must decide whether we are going to use alphabetical, numerical or alpha-numerical coding. Many companies use letters of the alphabet as initial letters for main groups of items but this practice usually results in confusion, as the number of groups increases and initial letters are duplicated for several groups. Furthermore, if it ultimately becomes necessary to mechanise the accounting, recording or control system, it is much more difficult to cater for letters than figures. In general, therefore, it is usually preferable to use numerical coding throughout.

Development of the Coding System

Having decided the main objectives our coding system is required to achieve and having determined the most suitable method of classifying the materials, we must now look at the type of code to apply. First we must consider the main principles to follow in the development of any system of coding.

- The system must be capable of covering all items likely to be used, both at present and in the foreseeable future.
- It must be designed to suit the particular organisation.
- It must allow for expansion without duplication.
- Each item must appear only once in the vocabulary.
- It must be easily understood by all those using it.
- There must be a constant number of symbols or digits in all code references.
- Each group of symbols or digits must signify only one object.
- Descriptions and specifications, upon which coding is based, should be as brief as possible, without affecting accuracy.

Any system of coding should be founded on these fundamental principles, whether it be a system of group coding or a system of digital significance, such as Brisch.

Group Coding

This method is one in which major commodity groups are given specific code references, for instance:

Example 1   01 = Steel
02 = Oils, greases and fluids
03 = Fixings and fastenings
etc.

The sub-group within each major group is then allotted a sub-group code, so that:

Within Group 01 Steel -

01 = Bar
02 = Strip
03 = Sheet
04 = Coil
etc.

Finally, we must code each item within the sub-group. This may be done by allocating numbers, in sequence, as the item arises, or the item number may be designed to indicate the qualities inherent in the item, such as size, quality, etc., by retaining certain series of numbers for certain item classes:

Within Group 01 Steel, and Sub-group 01 Bar

0001 - 0199 reserved for Mild Steel
0200 - 0399 reserved for 05/08
0400 - 0599 reserved for 08/13 Carbon Steel
etc.

Based on this coding system, 05/08 Carbon Steel Bar would have a code number:
between 01/01/0200 and 01/01/0399
depending upon the particular item number allocated to the size and length of the material in question.

If the items number 0273 has been allocated to $^1/_2$" Round in Random lengths then:

01/01/0373 - $^1/_2$" Round 05/08 Carbon Steel Bar, Random length.

Example 2

Similarly, within the next major group "Oils, Greases and Fluids", the following code may arise:

02/01/0071 = 20/50 Lubricating Oil,

because 01 has been allocated to the "Lubricant" sub-group, and within that sub-group 0071 has been allotted to 20/50 Oil.

Example 3

Within our third group, "Fixings and Fastenings", we may get a code number

03/16/1729 - 4 x $\underline{3}$ Hex Rd Hex Bolts & Nuts
16

because within main group 03, Fixings and Fastenings, 16 has been allocated to Bolts and Nuts, and within that sub-group 1729 has been allocated to 4" x 3/16" Hex Rd Hex Bolts and Nuts.

As can be seen from the foregoing examples, group coding has the following advantages:

● It is fairly simple to understand.
● It can be applied fairly quickly.
● It would cost less to implement.

Its major disadvantages, however, are as follows:

● Immediate identification from the code is difficult because the item codes do not represent specific features of the item concerned, they are merely allocated as the item arises.
● Group coding is less flexible than codes using "digital signifi-cance" and is more likely to break down when the varieties of groups, sub-groups and items become too great.
● Group coding is of less assistance in the maintenance of standardisation.

Digital Significance Coding

This type of coding system is used where it is considered important that the description and specification of an item should be clearly represented by digits or symbols making up the code number. Each digit has a particular significance and describes a particular factor of the description or specification. The best known method of digital significance coding is the Brisch system. In this system the code number is made up of a "surname", which broadly classifies the item concerned, and a "christian" name, which provides the detailed description of the item.

Example 1   "*Surname*" -   "*Christian Name*"
                                                    112   0120
which interpreted, means

1st figure - 1 = main classification = raw materials
2nd figure - 1 = secondary classification = steel
3rd figure - 2 = type of steel = bar
4th figure - 0 = specification of steel bar = mild steel
5th figure - 1 = diameter of bar in 1/16ths of an inch = $^3/_4$"
6th figure - 2
7th figure - 0 = lengths of material = random lengths.

Therefore: 112-0120 = $^3/_4$" mild steel bar, random lengths.

Example 2   "*Surname*" -   "*Christian Name*"
                                                    347   4036
which, interpreted, means

1st figure - 3 = main classification = piece parts
2nd figure - 4 = secondary classification = fixings & fastenings
3rd figure - 7 = type of fastening = bolts & nuts
4th figure - 4 = length in inches = 4 inches
5th figure - 0 = diameter in 1/16ths of an inch = 3/16"
6th figure - 3
7th figure - 6 = finish of product = galvanised

The foregoing examples simply indicate the way in which the digits in a Brisch code number may be interpreted to give a description or specification. When designing a coding system of this type it will be necessary first to decide how all items to be included in the system can be divided into ten or less main classifications, so that this factor can be covered by using figures 0 - 9 in the first column.

Then each of the main classification must be divided into ten or less sub-classifications – obviously the sub-classes under a "raw materials" main classification will be different from the sub-classes under a "piece parts" or "consumable materials" main classification. With ten main classifications and ten sub-classes under each, we can get as many as 100 sub-classes.

The third figure of the surname will be used to indicate type of item within each sub-class, and with a possible ten types of item within each of 100 sub-classes we can describe 1,000 types of item by just using the surname.

Should we require to identify more than 1,000 types of material we may need to increase the "surname" to four figures.

The christian name can then be used quite differently for each type of material described by the surname to provide detailed specifications of the item. The figure may be used individually or in pairs to represent some important factor of the description. The major advantages of the Brisch system are:

- Direct identification of any item from its code number.
- Much more flexible for expansion.
- As the code must be directly related to the description, it can be used to maintain a standardised range (code numbers not included in the standard range are not ordered or manufactured) - this advantage brings others, namely reductions in design costs, reductions in storage costs and reductions in tooling costs.
- Assists in location of equivalent or alternative materials, when out of stock.
- Is ideal when mechanising data processing.

The one disadvantage is that it takes a good deal of planning to devise a Brisch system and the personnel who do that planning need to be more than usually skilled in the planning process and knowledgeable about the materials and their descriptions and specifications.

The Stores Vocabulary

When materials have been coded, it is necessary to prepare a code book or manual, showing material descriptions and the codes which will represent these descriptions; this is called a stores vocabulary. The vocabulary has four main purposes.

- It provides the means by which all people, departments or functions are initially notified of the new codes.
- It provides a permanent record, against which additions or amendments to the materials-range are decided.
- It is a ready-reference book for day-to-day working for all departments.
- It provides a sound basis for future training of people concerned with materials.

To be of any permanent use the stores vocabulary must be properly prepared, designed and presented so that the people using it have confidence in its accuracy and validity.

Stages in Preparing a Stores Vocabulary

Earlier we determined that the stages leading to the development of an effective coding system were:

Identity   Specify   Classify   Code

These same stages are inherent in the preparation of a stores vocabulary, but we shall look in more detail at the practical situations in which this work is carried out.

It will be seen from the following that several departments or functions will be involved in the various stages of development and preparation of the vocabulary, which are as follows.

Preparing a Library of Information

As comprehensive a knowledge as possible will be required of all materials, components and supplies in use, or likely to be used in the foreseeable future. This will mean identifying potential material needs and filing each piece of information for use in later stages. The department given the responsibility for this task (usually a vocabulary or standards section, or stock control) can make a major contribution to the ultimate effectiveness of the system, if the collection of the information is done with care, and if the filing of the information is done efficiently. The information may be obtained from design, production, stores, inspection, maintenance, and purchasing departments, from outside suppliers, customers, trade or research associations or from the British Standards Institute.

At this very important stage it will also be necessary to prepare specifications for each item or range of items so that each is filled in an orderly fashion in readiness for subsequent classification and coding. In preparing the specifications it will be helpful if we adhere, as far as practicable, to the following basic rules:

- try to make descriptions or specifications simple, clear and specific;
- develop accurate physical descriptions;
- determine accurate performance requirements;
- determine inspections or tests that must be met for acceptability;
- determine any special marks to be used on materials for identification;
- indicate where specification will meet several alternative needs.

Consideration of Present Coding Systems

In some cases several attempts may have been made in the past to codify individual classes of materials; or supplier or customer codes may have been used. We must understand the nature and purpose of these past systems, and how they were used, so that adequate consideration is given to such requirements in our new classification and coding.

Consultation to Determine Coding System

When all the information has been collected, meetings should be held, at which all interested departments are consulted, to determine the coding system most likely to meet the most important requirements. Another purpose of these meetings will be to programme the work to be done and determine the contribution any department may have to make within the programme.

Preparation of "Originating Sheets"

The next stage is the actual classification and coding exercise. It will have been made very much easier if the first stage has been done well. In fact, if an excellent job has been made of "preparing the library of information", the preparation of originating sheets will virtually be a clerical task, as very few difficulties or queries of classification will arise.

An "originating sheet" is simply a record of all items in a particular classification of material. All the items are recorded in a logical sequence and ultimately a code of recorded against each, to provide to the stores vocabulary. The first originating sheet will show only the main classifications.

ORIGINATING SHEET 1   Main Classification

Material Group	Code
Raw Materials	0
Piece parts	1
Oils, Greases, Fluids	2
Consumable Stores	3
Tools, Jigs, Fixtures	4
Building Materials	5
etc.	

An originating sheet will then be prepared for each of the above material groups. For example:

ORIGINATING SHEET 2   Raw Materials - Code 0

Material Group	Code
Steel	0
Cast Iron	1
Copper	2
Brass	3
White Metal	4
Wood	5
etc.	

This process of preparing originating sheets will be continued in more and more detail as the classifications are broken down further.

In the more detailed originating sheets, where descriptions become more extended, drawings may be used to help in showing specification. For instance:

ORIGINATING SHEET 346

Salt Glazed Drainage pipes - Tees - Code 573-4...

Diameter A	Diameter B	Measurement C	Code No.
10cm	10cm	1 Metre	573-4441
10cm	10cm	2 Metres	573-4442
10cm	15cm	1 Metre	573-4461
10cm	15cm	2 Metres	573-4462

Finalising the Stores Vocabulary

The preparation of the originating sheets is the process of classification, and when the codes are allocated we have a stores vocabu-lary. In some cases, however, it may be necessary to show conversions from old code numbers, in old code number sequence, as an appendix to the new stores vocabulary. In other circumstances it may be only necessary to issue certain parts of the total classification to certain parts of the organisation, with one or two departments getting a complete copy. It is this preparation of the classification and coding, for general use throughout the company, which demands the finalisation of the stores vocabulary in a suitable format and using terminology that is readily understood in the explanatory sections.

Standardisation, Rationalisation and Variety Reduction

In manufacturing, variety on a theme is common – the basic car or van in a variety of colours, trims, equipment, engines, etc. Thus variety and marketing promotions and fashion trends encourage the ever-increasing requirement of stock range expansion. The problem is of course to balance the fulfilment of variety without overloading stores and stock costs.

One of the most effective ways of managing the range of stock in relation to variety availability is to operate a planned variety reduction programme. This should involve several departments and users in addition to stores and stock controllers. A typical group would include: stores staff, production staff, marketing, purchasing, finance. A variety reduction programme will involve a total and regular review of the range of stock within an organisation. The team should analyse its work into various categories. On the basis of such a team in a manufacturing organisation there will be categories such as:

- The range and variety of sales products.
- The range and variety of stock, components and parts to manufacture the sales products.

The process of review should be regular and ongoing if it is to be effective. The programme and the team need to have the direction and executive support of senior management. The review and reduction process is essential to the ongoing production of a viable sales range.

In most organisations and particularly if the organisation has been in existence for some time, a large number of parts, components and materials will be held in stock. A critical examination of these items will reveal that:

- A number of items, carried as different items, may in fact be the same.
- Many items are similar to other items and one may be used in place of two or more different items.
- Some items carried as "company specials" will be found to be similar to items covered by national specifications.

The advantages to be gained from a policy of standardisation and rationalisation, are:

- A reduction in stocks carried.
- Reduced inventory costs
- Costs of carrying stack lowered.
- More effective purchasing and stores procedures as they can concentrate on fewer items.
- Design department can reduce their range of products and adopt a more positive attitude to design.
- Quality control can be more effective.
- Production methods can be simplified and improved.

In order to prepare our store vocabulary it was necessary to prepare a library of information; we now need this information to assist in deciding those items which will become our standard range. We shall also need to examine carefully each item currently carried in stock, and to compare our range of stack items with actual requirements. The next steps are to:

- Identify each item and its purpose or use.
- Eliminate from the stock range those items not essential or duplicated.
- Examine critically those items which have similar features; it may be possible to reduce the list even further.
- Make a list of items and components that are to be carried as a standard stock range.
- Decide size range, standard pack sized, methods of packaging, for the standard stock range.
- Specifications can now be entered against each item in the standard range.
- Arrange for publication of the list of standard items, and its issue to all interested departments (eg design, production, purchasing, stores, costing).

There will always be a need for certain items not in the standard range to be carried. However, these must be strictly controlled and only allowed in particular circumstances. A written procedure for obtaining authority to purchase non-standard items should be issued, as part of the "standards list". Those persons authorised to allow the purchase of non-standard items should be named, so that the responsibility for carrying a non-standard item can be clearly seen.

In a similar manner, a written procedure must be laid down for amendments and changes to be standard list. This will obviously be necessary since lists will need up-dating to cater for new requirements and to delete items no longer required. Again we cannot have just anyone altering standard lists, as this would make a nonsense of the system. The following must be clearly stated.

- Those persons who may request an amendment to the standard range (named by their appointment).
- That all interested departments must be consulted on any proposed amendment and a system for ensuring this must be built into the procedure.
- It must be shown who has the final authority to permit any change in standards.

- That no change may be made in the standard list unless properly authorised.

The standards list when published has the following advantages.

- There is available throughout the enterprise, as a handbook, a record of all standard stock items. This will assist all departments, particularly design, production, stock control, stores and purchasing.
- It is a method of informing everyone of the enterprise's authorised standards.
- It is the means of ensuring that the company's standards policy is carried out.

Specifications

The more widely accepted the specifications we use in adopting our standards, the easier will be our task in obtaining the items concerned. In fact, life is simpler if we can quote a specification, in the confidence that others will know exactly what is required. Consider the problems if there were not national specifications for items such as bolts and nuts; every manufacturer would use a different thread form. It was to avoid such problems that organisations like the British Standards Institute were set up. Among specifications in wide use are :

- British Standards Institute (BSI)
- International Standards Organisation (ISO)
- British Pharmaceutical Commission (BPC)
- American Society for Testing Materials (ASTM)
- American Petroleum Institute

Wherever possible specifications such as those above should be used. The benefits are likely to include:-

- Lower costs, since the items will be manufactured on a large scale for several users.
- Easier availability of components and items, since they are not specially made.
- Avoidance of the need to draw up specifications on each occasion an item is required.

There are instances however where the company must issue its own specification; where, for instance, no specification is available. If a company wishes to ensure that its designs and products are not copied, it may also decide to issue its own specifications. All specifications and drawings must be entered on the standards list against each item.

Inventory Reduction

To illustrate the principle of inventory reduction, if a project involves a cost reduction, not only does this result in an ongoing cost saving but it will also be reflected in the fact that the book value of the components concerned will be reduced when standard costs are next revalued. This means that any of the components being held as stock (including WIP) at the next annual stock check will have a lower asset value, resulting in the value of assets in the company's accounts being reduced. This reduction will be additional to any changes in asset value caused by changes in stock levels.

Although the aim of any cost reduction project is to increase profits, and the ongoing cost savings will do this, the reduction in book value caused by revaluation will appear in the accounts both as a reduction in assets and a corresponding reduction in profits. Although this reduction in book value does not itself represent a change in cash flow, the reduction in reported profits represents a reduction in tax liability which does provide a cash flow gain.

Taking an example of a component which used to have a book value of £100.00 and which has been reduced to £75.00, the effect will be:

	Old Cost	New Costs
Material	£ 40.00	£30.00
Labour and variable cost	£ 20.00	£15.00
Manufacturing overhead	£ 40.00	£30.00
Book value	£100.00	£75.00
Reduction is asset value	£25.00	
Corresponding reduction in reported profit	£25.00	
Saving in tax liability (resulting from reduced reported profit) (£25.00 @ 35 per cent)	£ 8.75	

Stock revaluation results from a change in the standard cost value of components, not from a reduction in stock levels. Thus, for a project which involves a reduction in both the value and quantity of stock, there are four elements to be considered:

- One-off cash flow saving from curtailing the supply process to reduce the quantity of stock.
- One-off reduction in tax liability resulting from having a lower quantity of stock at annual stock check.
- Ongoing cash flow savings resulting from the reduction in cost of manufacture or purchase.
- Reduction in tax liability as a result of stock having a lower book value at annual stock check.

However, if a project involves both a major cost reduction and a major reduction in stock levels, care must be taken in deciding how the reduction in stock levels is to be valued. It is necessary to decide whether the cash flow element (eg material, labour and expenses) in the saving from reducing stock quantities is to be valued on the basis of the old method of manufacture or the new method. Two different situations may exist.

- Little risk is perceived in the introduction of the new process, so stocks are allowed to run down before the new process is fully commissioned. In this case it is the old supply process which is curtailed and savings would be valued using the old costs.
- Where there is risk of uncertainty regarding the new process, it may be decided to have it fully commissioned before starting to run down stock levels. Full production would be achieved to use up stocks. In this case the savings would be valued using the new stocks.

Because the saving comes from curtailing the supply process for both material purchase and manufacture rather than from the sale of the excess stock, the valuation of the cash flow element of inventory reduction must be based on whether it is the old or new process which will be curtailed.

Although this cash flow saving will occur at the time when the supply process is curtailed, such as by avoiding the purchase of raw material, the reduction in asset value in the company accounts may not be reported until the stock level check at the end of the financial year. By this time the inventory may have been revalued on the basis of the new cost of manufacture.

The importance of inventory revaluation will be dependant on the magnitude of both the stock reduction and the cost reduction. The way any evaluation is done will depend on the nature of the project, the timing of the changes and the way the company records changes in inventory levels and book values.

For any project where there is a reduction in inventory levels or a change in the value of inventory is going to be a major factor, it is essential to investigate in detail how the changes will be costed and what effect any changes in the value of assets will have on the company's balance sheet. Any reduction in inventory values in a company's accounts will not only produce a cash flow saving but also a change in asset values which will be reported as a reduction in profits. There is a paradox in that while inventory reduction is always portrayed as an ideal objective, achieving the reduction may appear to have had exactly the opposite result to that originally intended. Because of this, any project involving a planned change in inventory values must take into consideration the effect on the company's management of having to report to shareholders an apparent failure to meet profit forecasts.

Although high inventory levels are always portrayed as being a symptom of inefficiency, there is no such thing as a correct level of inventory. The optimum required level is something which is dependant on many different factors, such as market requirements, manufacturing facilities and product design.

High inventory levels themselves are not a basic problem, only a symptom of other problems. There is a danger that if the real reason why the inventory is there is not understood, the action taken to reduce stock may not be solving the real problem. It is important to start by identifying and changing the basic reasons why inventory is there; only then should stock levels be reduced.

Carrying stock is an integral part of a company's manufacturing operation and stock is there to help iron out problems in both the supply process and the sales function. The supply problems may be due to the length and uncertainty of the process or the inflexibility and unreliability of the ordering and scheduling procedures, while the sales problems can be caused by fluctuations in sales volume and product mix. The combination of these problems can result in the production process being too long and inflexible to satisfy the market requirements for variations in product specification and delivery. Holding stock at various stages in the manufacturing process is used to overcome these problems, and different types of inventory can be there for different reasons. High WIP may be a result of long lead times and uncertainty of supply, such as can be caused by the problems of scheduling work in batch manufacturing environment where there is the possibility of scrap and rework if the manufacturing process is not completely reliable.

It is unrealistic to expect marketing to forecast short-term order input with any accuracy so that manufacturing can plan a uniform throughput. Therefore, to obtain orders, companies may either have to carry finished or semi-finished stocks or change their manufacturing process to provide the flexibility quickly to change output in response to customers' needs. Changing the manufacturing process to reduce the need for stock, such as WIP, will not in itself bring about a change in stock levels; making a permanent change in stock levels requires a change in the way that the stock is ordered in the material control system. While large sophisticated material requirements planning (MRP) packages may contain a number of different sets of ordering rules which can be used simultaneously for different components, some MRP packages may have little flexibility for rule changing.

If the change in manufacturing required to reduce stock levels is such that the ordering rules within an MRP package need to be altered, there is a danger that unless there will be a major saving in inventory value, it may not be worthwhile making the change. For example, inventory reduction is often portrayed as an objective for investing in CNC machining centres because the number of operations can be reduced. However, the introduction of a single machine may only affect a relatively small percentage of components and without a change in ordering rules; all that will happen is that some lead times are reduced and the components put into finished part stores at an earlier date, in effect increasing the value of inventory.

In evaluating the benefits of inventory reduction it is important to identify the way in which the supply process will be curtailed to bring about the stock reduction. In reducing brought-in components and the raw material content of WIP, it is likely that material purchases will be reduced for a short time to use up existing stocks. However, in order to reduce WIP the manufacturing process will be restricted only for a short period of time. As a result, there is a danger that the labour element will not be curtailed because, unlike material purchases, labour cannot easily be turned off and then turned back on again.

It is unlikely that operators' wages will be stopped so that unless specific plans are made which identify how the labour savings are going to be implemented, it is possible that Parkinson's Law will operate, with work expanding to use the labour available. As a result there will be no cash flow saving in labour costs at all. If the planned labour savings does not occur, the forecast cash flow element will be reduced while both the reduction in asset valued and corresponding profit reduction will be increased.

A commonly-suggested method of reducing inventory is to have smaller batch sizes by reducing ordering quantities. This will only be economical if changes can be made which will reduce ordering costs, such as batch set-up times, thereby reducing the cost penalties of smaller batch sizes. However, consideration must also be given to other problems which can arise from an increase in the number of batches.

Review of Recent Concepts

Arising from issues such as sourcing and how to control stock will be less standardised approaches requiring less rigid purchasing methods with more thinking about strategy and less fire fighting. In order to examine the strategy and draw a considered conclusion it is necessary to establish typical views with regard to sourcing policy and examine some recent concepts. Of major concern to managers at the present time is the perceived challenge to the West from Japanese manufacturing industry. Kanban, Just-in-Time, FMS, robotics, CAD/CAM : a whole new vocabulary has been devised to describe differing aspects of the changes that are taking place. It is necessary therefore to focus attention on the implications for the purchasing function of these developments, impact on buyer behaviour, collaboration and the actual effect on industrial sourcing policy in Europe. Looked at from the purchasing viewpoint Just-in-time has the following objectives:

- reductions of raw material stocks;
- improvement of input quality;

- achievement of greater schedule flexibility;
- reduction of bought-in costs through long-term cooperative contracts with suppliers.

These objectives require a number of changes in purchasing practise:

- highly reliable material planning;
- vastly improved supplier quality performance;
- reduced delivery lead times;
- smaller delivery quantities;
- greater increased delivery frequency;
- creation of long-term contracts with suppliers;
- a shift from competitive price reduction to long-term cooperative cost reduction programmes with suppliers;
- an increase in the level of single sourcing.

Criticism of Just-in-time (JIT) has focused in the UK on its reliance on a policy of single sourcing. Such a policy is essential to the implementation of JIT because the technique requires suppliers to make a number of significant changes to their operating procedures. They must, for example, change from a batch to a smooth continuous form of production to match the change in the buyer's demand pattern. They must achieve enormous improvements in quality control and implement major changes in transport operation. Few suppliers are likely to be willing to contemplate making such fundamental and expensive changes without the stability and certainty that long-term, single-sourced contracts provide. Single-sourcing is an essential pre-condition for the successful implementation of JIT. Awareness of this fact has stimulated warnings about the effects of single-sourcing on continuity of supply.

Moreover, the cost benefits of single-sourcing are undeniable. On the face of it, the car industry would appear to have confounded its doubters and critics. Appearances can be deceptive however, and the truth may be different. Companies adopting JIT may well be storing up a uniquely devastating kind of trouble for the future.

The source of this threat is to be found in the combination of JIT's requirement of single-sourcing with its objective of stock-minimisation. Not only does JIT seek to reduce finished goods, work in progress, and bought-in stocks within the organisation itself, it also demands similar reductions from the organisation's suppliers. The effect of failure to achieve this goal has been spelled out by *Fortune* magazine commenting on the experience of American companies that have tried to implement JIT: "... the auto companies are forcing suppliers to eat inventory. In other words, much of the inventory still exists, but instead of being in the manufacturers' warehouses it has been pushed out to the suppliers". A mere shifting of inventory, of course, will largely defeat the goals of Just-In-time. Over the long run, the suppliers will find a way to get manufacturers to pay for it.

With very little, or (ideally) no safety stock in the system, companies using JIT become extraordinarily vulnerable to supply stoppages. Certainly they are much more vulnerable than companies running a single-sourcing policy in conjunction with conventional inventory control policies. The longer the system is in operation, the lower the total stock levels become, the smaller the total number of suppliers, the larger the amount of investment the remaining suppliers are persuaded to make, the more difficult and time-consuming it becomes to re-source, and the more vulnerable to collapse the system becomes. It can be seen that the nearer an organisation approaches the JIT ideal, the more exposed it becomes to the effects of stoppages down its own supply chain.

Why have the Japanese devised and embraced such a potentially unstable system? It cannot be because they are stupid or irrational. As we all know, their success in the field of manufacturing is unrivalled. The mystery deepens if we consider the conventional responses to the kind of high-supply risk situations that JIT creates. In the West, companies typically follow one of two courses of action. Firstly multi-sourcing and secondly vertical integration. Multi-sourcing is clearly not a Japanese favourite and the evidence on vertical integration appears at first sight to be equally unpromising: "Many operations which, in Britain, would be undertaken by enterprise employees, are performed in Japan by sub-contractors outside the factory gates ... Each major Japanese enterprise swims in the economy like a shark with its cloud of pilot fish, surrounded by voluminous sub-contractors ......".

This description looks like the very antithesis of vertical integration in which organisations acquire their suppliers and in this way secure their sources of supply. The truth is more complex. The

Japanese industrial scene is not what it appears to be.

The principal stockholders of Japanese companies are normally other companies. Individuals hold less than 10 per cent of the stock in 97 per cent of the companies listed in the first section of the Tokyo Stock Exchange, which includes the 1005 largest publicly traded companies in Japan. It seems plausible that in many markets these patterns of inter-locking directorships improve the allocation of resources. In some respects companies with inter-locking directorships can mimic the resource allocation decisions of vertically integrated companies.
(Institute of Purchasing & Supply ((1990) *Just in Time: The Purchasing Viewpoint*)

We can now see that although the large Japanese corporations are devotees of subcontracting, they have also developed a method of obtaining the benefits of security and supply certainty that accompany Western-style vertical integration without resorting to outright acquisition of their suppliers. This begins to explain the Japanese enthusiasm for single-sourcing and their willingness to abolish safety stocks. It is perfectly safe and rational to become dependent on a small number of suppliers if you are directly represented on the boards of those companies and have some control over the way they are run.

The second relevant major difference between Japan and the UK is frequently dismissed by JIT supporters as being old news and therefore worn out and of no significance. It is true that we have known for some considerable time that Japanese industrial relations are positively tranquil compared to the UK, but the age of that knowledge does not dilute its relevance. Japanese companies face significantly lower risks of supply stoppages caused by strikes than do their UK competitors. It is also true that the current levels of unemployment have had a pronounced emasculating effect on trade union activity in the UK. However, it is a brave man who predicts that this state of affairs will persist.

Another negative factor of JIT is that, in order to achieve management effectively and a JIT network, the Japanese tend to focus production of similar items in small factory units of under 300 each. This is fine in Japan where two-thirds of the 240,000 manufacturing corporations have fewer than 30 employees and where indeed the culture is far different from UK. The combination of minimal safety stocks and single-sourcing is perfectly rational and desirable for Japanese purchasing techniques; without first creating conditions in the European economies comparable to those in Japan appears foolhardy. Single-sourcing per se is not the problem. The European car industry has already convincingly demonstrated the cost advantages of volume concentration on a small number of suppliers, but single sourcing plus a Just-In-time stock-holding policy looks like a recipe for disaster.

Within the European industry the supply sources of the often highly specialised materials and components needed are not numerous. Aerospace for example is to some extent unusually vulnerable to supply disruption and the costs effects of a fairly narrow field of market competition. However, a sensible policy of dual sourcing together with good order and market intelligence, is an essential part of overall purchasing strategy.

Materials Requirements Planning (MRP)

It is rarely the case that the demand for an item is smooth and at a constant rate. In manufacturing it is more likely that the demand for an item will occur in large increments at varying points in time, a characteristic referred to as "lumpy" demand. In such situations the MRP approach has been developed as a means of managing inventory. The MRP system is for controlling inventories of raw materials, work-in-progress, component parts and sub-assemblies. A further characteristic is that as far as possible production takes place only for actual sales. It has proved to be a very powerful tool in the planning and control of manufacturing industries.

In a "nutshell" you could describe MRP as a system for supplying the number of components required to produce a known quantity of finished assemblies. The three ingredients of an MRP system are the bill of materials (BOM), the inventory status file and the master production schedule. These ingredients are fed into a computer system. The system begins with a production plan and schedule and ends with orders being placed on suppliers and the receipt of those materials.

In comparison to traditional systems, MRP seeks to control inventory by what is occurring or is going to occur, rather than by what has occurred. Thus, the order sizes are linked to needs and the delivery becomes paramount. There may be a tendency to over-emphasise expediting incoming deliveries from suppliers. Of course, any halt to production calls the cost-effectiveness of the system into question with a nasty jolt. On the other hand, production plans have been known to change!

In the context of supplier relationships, it is quite possible for customer and supplier organisations to be computer-linked, giving access to production schedules, which allows suppliers to increase their own effectiveness by being able to plan and schedule their work. MRP pushes organisations into the realisation of a materials management function, whereby the overall responsibility for the control of materials from the point of leaving the supplier, passing through the organisation and finally reaching the customers, resides in the hands of one person. This is often cited as a crucial stage in the progression of an organisation towards realising its full performance potential, particularly in manufacturing industry.

Take, for example, a product which has components, none of which are manufactured, but are all bought from various suppliers. The organisation only assembles the bits to make the produce, and there is also only one product. (In such a situation in real life, a traditional control system would probably prove quite effective).

The first item is the bill of materials, which is a schematic listing of all the components that go into making the product in the sequential order of production, or build. The product is "exploded" or "cascaded" into its various assemblies, sub-assemblies and components at various levels. Some items, such as a nut and bolt, could appear at various levels. If this were the case, it could be allowed to filter through these levels and accumulate at the bottom. It may be a cheap item, but it could well be crucial to production and therefore it might be subject to a separate traditional system of control, such as re-order level.

Suppose the master production schedules calls for 150 product A's to be ready for delivery in week 17. Then an MRP plan can be developed. The plan is constructed by combining the information contained in the master production schedule, the bill of materials, and the inventory status file. This file shows what materials, components, sub-assemblies, etc, are already held in stock together with their lead time.

This simple example indicates the large number of combinations and calculations facing the computer, where a large number of complex products are produced to meet continually changing demand. MRP appears quite complex but to assist you a summary list of the stages is given below plus a flow chart.

- Sales forecast, updated with latest actual sales information.
- Sales forecast, customer orders and production policy used to produce master production schedule (MPS).
- MRP programme computes how many of each component and raw material are needed by "exploding" end product requirement into successively lower levels in the product structure.
- Net requirements calculated utilising inventory status file, ie stocks and current orders deducted to give net requirements.
- Net requirements adjusted by lead times to determined.
- Purchasing place order.
- Goods received.

Reported benefits from MRP include the following:

- Reduction in inventory
- Improved customer service
- Quicker responses to changes in demand
- Greater productivity
- Better machine utilisation
- Reduced set-up times and changeover costs.

MRP is therefore a useful technique in manufacturing industry for overcoming the problems of inventory management for components which are in dependant and lumpy demand.

Manufacturing Resource Planning (MRPII)

MRPII is an extension of MRP. The first stage in the conversion of MRP into MRPII is the development of a "closed loop" MRP system. Closed loop means that the various functions in production planning and control (capacity planning, inventory management and shop floor control) have all been integrated into a single system. This represents an improvement over MRP because it provides a number of additional features:

- Priority planning: "rush" jobs, can be brought forward in time and others put back in time and the necessary adjustments made to material delivery schedules.
- Integration of related functions into the system allows feedback from them, making sure that the production plan is constantly kept up-to-date. In particular capacity planning, inventory management and shop floor control.
- There is feedback from vendors, the production shop, stores, etc when a problem arises in implementing the production plan which enables adjustments to be made to overcome these problems immediately, that is before they become insurmountable.

The tying together of these various functions as a closed loop MRP system represents a considerable improvement over the basic MRP system. However, it is the final step which is the essential one. This converts the closed loop MRP system into a full MRPII system, linking the closed loop MRP system with the financial systems of the organisation.

A closed loop MRP system + financial system = MRPII. The inclusion of the financial systems in the operation of MRPII gives it two invaluable characteristics which represent a significant improvement over closed-loop MRP.

- It is an operational and financial system.
- It can be used for simulations.

MRPII is in fact a company-wide system which is concerned with all aspects of the business and includes purchasing, inventories, production, sales engineering and cash flows. All departments operate with the same data and a common database. This recognises the interaction of all business activities; what happens in one area has direct effects elsewhere and these affects are captured by the system which adjusts throughout each area. In all areas the data is reduced to the common denominator of financial data which provide management with the information it needs to manage the business successfully; for example the values of inventories, work-in-progress, finished goods, etc are known at all times. MRPII is a total management control system.

Another benefit which can be derived from an MRPII system is that it can be used for simulation purposes. This can be done by taking a "cut" or section across the database and posing "what if" questions. For example we may wish to bring forward a production date so we pose the question "What if we work an extra shift?". The system will simulate the consequences for order releases, current order schedules, inventories, work in progress, finished product, labour costs and cost flow. If this is not a viable proposition then an alternative can be tested, and once a solution is found the necessary adjustments can be made throughout the system. The same approach can be used with financial plans, production plant, inventory levels and so on. It is of course vital that the data within the system is completely accurate otherwise the results will not be reliable.

MRPII is obviously a computer-based system and simulations utilising visual display units can be a most helpful aid in planning as the alternative "scenarios" can be tested during management meetings.

The objective of systems such as MRP and MRPII is really quite basic: it is to give greater control and accountability but also to reduce inventories to a minimum and reduce the length of time between identifying and need and fulfilling it to the customer with ultimate aim of improved cash flow and profitability.

CHAPTER 9

Stores Management

Stores Management Objectives

The stores function is concerned with holding appropriate levels of stocks of the required quality and under the correct storage conditions, for use by other departments. To realise these objectives stores management has a number of duties including:

- receiving, storing and issuing stock;
- controlling the movement of stock;
- control of all storage units;
- material handling procedures;
- quality and quantity control;
- staff training;
- clerical administration duties.

The Stores' Function

The stores have a wide range of functions which must be carried out efficiently and logically to ensure the smooth ruining of the department including:

- receiving and maintain the quality of all incoming materials;
- supplying materials to user departments to ensure continuation of production;
- storing, control and issue all items in stock quickly and efficiently;
- issuing any tools or spare parts that may be required by the departments;
- ensuring that all health and safety regulations are followed;

- undertaking training of all stores staff;
- complying with the Control of Substances Hazardous to Health Regulations 1989.

The stores provide a service to the company as a whole and to individual user departments. Obligations to particular departments are as follows.

- *Production department:* to ensure that materials are available as and when needed.

- *Distribution department:* to ensure that all finished products are marshalled ready for dispatch.

- *Sales department:* to ensure that stocks for sale are stored and issued correctly.

- *Accounts department:* to ensure that information on the value of stock, goods received and invoice queries is provided promptly.

In turn, the stores rely on other departments. For example, purchasing department must ensure that all goods required by the organisation are purchased, are of the correct quality and at the right price, for timely delivery to the stores. For any stores management system to function efficiently, considerable time and attention needs to be given to:

- siting of stores;
- construction of buildings;
- stockyards;
- internal layout of stores;
- types of stores;
- storage equipment.

This chapter deals in turn with each of these critical matters.

The Siting of Stores Buildings and Stockyards

We must usually settle for a site that is less then ideal but it should be one which, as far as possible, meets the following requirements:

- Clear, level, well-drained land capable of providing foundations suitable for the building or stockyard required.
- Of a size sufficient to accommodate stores buildings, stockyards, access roads, car and lorry parks and possible future expansion.

- Site convenient for main services, such as drainage, water, electricity and gas.
- Convenient for transport facilities, for example motorways, rail points, airports and docks.
- Away from congested urban areas, where traffic may have difficulties, collecting or delivering.
- Close to user departments or centrally situated to serve a number of units. Planning permission will be required and buildings must conform to local authority specifications.

The site will also have to be within the limits of finance available for purchase, or obtainable on a satisfactory leasing agreement. The purpose of the building of a stockyard must be borne in mind and the following matters taken into account:

- The size, weight and handling characteristics of goods and materials. Nature of the goods is very important since this will determine the structure of buildings and the site. Consider particularly explosives, petroleum spirit, deep-frozen food.
- The location of the user departments and depots to be served from the stores building. Quantities of goods likely to be stored and the rate of turnover.
- Methods of transporting goods to and from the building, such as palletisation, containerisation, etc.
- Loading and unloading facilities required, with special regard to maximum weights to be handled, and maximum size of containers, etc.
- The traffic volume anticipated. This will influence the type of handling equipment for which provision will have to be made.
- Storage methods and equipment that will be required.
- Any security systems that will be needed.
- The number of staff that must be provided for in operating the building.

Construction of the Buildings and Stockyards

When deciding upon the construction of the building and stockyard, certain basic matters require consideration, these are:

Type of Building: Single or Multi-Storey

Single storey buildings are cheaper, a lighter shell is possible, ventilation and lighting are easier, materials handling presents fewer problems. Multi-storey buildings make the best use of a restricted site, and may be necessary when an existing site must be re-developed.

Type of Structure

Steel frame or brick pillars; the type of infill must be decided. Here the load bearing of the framework is the main factor, based on suitable foundations. In a stores it may be necessary to support additional floors, overhead cranes and other equipment. The stacking height and free movement of materials are the factors that affect internal construction.

Load Bearing of Floors

This must be carefully considered, so that it is suitable for the goods to be stocked. Floors will also need to be dust free and non-slip.

Receiving Bags and Loading Docks

These will need to be of correct size, type and height to suit vehicles using the stores.

External Doors and Windows

These will need to meet security requirements. At the same time doors must provide an adequate means of entry and exit, for example power-driven roller doors, with at wicket gate. The larger doors can be raised for vehicles and the wicket gate for personnel. Draught-proof screens of polythene or other plastic strips help to conserve heat. Internal rubber doors provide the same facility and allow movement of fork lift trucks. There must also be doors and screens adequate to prevent the spread of fire. Internal partitions should be of a type that can be easily moved around, to give the greatest flexibility in the use of space.

Heating, Lighting and Ventilation

In a stores building much planning should go into these aspects. Some form of heating will nearly always be required; the problem is to provide a source of heat that is sufficient, economical and does not interfere with the storing of materials. Many buildings use fan-heaters for this purpose. Adequate ventilation must be provided. Air conditioning may well be required so that stock is kept in the best condition. A specialist should be consulted if this is the case. Natural lighting is the best form and should be provided if possible. Roof lights are a convenient method of doing this. Fluorescent lighting is effective and cheaper than tungsten lighting.

Welfare Facilities

It is essential to provide for facilities such as a canteen, first aid post, toilets and garages. Suitable welfare facilities will be required and provision must be made for them.

Stockyards

These provide a means of storing certain classes of materials more cheaply then in an enclosed building. Those materials include such items as bricks, sand, gravel and timber; in fact any materials which do not deteriorate in the open. A firm surface area will be required for vehicles, and handling equipment, such as cranes and fork lift trucks. These areas are usually concrete or tarmac. Stacking areas may be of ash or shale.

Adequate lighting will be required, particularly if work is to be carried out in the hours of darkness. There are several types of tower floodlighting available. Security fencing and goods gates will be required for stockyards.

Internal Layout

Before planning the layout of any store with any degree of certainty, to provide the most satisfactory base for efficient operations we must determine all storage needs very carefully and then decide:

- The best that can be done in terms of grouping stocks.
- What can be provided in the way of a building or site for each group.
- Exactly what type of service the store will provide.
- What kind of supporting facilities a particular stores area will require.

Disjointed planning of stores layouts, where each section does not form part of an overall plan, is likely to result in poor service, inadequate control, costly administration, unnecessary duplication of equipment and facilities and frequent emergency re-arrangements to meet unforeseen circumstances. The factors which will form the basis for our overall planning of storage facilities throughout the company are, therefore, vitally important and must be carefully considered.

- What types of service can we reasonably afford?
- What materials must be handled at each location?
- How will they be constructed?
- What kinds of equipment will be needed at each location?
- What provisions, if any, must be made for overall "work flow" throughout the company?

Detailed Planning of Layouts

Now we should have a clear picture of overall requirements, and we can begin to plan the facilities at each of the designated locations, and then the layout of those facilities to give the greatest possible efficiency. Whilst satisfying the needs of our overall plan for stores, the layout at each location must be dictated by the particular requirements of individual stores areas. These requirements will be influenced by the following characteristics:

- Determination of material needs.
- Receipt and inspection of incoming materials and supplies.
- Storage, safekeeping and issue of materials and supplies.
- Centralised or decentralised storage of materials and supplies.
- Recording and administration of stocks.
- Handling and transportation of materials.
- The need for "work flow" to be considered in the particular location.
- The working space required by each of the functions involved.
- The type of materials involved and the "mix" of materials in the particular location such as raw materials, piece parts, bought-out parts, work in progress, tools and patterns, jigs and fixtures, equipment and spares, general stores, packaging materials and finished products.

The nature of certain materials requires special consideration:

- Those which are valuable or attractive to pilferers.
- Fast-moving or slow-moving.
- Requiring special means of storage (eg liquids) and the type of freight containers used such as those shown at Figure 34.
- Bulky or awkwardly shaped items.
- Dangerous materials.
- Identical components which must be stored in two separate areas for different purposes, such as production supplies and supplies of spares.
- The gangways, corridors or free areas necessary for the "lift" or travel of overhead cranes or the movement of other materials handing equipment.
- Areas for the receipt or dispatch of internal or external transport.
- The need to assist administration and supervision to maintain control efficiently.
- The need for flexibility, so that the facilities can be adjusted to meet changing circumstances.

Types of Stores

It may well be that, in a small company, all stores facilities must be provided in a single building, and if an efficient service is to be provided, all the above factors must be considered when planning the layout of that building. The larger the company one is dealing with, however, the more fragmented the stores facilities become, and the more specialised become the activities of each stores location. Whilst this may simplify the layout of individual stores locations, it demands a more detailed consideration of the function or purpose of each. Some of the more specialised applications which justify individual consideration are:

- Centralised goods receiving
- Centralised storage
- Special storage facilities
- Popularity storage

In considering these we can examine specific needs as far as layout is concerned.

Figure 34 Typical Freight Containers

Bulk Liquids

Half-height Soft Cover

End Opening

Bulk Solids

Centralised Goods Receiving

Firstly, it is essential to recognise that control over the material assets of any organisation is very difficult to achieve or maintain unless it occurs as soon as the material arrives on the premises. If that initial control is lacking these is a considerable danger that materials will be "lost" or misused and their cost may eventually prove an insupportable burden on the company. The first step in the application of this control is to limit the number of points at which materials may be received, if possible restricting receiving points to one. It is necessary to consider the nature of the function being performed, and the activities involved at such a point.

- Receipt of transport of various kinds.
- Unloading and subsequent re-loading of materials of various classes.
- Initial checking of goods for damage in transit.
- Recording and documenting goods received.
- Provision of facilities for the "technical" inspection of those goods requiring it.
- Provisions for goods awaiting distribution to user departments or storehouses.
- Provision for goods awaiting return to suppliers.

The nature of the function being performed will tend to decide the general location and pattern of layout, which will then be varied by certain other factors:

- The need for "work flow".
- The volumes of work being handled.
- The types of materials.
- The nature of certain materials.
- The working areas needed.
- The need for flexibility.

Bearing in mind the importance of goods receiving and recognising its purpose in the overall scheme we can design this department's internal layout to achieve its purpose in the most efficient and economical manner. If the centralised goods receiving department occupies part of a building, the remainder of which is a storehouse, this is a further factor to be considered in our layout.

Centralised Storage

There are four quite different interpretations to the term "central stores", and it is most important that we appreciate the meaning and significance of each before we consider their application or their overall effect on the layout of storage facilities.

Central Stores Only: this type of central stores will exist where only one storage point is justified in a factory, and all supplies are provided from that one point. In addition, probably all other storage activities will be carried out at that one location.

Central Stores Supported by Sub-Stores: where stores facilities are organised in this way, all requirements are controlled and ordered by the central stores where the materials are received and stored. Normally, the sub-stores are located adjacent to the operating departments they are designed to serve, and the stocks held in them are limited to reasonable operating levels. Stocks in the sub-stores are replenished at intervals from the central stores.

Figure 35 Example of Central Stores Organisation

This type of central stores organisation may be used in a large company where there are many departments to be served within the one premises, and where many of the materials used are common to all departments.

Central Stores in Addition to Departmental Stores: when stores are organised in this way the departmental stores operate independently, ordering, receiving and storing those materials which are used only by the department served by that departmental stores. The central stores is responsible only for providing supplies of those items which are common to more than one department. The central stores will order, receive and store common items and departmental stores will replenish their stocks of such items by requisitioning their requirements from central stores. This type of central stores organisation may be used where the factory departments are widely dispersed geographically, and transportation costs only make it worthwhile to centralise those items common to all departments, and which can be bought and stored in bulk. Another justification may be that the work of the various departments is so diversified that it would be unreasonable to bring highly specialised materials into a central point merely for them to be distributed to one department.

Central Stores (Main Distribution Warehouse) and Depots: sometimes the term "central stores" is applied to a main warehouse in which the finished products of a company are held prior to distribution. From such a stores the products may be distributed to sub-stores or depots which are located at strategic geographical points from which the best service can be provided to customers. Such depots may operate with or without the control of the central warehouse, but as with all centralisation a central stores does tend to ensure closer management control over distribution priorities whilst a depot reduces the transportation problem within its own area, in addition to providing quicker service.

Advantages and Disadvantages of Centralised Stores

Both centralisation and decentralisation have their advantages, and there is an unfortunate tendency to rush to obtain the advantages claimed for centralisation without giving any consideration to its disadvantages or the equally strong claims of decentralisation in certain circumstances.

Advantages of Centralised Stores

- Allows closer management control.
- Justifies the use of more advanced control methods and techniques.
- Creates economies in storage space because quantities held in stock can be proportionately smaller. For example five separate stores may need to hold twenty each of a particular item: if centralised it would not necessarily mean that a hundred of the item need be held.
- May justify the use of better storage, handling and transportation facilities.
- Better facilities may be provided for receipt, inspection and testing of materials.

- Stocks will be "turned over" with greater regularity, thus avoiding depreciation or obsolescence.
- Allows for more specialisation by stores personnel.
- Reduces the number of orders placed for the purchase of particular materials thus facilitating quantity buying.

Disadvantages of Centralised Stores

- Involves extra handling and transportation costs.
- Requires a much stronger organisation or inefficiencies may arise.
- Will involve more documentation if it involves distribution through sub-stores.
- Greater dangers of shortages and loss arise if the central store is badly managed.
- Bad management of any kind will have more serious repercussions and be more costly.
- Central stores personnel may be less concerned with local needs in the factory and so deal less efficiently with them.

If one is considering the claims of decentralisation the advantages and disadvantages tend to be the reverse of those for centralisation.

Special Storage Facilities

In listing the factors to be considered in the detailed planning of layouts we mentioned:

- The nature of the functions being performed.
- The need for "work flow".
- The volumes of materials to be handled.
- Greater dangers of shortages and loss arise if the central store is badly managed.
- Bad management of any kind will have more serious repercussions and be more costly.
- Central stores personnel may be less concerned with local needs in the factory and so deal less efficiently with them.

If one is considering the claims of decentralisation the advantages and disadvantages tend to be the reverse of those for centralisation.

Special Storage Facilities

In listing the factors to be considered in the details planning of layouts the following were mentioned:

- The nature of the functions being performed
- The need for "work flow".
- The volumes of materials to be handled.
- The working areas necessary for each function being performed and for the volumes of materials.

These factors are considered again for effective layout in a central goods receiving department. The factor listed earlier which has special relevance when considering the layout of facilities specifically for the storage of supplies was: the nature of the materials. Whether a company or its stores function is large or small, whether or not it justifies central goods receiving and whether it uses a centralised or decentralised stores organisation, there will invariably be some materials which require special consideration as far as storage is concerned. There will be those materials which may be better controlled if held in different storehouses, such as:

- *Raw Materials:*(ferrous or non-ferrous metals, etc, in bars, strips, coils, sheets, etc.)
- *Component Parts:* (piece parts or bought-out parts stored for final use).
- *Engineering Supplies:* (tools, jugs, fixtures patterns, equipment and spares).
- *General Stores:* (consumable materials, small hand tools, protective clothing, packaging, etc).
- *Finished Goods.*

There will also be those materials which may be stored more suitably in stockyards, for example:

- *Raw Materials:* (ingots, billets and slabs of ferrous metals, timber, etc).
- *Solid Fuels:* (coal, coke, etc).
- *Building Materials:* (bricks, sand, gravel, stoneware, etc).

Then there will be those materials which require special consideration either because they are dangerous, or because there must be
special means of dispensing or controlling them:

- *Oils:* fuel oils may need to be stored in containers, above or near
  to the boilers or furnaces using them. Lubricating oils may be
  stored in reservoirs above or below special purpose or automatic
  machinery.
- *Petrol:* this may be stored in underground tanks in or near to a
  company garage or maintenance shop, but in an accessible
  position for all vehicles requiring supplies.
- *Dangerous Goods:* goods such as explosives or highly inflammable
  materials, which may have to be located at safe distances from
  normal working areas, need specially-constructed buildings with
  protective earth mounds or baffle walls.
- *Solid Fuels:* some of these may weather badly or may be subject to
  spontaneous combustion so that protective measures may be
  necessary to avoid physical or chemical changes taking place.
- *Valuable or Attractive Goods:* these are especially prone to pilferage
  and require special protection.
- *"Clean" Goods:* these must be stored in a manner which prevents
  their becoming contaminated with other materials.
- *Specially "Bonded" Materials:* this category covers a wide range of
  materials which must be segregated from other similar materials
  because they are "free issue" materials which are a customer's
  property; approved or tested materials which must be segregated
  from non-approved materials; materials which are subject to a tax
  or duty which has not yet been paid; components designated as
  spares for customers and which must be held separately from
  production supplies.

Finally there are those materials requiring special consideration in
order that they may be made immediately available to user departments to avoid unnecessary handling. This may occur in:-

- *Work-in-Progress Stores:* it may be necessary to provide work-in-
  progress quarantine areas in appropriate locations in the factory
  if it is impossible to maintain a balanced flow of production from
  machine to machine or department to department in the factory.
  It may be inadvisable or impossible to allow the work in progress
  to remain scattered around production departments, but where

it is undesirable to bring large volumes of materials back into stores for short periods of time. These "stores" will provide control and safekeeping of materials and components, but may not be the responsibility of the stores manager. However, they will influence the planning of storage facilities throughout the company.

- *Open Access Stores:* where items of relatively low value are being used on a continuous basis at a rapid rate, and where the handling and control costs are disproportionate to their value we may decide to make them freely available to the user departments from an open access store within that department. Similarly where sets of components have been kitmarshalled for subsequent assembly departments, the sets may be transferred to open access stores ahead of the assembly production programme.

- *Popularity Storage:* the final factor to be considered under the general heading of "nature of the material" is the rate of usage. Some materials are fast moving since they are used quickly and regularly; other materials are slow moving, and whilst their usage may be regular or intermittent they tend to stay in stores for long periods of time.

This "popularity" of certain materials will affect not only the ordering policies or stack levels, but also will need to be considered when planning the layout and location of supplies.

Fast moving materials are less likely to deteriorate, but they should be as near to the issue point as possible to reduce the distance travelled by personnel responsible for issue. Slow moving materials can be stored further from the point of issue but are likely to be more prone to deterioration. These points must be taken into account in stores layout.

Planning Storage Equipment

There are a number of basic principles which should be considered whenever we are planning storage equipment. They are:

- Are we making the most economical use of the space available?
- Are we achieving the greatest overall benefits for the storage costs incurred?

- Are we paying the most economical prices for the most suitable equipment?
- Will the equipment help to provide the most efficient service?
- Will the equipment assist in the handling and controlling of stocks?
- Will it help to provide the right conditions in which to hold stock?
- Will it present any dangers to premises or personnel?
- Will it provide the right degree of security for the stocks?
- Does it give us flexibility in use?

Consideration of the general principles above would enable us to arrive at a general policy for selection of stores equipment but this does not mean that we can then proceed to purchase a standard range of equipment to meet all needs effectively.

A very wide range of storage equipment is already available, and is being continually expanded. In most cases it has been designed to meet the widest range of "standard" needs without necessarily meeting any particular need with complete satisfaction. One danger of such standard equipment is that it appears to be less expensive in the short term, while in the long term it may turn out to be more costly and probably involve some insurmountable space, flexibility or manoeuvrability problems.

This does not mean that all our storage equipment must be special purpose or custom-built; what it does mean, however, is that we must give the fullest consideration to our equipment needs if we are to get the best possible results at the most economic cost. Firstly we must look at the materials that have to be stored, and the locations at which they will be held, to determine the types of equipment necessary, based on factors such as:

- The nature of the material: size, weight, shape.
- The volume to be held.
- The degree of protection required from pilfering, from dirt and from atmospheric conditions.
- The problems of handling the material.
- The needs for physical or administrative control over quantities, flow, etc.
- The nature of the building being used.
- The location of the stocks in relation to their point of use, and the space available.

- The handling methods or facilities available or necessary.
- Whether materials are received, stored and issued in unit quantities.
- Rapidity of turnover of the stocks of individual materials.

Consideration of these factors will outline certain requirements which must be met in selecting the equipment which will satisfy our needs, such as:

- Strength - to support weight.
- Durability - to withstand constant wear.
- Ease of operation - to assist efficiency.
- Flexibility - suitability for a variety of uses.
- Protection provided - against, for example, dirt or misappropriation.
- Adaptability - for different locations.
- Safety - for premises, materials and personnel.
- Manoeuvrability - for swift re-arrangement of storage areas where necessary.
- Cost - giving the greatest value for money spent.
- Dimensions - to fit the space or headroom available, or to contain the volume required.
- Suitability - to the method of handling or type of material held.

Careful consideration of the basic principles of effective storage, together with clear recognition of the practical requirements to be satisfied, will enable us to determine the best methods to adopt, and most suitable equipment to use. Any efforts we exert in this direction will help to provide maximum flexibility, and fullest utilisation, both now and in the future, within the economic and space limitations imposed upon us, avoiding:

- uneconomic use of space;
- unnecessarily high storage costs;
- unnecessarily high costs of equipment;
- inefficiency in providing a service;
- difficulty in controlling stocks;
- detrimental effects on the condition of stocks;
- dangers to premises and personnel;
- lack of security for stocks;
- lack of flexibility in use.

Handling Equipment

Goods Movement Theory

The first thing one must remember about the movement, handling or transportation of materials is that they add to the cost without adding in any way to the value. It is important to bear in mind that basic principle when planning the primary activities involved, so that unnecessary movement is eliminated. Even then we cannot assume that, whatever handling methods we employ, we shall achieve the best results at the lowest cost; we must plan them carefully, considering the following principles.

- Major handling or movement should be restricted as far as possible by siting incoming and outgoing materials correctly prior to any operation, and using the most helpful methods for holding the materials at any point.
- Try to plan the work on a "flow" principle which will involve correct routing of materials; correct movement of personnel involved in the activities; proper designation of working areas and working groups; suitable arrangements being made for obtaining and disposing of containers; proper routing of documentation.

Frequently these factors are determined prior to considering materials handling, and unnecessarily expensive handling methods have to be adopted as a result, whereas if they had been considered with the handling problems in mind, the handling methods could have been much simpler and the whole operation much less expensive.

- Eliminate wasteful methods wherever possible by employing unit loads to reduce handling and perhaps counting individual items; use pallets where frequent movement is involved; use the force of gravity wherever possible to add movement.
- Where mechanised methods of handling are necessary, select the most appropriate equipment, carefully considering what degree of flexibility is required from the equipment purchased. Can some form of standard equipment be used? Does the volume of work involved justify special purpose equipment? Can some conveyor system by employed in place of handling?

- Do we need to provide alternative methods of handling in the event that our first choice equipment breaks down? If so, will the layout adopted allow the alternative methods to operate?
- The methods adopted should be designed in the interests of safety, firstly of personnel, then of property.
- Equipment should be designed and installed for safe and efficient operation, and where operators are required they should be properly trained for the job.
- The environment in which the materials will be handled will affect our choice of certain equipment (see Layout Considerations).
- We must compare the overall benefits of alternative methods with the costs of employing those methods.

Investment Justification

The investment and running costs of different handling methods can easily be computed, and these costs must be set against potential benefits of each of the alternative methods. The potential benefits may include:

- savings in time and labour;
- reductions in damage or breakages;
- increases in output or turnover;
- more efficient use of space;
- reductions in risk to life or property.

The majority of the above benefits can also be quantified in terms of money, and cost comparisons between a number of alternative methods will show the type of handling which will more readily justify investments and give the greatest profit.

Example:

METHOD A	Cost per Annum
Depreciation on equipment	Nil
Labour cost	£6,000
Space cost	£1,000
Potential cost of damage goods	£200
Potential "profit" on turnover in this area before handling costs	£18,000

METHOD B	*Cost per Annum*
Depreciation on equipment	£1,000
Labour cost	£4,000
Space cost	£2,000
Potential cost of damaged goods	£500
Potential "profit" on turnover in this area before handling costs	£19,500

METHOD C	
Depreciation on equipment	£5,000
Labour costs	£2,000
Space costs	£3,000
Potential cost of damaged goods	£700
Potential "profit" on turnover in this area before handling costs	£20,500

Method B is a more profitable one to employ, although it is not so highly mechanised as Method C, nor does it achieve the same level of output or turnover. However, Method B does maximise profit on the operation.

Reduction in overall costs of operations is the same as "profit" in circumstances where "profit" cannot be measured as return in excess of costs on output or sales.

Layout Considerations

Layout, of course, is one of the fundamental principles to be considered in planning materials handling, but it is a factor which deserves more detailed consideration since space utilisation is an inherent problem in all materials movement.

The planning of the layout and the best use of space must be accomplished along with the determination of the best possible handling method, not after equipment has been purchased and has all to be fitted in somehow. The main considerations will be:

● The use of the flow principle as far as possible in the siting of incoming materials, the holding areas for materials, obtaining or disposing of containers, the routing of materials through the process, designation of working areas, correct movement of the people involved, implementation of alternative methods in case of break-down, siting of outgoing materials.

- Maximising the use of the space available in relation to the type of equipment under consideration by the holding or storage of materials at the right levels to assist operations and avoiding the storage of fresh air.
- The provision of adequate room to manoeuvre by the provision of gangways, providing sufficient headroom or clearance for conveyors or overhead handling, access to and from all points for equipment and personnel and the provision of suitable surfaces for floor operating equipment.

It is worth repeating that these factors should be considered *before* methods or equipment are selected, otherwise the best possible choice cannot be made to give flexibility, adaptability and ultimately profitability in the handling of materials.

A recent example of layout flow problems can be found in former Eastern bloc countries although it may not be uncommon in Western nations. Inefficient manufacturing is one problem facing Russia and its former satellite countries, but perhaps an even bigger obstacle to their future prosperity is widespread ignorance of efficient warehousing and distribution methods.

One company which helped to solve this problem is Mieback Logistics, Oxford. Partner Michael Boos and his team designed a new multi-million pound warehouse for a distributor in Moscow which supplies goods to Western embassies in Russia and former Eastern bloc countries, as well as to their embassies in the West. The existing manual warehousing system involved 50 people picking and 25 people keeping records of stock movements. Lead time to locate and pick some items could take up to six months. The Russian distributor needed a reliable warehouse, built on a greenfield site to Western standards, which would double throughput and achieve at least 95 per cent order fulfilments at the outset. They also needed room for expansion.

Another key requirement was for a flexible warehousing system, owing to the enormous diversity of products to be stocked. These ranged from washers and light bulbs to construction materials and 10-tonne steel coils, and included such items as office furniture, safes, carpets and washing machines. Miebach's concept study involved storing the stock items on one-ton single and two-ton double Europallets in a 24 metre high-bay store. Compared with an earlier Russian concept, the floor area used has been reduced to 15,000 square meters, incorporating an additional 2500 square meters for handling, leaving enough space on the site to expand the warehouse by 60 per cent. A typical warehouse design is shown at Figure 36.

Figure 36 Warehouse Design

Robustness and simplicity in operation was a further requirement. Although the system normally runs under computer control, it is designed to be operated manually in the event of computer failure. Every item has been specified primarily for its reliability. For example, manual stacker cranes are used instead of fork lift trucks. The job of any piece of equipment can be taken over by another in case of breakdown.

Types of Handling Equipment

Apart from the normal methods of handling, such as lifting, carrying, pushing, shovelling, etc all of which may be quite adequate in some circumstances there is a wide variety of mechanical methods which fall into four categories: industrial trucks, cranes and hoists, conveyors and pumps, pipeliners and feeder systems.

Industrial Trucks (Manual)

This range of equipment is designed to provide simple mechanical assistance in the operations of lifting, moving or transporting loads which are too heavy to man-handle, or which can be handled more economically in bulk lots. Into this category falls such equipment as:

- Sack trucks
- Platform trucks (manually operated)
- Platform lift trucks (manually operated)
- Drum lifts
- Cylinder trucks
- Pallet trucks (manually operated)
- Carboy tippers
- Lifts or mobile ladders (manually operated)
- Special purpose trucks and trolleys

Industrial Trucks (Power-Driven)

Power-driven trucks have been designed for a wide variety of applications. Basically their purpose is to handle loads which cannot be man-handled even with the assistance of the simple mechanical aids, or to transport loads over longer distances at greater speed. Into this category falls such equipment as:

- The fixed platform power-driven truck
- Power-driven platform lift trucks (such as a 4-directional truck shown at Figure 37)
- Tractors and trailers

As the volume of materials to be handled has increased, the problems of double-handling have demanded new methods of storage which, in turn, have led to the need for new ways of handling. As a result we have the various types of pallet and stillage, and a wide range of fork-lift trucks to handle them. Before dealing with the applications of such trucks we must consider the following factors.

- *Pedestrian or Diver Operated:* this will depend upon the loads to be carried, the space available and the distances to be travelled. A typical example is shown at Figure 38.
- *Petrol, L.P. Gas, Diesel or Electric Driven:* here consider whether for internal or external use, economy of running, economy of maintenance, capital cost, and mechanical reliability and availability.

- *Solid or Cushion Tyres:* this will depend upon the loads to be carried, the nature of the application and the surfaces upon which it is required to operate.

Figure 37: Four-directional truck

Standard or special fork-lift trucks designed to cope with a wide variety of applications are:

- Normal or high lift.
- Reach trucks - with forward movement of the forks as shown in Figure 39.
- Straddle trucks.
- Lifting attachments for special purposes eg Ram - for .
- Coils, clamps - for drums
- Side-loading trucks as shown in Figure 40.

Figure 38: Pedestrian Stackers

Pedestrian Pallet Stacker   Pedestrian Counterbalanced Truck

Another development in the field of power-driven industrial trucks is the automatic or robot system, the main purpose of which has been to reduce the manpower requirements in warehouses or stores, for collecting or distributing large volumes of many items of stock.

The robot trucks are loaded at and controlled from a central point and are directed electrically along pre-wired gangways to the points within the warehouse where the goods are to be unloaded and stored. Similarly, goods from stock can be loaded on the trucks which are automatically directed to a central point for issue, packing for despatch. Such a system is expensive to install and demands extremely careful planning of storage locations for fast and slow moving items and the balance between them; "traffic jams" of robot trucks would cancel out the benefits that the system was installed to obtain.

Figure 39: Reach Truck

Cranes and Hoists

There are certain circumstances in which cranes or hoists are preferable to other forms of materials-handling equipment. These include:

- where heavy materials must be lifted for loading on to trucks or other vehicles for transportation;
- where heavy materials need to be lifted and moved only a short distance for further processing;
- where awkward loads are involved which cannot be handled or industrial trucks;
- where the movement involved is between two or more constant points;
- where insufficient space is available on the floor to allow materials movement.

Figure 40: Side loading truck

The following are examples of the various types designed to meet the problem.

- *Pull-lifts:* a hand operated chain-block at a fixed point to lift heavy materials for loading on vehicles or machines.
- *Electric Hoists:* an electrically operated version of the Pul-lift for basically the same purpose.
- *Monorail:* a single overhead rail from which a Pul-lift or electric hoist is suspended on rollers, to allow loads to be moved to any point over which the monorail passes.

- *Swinglift Jib:* a swinging arm on which a Pul-lift or electric hoist is attached to allow loads to be moved to any point within the arc of the job.
- *Mobile or Rolling Gantry:* a steel structure which straddles the working area and is mounted on rollers and rails. A Pul-lift or electric hoist is suspended on rollers from the gantry which then allows manual movement from side to side, as well as along the length of the working area.
- *Overhead Cranes:* a power-driven vehicle which is mounted on a fixed gantry running the whole length of the working area. The lifiting apparatus can be power-driven from side to side across the working area, as well as along the length of the gantry. The lifting is also electrically powered and can be controlled either from an overhead cavin attached to the vehicle, or form ground level by hanging controls.
- *Jib Crane:* a lifting arm which is fixed at one point; both the arm and the lifting apparatus are power driven and usually controlled from a cabin which rotates with the arm. It is usually used for lifting heavy loads to considerable heights.
- *Mobile Crane:* a jib crane mounted on a manually operated or motorised vehicle; usually used for lifting and transporting occasional awkward loads over reasonable distance, or where an overhead crane cannot be erected.

Conveyors

Where a continuous flow of goods or materials is passing between two or more fixed points, and the cost and utilisation of space can adequately be justified, a conveyor may be installed. Usually the expense that a firm is prepared to incur in installing conveyors will be in direct relation to the volume of goods or materials involved. The type of conveyor selected must obviously depend upon the type of materials to be handled, but wherever possible one should use gravity to drive the conveyor and thus avoid the cost of power and driving plant. Within the general classification of conveyors, therefore, we include the following:

- *Slides and chutes:* for parcels and cartons.
- *Gravity roller conveyors:* used for many purposes from the movement of hot-rolled steel bar or strip, to the movement of packing cases.

Then there are the power-driven conveyors, chain-driven from electric motors:

- *Live Roller Conveyors:* in which some of the rolls in each section of track are driven by chain as with the wheel of a bicycle; or there is the tow-line principle in which cog-wheels, driven by electric motors, tow an endless length of conveyor.
- *Overhead Conveyors:* for carrying materials or goods suspended above the working areas in which they are to be used, or through process areas such as paint dipping or heat treatment.
- *Sub-floor Tow Conveyor:* an endless chain below floor level onto which carts or trucks are hooked to tow them to the point at which the materials they contain are required.

Another conveyor system is the pulley-driven conveyor, an endless belt moved by power-driven pulleys or rollers positioned at one or both ends of the conveyor system. Such a conveyor can be either:

- *A Belt Conveyor:* mainly used for transporting small items which must be "contained" by the conveyor itself, such as small components, solid fuel, ashes, etc.
- *A Slat Conveyor:* where the "containing" ability of the belt conveyor is not necessary but where a flat surface is desirable.

Pumps, Pipelines and Feeder Systems

In circumstances where the materials to be supplied are in gaseous or liquid form, or are solids in powder or fine grain form, and where large quantities of such materials are involved, it may be advantageous to handle or transport them via pipelines or feeder systems. In this way the materials are enclosed in pipes or ducts giving the following advantages:

- easier control of material movement;
- less likelihood of waste;
- protection from contamination is facilitated;
- flow of materials is more easily regulated;
- sometimes provides the easiest method of connecting the storage unit with the user location.

Where the storage unit can be located above the user unit it may be possible to use gravity feed, which saves the costs of providing power. Examples of this situation are:

- fuel oil from tanks above furnaces;
- lubricating oil from reservoirs above machines;
- grain from silos to road transport.

In other circumstances it may be necessary to introduce pumping units to "push" materials along the pipelines, or vacuum units to "suck" the materials along. This method of handling is now being applied to moving solids which can suitable be suspended in a liquid "transporter" (eg coal suspended in water or ore-bearing earth suspended in a suitable fluid).

Pipelines and feeder systems have a wide variety of uses which can prove more profitable or less costly than more conventional forms of handling, but the same "benefit to cost" analysis must be applied, and invariably the main factor justifying their use is the volume of materials to be handled.

Security

Stock is often a company's greatest asset. Bearing this in mind, compare the level of security afforded to the collection of one week's wages, with that usually devoted to safeguarding the stores! The security of stores buildings and stockyards is a natural base from which to start discussing security. Particular factors to consider are:

- A strongly built store, with security fencing in cases where the store is not part of the main premises. In case of stockyards, adequate security fencing is an essential requisite. Security lighting may also be considered in some locations.
- Weak points are doors and windows, therefore doors should be kept to a minimum. Proper locks and bolts should be provided to all doors. In the case of large doors necessary for vehicle access it is good practice to have a small wicket door for everyday use. Windows should also have locks if they open and have wire mesh or bars, for protection against forced entry.
- Burglar alarms of various types are available and thought may be given to installing them.
- Security patrols should of course include stores on their irregular patrols. The local police will usually have a crime prevention officer who will advise on security matters.

Keys are a weak point in any security system, and should only be issued to authorised personnel. The keys should be numbered and, when issued, the name of the authorised person receiving the key recorded. Duplicate or master keys should be kept in a secure place in the charge of a responsible person.

Access to stores be limited to authorised personnel under the control of the stores officer. Particular care must be taken to see that people such as drivers, maintenance fitters and the like do not get into the stores. Out of hours issues are a problem for security, since quite often stores staff are not available. The best solution is preparation through avoiding the need for out of hours issues, by planning and issuing in advance of requirements. If it is essential to make an emergency issue, a named official should be made responsible.

In any stores, there are items attractive to a potential thief. Secure areas within the stores should be provided for these items. Scrap and redundant materials are often a security risk, since they are often segregated from the main stores. This also applies to returns, awaiting despatch to suppliers.

Fire is always a hazard and the installation of fire fighting equipment is a necessity. This must be maintained at regular intervals.The local fire brigade should be consulted on fire precautions.

Safety and Safe Methods of Working

It makes good sense to have safe methods of working both in order to avoid personal injury and to safeguard the company's interests. In cases where personnel are injured at work the manager responsible may well face prosecution under the Health and Safety at Work legislation, if he or she has failed to ensure that safe working conditions and practices are maintained. The particular points to which the stores manager must pay attention are:

- Good layout of the stores, providing for clearly designated gangways, marked with white lines or similar methods. These gangways must be kept free from obstructions at all times. Areas for receipt of goods, inspection, returns to stores, scrap and redundant stack, as well as storage areas should be properly designated.

- Stores must be kept clean and tidy; what is generally called good housekeeping is an essential element in providing safe conditions of work. Many accidents are caused by tripping and falling over obstacles and the like. Piles of inflammable rubbish such as empty packaging are also a real hazard.
- Cleanliness must be enforced by management. This can be aided by the sealing of concrete floors, the provision of sheets and dust covers where required. The Factory Act lays down minimum standards for cleaning down premises, and for paintwork.
- All rubbish and arisings must be segregated and proper facilities provided for temporary storage until removal. This removal must be on a regular basis, since old containers, paper cardboard, wood wool and so forth soon accumulates in any stores.
- Storage equipment must be properly used and goods stored in it correctly. Particular care must be taken to ensure that the weight limits and capacity of all equipment is known, and not exceeded. In a similar way, the load bearing capacity of floors and maximum storage heights must be known.
- Lighting is an important factor in safety; all working areas must be adequately lit. The actual lighting required will depend upon particular circumstances. Where, for example, selection of small items is carried out, very good lighting will be needed. All passages and alleyways must be lighted to prevent accidents.
- Provision of handrails is required where gangways are above ground level, or the worker may experience difficulty in walking.
- The Health and Safety at Work Act requires the guarding of moving parts of equipment and machinery, and the stores manager must ensure that all equipment under his control is properly guarded. Fork lift trucks will need overhead guards to prevent loads injuring the driver in the case of accidents.
- Where there is a possibility of slipping (ramps, sloping paths, etc) non-slip surfaces should be provided.
- Areas of particular danger in a stores are loading and un-loading docks and wells. Removable handrails will be required, as will curbs or stops to prevent forklift trucks running over the edge of the dock.
- Warning and informative notices are an essential aid to safe methods of working. Many will be familiar, such as "Petroleum Spirit", "No Smoking", "Exit", and so on. These are available as standards from suppliers. Other signs to suit your own particular

requirements are available and can be made to your specification. In some cases such signs must be displayed. Colour is a useful method of conveying warnings or information. Danger signs and fire equipment are red and yellow, indicating caution, and fork and lift trucks are normally this colour.

- Protective clothing and equipment must be provided in appropriate situations and worn. It is the responsibility of management to ensure that safety helmets, goggles, gloves, overalls, safety shoes and boots are provided. The more difficult task the management must carry out is to make sure that the equipment is used properly.
- The organisation will have a safety officer, and the stores manager must consult him on safety matters and take his advice. Instructions regarding the safety of equipment and practices should be issued in writing by management to all personnel working in the stores. It is important that people such as crane drivers, forklift truck operators and slingers are aware of safety regulations.

Remember, it is the responsibility of management to provide safe working conditions and that under the Health and Safety at Work Act the manager is personally liable to prosecution for failure to take proper steps to ensure safety. Legislation moves on quickly and the need to keep up to date is paramount.

Food for Thought

Most materials will deteriorate in store, in the course of time. Steps need to be taken to prevent deterioration and these include the following measures:

- *Suppliers Deliveries:* packaging must be suitable for product and on arrival should be thoroughly checked. Most suppliers want their goods to arrive fit for use, for example sterile goods in hospitals.
- *Order of issue:* rate of deterioration varies. The longer a product remains in stores the more the risk of deterioration. Stock rotation (first in, first out) and shelf life are all important considerations, for example photographic materials.
- *Heating and Lighting:* damp is the supervisor's worst enemy.

Correct and adequate heating is essential; especially for products such as textiles. For some specific products light sensitivity can also be an issue, for example, drugs and dressings.

- *Stock Preservation:* some stock needs to be preserved against premature deterioration. Packaging, apart from its basic function of protecting goods in transit, also assists in preservation. Stores may also add packaging as protection for goods in store. Specific areas including dust-proofing, waterproofing, vapour-proofing/sealing, rigid packing for efficient stacking and packing in small boxes to keep items tidy. For example, canned goods need to be stable, stationery needs to be dust-proof, and electronic equipment needs to be water and vapour proof.
- *Specific Protective Measures:* if stores is adequately heated and ventilated then the majority of items will require no special treatment. But some materials are special and present their own problems. These could include cement, timber, textiles, crops, metal and machinery and equipment. All detailed protective measures need careful and constant watching.

The stores-issuing section is a key activity; its objectives should include the following:

- All requests must be authorised and issued in accordance with agreed procedures.
- Appropriate documentation must be raised and, subsequently, posted.
- Stores systems must be updated.
- Issues should be made promptly and in accordance with agreed standards of service.
- Staff employed on issuing must be trained and effective.
- Where possible, with customers agreement, issues should be pre-planned to even workload.
- Stores location system and layout of racking should ensure fast moving items are located to ensure efficiency.
- Staff must be aware of the necessity of security of goods when awaiting collection or delivery.

Stores Manuals

Many organisations produce a manual detailing the stores policies and procedure. There are advantages and disadvantages.

Advantages

- Provides, in written and accessible form, a record of all standing instructions and procedures.
- Assists with training, particularly new staff.
- Assists with standardisation of procedures and paperwork.
- Ensures stores are easier to audit.
- Can be used as a basis for performance measurement.
- Defining the duties of staff and supervision becomes easier as does standardisation of staff behaviour.
- Required for BS 5750/ISO 9000 and IIP approval.

Disadvantages

- Can be very time consuming to produce and therefore can be costly.
- Needs regular updating to be effective.
- Sometimes not read by all staff and therefore not followed.
- Can stifle individual initiative and creativity.

There is no right answer here but logic suggests the advantages outweigh the disadvantages.

Case Studies

The Problem: some years ago Iceland installed an automated sortation system fed by a pick-by-light to belt system into one if its frozen food depots. However, more recently, changes in the pattens of business have taken place and this has resulted in a belief that the system is no longer able fully to meet Iceland's needs. Also reliability has become more of a problem and support for the control system difficult. As a result of the above problems Iceland decided to call in consultants to advise them on how best to proceed. Because of their experience of retail warehousing and distribution and particularly of warehouse automation Iceland chose the Logistics Business to undertake the investigation.

The first step taken by the Logistics Business was to spend time with all the people directly involved in the use and operation of the system to understand the problems as well as any further changes in the business that might affect the performance. As is often the case they found they were usually hearing about symptoms and they therefore followed up with a structured investigation to understand the causes of the problems. By combining the information gathered with their experience of other warehouse operations they were able to match symptoms and causes and identify solutions.

The Solution: they concluded that the sortation system could meet the needs of the business if certain steps were taken. These included changes to the way product was zoned and picked, changes to the strategy adopted for use of the sortation output lanes, and adoption of new picking methods, not involving pick-by-light. They also recommended changes to workload balancing and to the frequency of store deliveries. Estimates were made for the cost of improvements to the control system which were shown to be favourable in comparison with the cost of other proposed changes.

The Success: Iceland was given clearly documented options to use as the basis for decision making. Discussions on the future of the sortation system were no longer based solely on opinion but upon clearly presented factual information.This demonstrated how success with automated systems is not dependant on the equipment alone. Performance is greatly influenced by the strategy adopted for operation of the system and by day-to-day management skills.

The Problem: Barclays National Records Centre (BNRC) holds some two million boxes of documents of varying types and moves up to 7,000 of these boxes per day. Growth over recent years has been very great as more activities have been centralised and this had put pressure on people systems and equipment. The starting point was a thorough review of activities using an unique health check. By involving employees at all levels this allowed a focus on the issues most likely to bring immediate benefits, in particular more thinking about internal customer service and service level as a means of measuring performance. Then specific areas were addressed where changes to layouts, equipment and systems could improve performance.

The Solution: In some areas the Logistics Business recommended the use of bar code identification as well as the introduction of radio data terminals. Specifications were prepared for new software to manage some expanding part of the business and they then managed the writing of this software and its implementation. In one area of the business where particularly high growth throughput was expected they designed new mechanical handling systems and managed the introduction of carton conveyor.

The Success: Managers and other staff are more focused on giving good service to their internal customers. Continued growth in handling requirements has been accommodated whilst service levels have been maintained or improved. BNRC has been more able to fulfil its role as an extension of the activities of the Bank's branches. New technologies have been introduced into areas which had previously operated using very conventional methods.

The Problem: The question facing Boots the Chemist when it came to consider the refurbishment of one of its larger warehouses in Nottingham was whether or not to replace the existing equipment on a like-for-like basis or seek another solution. The main consideration was how to maximise the use of space in the existing 35,000 square metres. Although Boots has its own in-house project team, this was already heavily committed so it was decided that on this occasion outside help would be sought. The Logistics Business was chosen for this task.

They worked very closely with Boots' team. Problem definition was not merely a question of data analysis. Whatever solution was arrived at, it would have to last for at least 20 years and Boots, in common with most major retailers, do not know what their business will be like over that time scale. Consequently, the solution would have to be flexible and capable of adapting to a range of situations. A number of options were explored ranging from straight replacement to more novel satellite and shuttle systems. They took responsibility for preparing the detailed presentations of the options and put these forward to the team for evaluation. They then developed the chosen option and prepared detailed invitations to tender. Following receipt of tenders they formed part of the evaluation team that made the final choice of supplier.

The Solution: An automated system was chosen. Aisle-changing stacker cranes fed by conveyors and shuttle cars form the basis of the solution and, as a result of recommendations made, overall storage capacity has been increased. A major factor affecting the refurbishment was minimisation of disruption to the existing warehouse operations. Designing an implementation method whereby operations could continue whilst installation was carried out was a major challenge where the experience of the Logistics Business brought some particular benefits. The contract for the refurbishment, worth some £7million, went ahead smoothly and on time. The project is rated as highly successful.

The Success: The Boots' team has benefited from the wider experience of the Logistics Business to add to its own in-depth knowledge of the Boots business. Options have been evaluated objectively with unanimous agreement that the most appropriate solution has been adopted. The refurbishment has gone ahead with minimum disruption. Storage capacity has been increased and flexibility maintained.

Details of these case studies and services available can be obtained by contacting the Logistics Business Limited, Aston Science Park, Birmingham, B8 4BJ, United Kingdom. Tel: 0121 333 6303. Fax: 0121 333 6407.E-Mail: HYPERLINK mail to: Info@logistics.co.uk Info@logistics.co.uk. HYPERLINK http://www.logistics.co.uk http://www.logistics.co.uk. In the next chapter we will overview transport and distribution of those items we have now successfully stores-managed!

CHAPTER 10

Transport

Shipping, transport and distribution can be grouped under one heading: logistics. Logistics planning involves not only the transportation side of distribution but also provides the "place element" in the marketing mix by helping to ensure that products arrive in sufficient quantities in saleable condition at points where the consumer can most easily buy them. Thus logistics management includes forecasting demand and matching supply to meet that demand through procurement of materials, production scheduling, inventory management, order processing, warehousing and transportation.

In international systems the logistics planning function involves a number of sub-systems which have central points of reach territory. There is a further sub-system for the management of local logistics, that is the transport and distribution systems used by the importer to move your products to customers in the market concerned.

Logistics, as well as being essential for moving goods to their destinations, is also a key marketing activity. As such it requires marketing management's attention. Logistics contributes to a major portion of costs, particularly in international business. Logistic planning plays a major role in creating a good relationship with customers, ensuring that sales opportunities are not lost because of stock-outs (which allows competitors to eat away at the company's market share).

In assessing the real cost of transportation you should be concerned with factors relating to reliability, time and price. Therefore, your decisions in choosing methods of transport and distribution will be based on trade-offs between these factors. Transportation costs are often peculiar in that they frequently bear little relation to distance. The key factors in cargo pricing are competition and volume. For example, goods going from the Far East to the East Coast of the USA pay less than 30 per cent of the rate of goods going the other way. Costs from the USA to South America are frequently lower than among South American countries.

In planning transportation the problems can be enormous and considerable hidden costs can be concealed, for example the costs of out-of-stock positions which lose you business, or delays over insurance claims which you have to finance. Transport is clearly a critical function within the overall logistics discipline. This chapter looks at the component parts of transport consisting of:

- Fleet management
- Vehicle replacement
- Vehicle scheduling
- Maintenance and security
- Containers
- Loading equipment
- Road vehicle design
- Haulage
- Rail freight
- Air freight

Fleet Management

The main duties of the fleet manager are comprised of the efficient operation of his or her fleet and, in addition, the attainment of any further objectives laid down by top management. This is done by first achieving maximum utilisation of the vehicles operating and by setting and maintaining correct weight/distance standards. It is also essential to keep within budgets and make sure vehicles are properly maintained.

There are probably more Acts of Parliament and Statutory Regulations concerning road transport than any other activity. This is now being further complicated by EC Regulations. The fleet manager will need to be aware of these, for example:

- The Highways Acts
- Road Traffic Acts

- Transport Act
- Vehicles and Driving Licenses Act
- Heavy Commercial Vehicles (Control and Regulations) Act
- Motor Vehicles (Construction and Use) Regulations
- Goods Vehicles (Plating and Testing) Regulations.

Note the foregoing is by no means exhaustive and the fleet manager must be aware of all present and relevant legislation. A whole host of matters arise from this legislation which impose duties upon fleet managers. Among these matters, some of the more important are to ensure that:

- vehicles are not overloaded;
- vehicles are not loaded in such a way that the load is unsafe;
- vehicles are properly maintained to the standard required by law;
- vehicles are correctly tested and plated as stated in the Regulations;
- drivers do not exceed permitted hours of work;
- a record of work is kept by all drivers;
- drivers hold a current driving license of the appropriate class for the vehicle to be driven;
- the licensing authority is advised of any change in company ownership.

An important aspect of every manager's job is to control his or her function. This means setting standards, measuring actual performance and, combining the two, enabling correction to any deviations. A convenient and effective method of control is budgetary control. This can, of course, be equally well applied to fleet management. It is these costs which provide the fleet manager with the information needed to control the department.

Other information required will be mileage: average operated per day, average mileage maintained per day and tonnage or volume equivalent carried. The following indicators will be needed to measure performance:

- Total operating costs per period (usually one month).
- Cost per hour.
- Cost per mile.

- Cost per ton (or volume equivalent).
- Cost per day operated.
- Cost per day maintained.
- Cost per depot.
- Cost per vehicle.
- Cost per vehicle class.

You will see from the above that the manager can establish the cost and efficiency of the department and its individual depots, where applicable. The performance can be checked of types of vehicles or even an individual vehicle, if required.

Vehicle Replacement

Any of us who owns cars, knows how quickly they need replacing and the problem of financing the purchase of a new model. This is, of course, a much greater problem for a fleet manager who has to maintain a definite number of vehicles on the road to keep the company's goods moving. The first necessity is to establish a clear company policy on replacement, based not only on the need to replace vehicles at the end of their economic life, but upon such factors as:-

- Long-term strategic planning (what goods will be transported in the future, and where they will be sent).
- Capital resources available.
- Any legal requirements at home or overseas, or any impending legal requirements.
- The government's transport policy (for example programme of motorway building, or a decision not to build new roads and so on).
- Economic loads, unionisation, containerisation.
- Design and construction of vehicles.
- Vehicle maintenance needs.
- Vehicle depreciation.

Having decided that we must renew fleet according to a planned policy and having decided which vehicles we need for our replacement programme, we come to the question raised earlier: how to finance the purchase of new vehicles. Among the methods available to companies are:

- *Outright Purchase:* this is simple if the capital is available at a reasonable price (remember the price of borrowing money is the interest paid). Capital allowances are available which can be set against the purchase.
- *Hire Purchase:* this is often favoured since it avoids the need to find large capital sums. At the same time a tax allowance is given as if it were an outright purchase. Hire purchase rates are the price of borrowing the money, and must be studied before entering into an agreement. It is also worth noting that the purchaser does not obtain ownership until the last instalment is paid.
- *Lease:* this method avoids the need to provide working capital, and since the vehicles are on lease the operator does not have to worry about depreciation. However, there are problems to be considered. One important point is that the vehicles will never belong to you. Leases are usually for a fixed number of years, and you are obliged to have a vehicle for that period of time. Lease charges will need to be studied, and you will also have to take into account operating and repair charges, which are often additional to the basic charge.
- *Contract Hire:* details of the contract must be studied carefully, to ensure exactly who is responsible for insurance, maintenance and supplying replacement vehicles, etc. The basis of charging and the rates of charge also require careful investigation.

Choosing the Right Policy

As has been indicated this is not a straightforward decision, many factors have to be taken into account. A detailed analysis of quotations for each method will have to be made; remember that it is not only the immediate replacement cost that has to be taken into account, but also the cost of operating over a number of years. An analysis must also be made between the various methods of replacement, and such matters as tax allowances and inflation taken into account. This will give you the true cost of each method, and taken together with the company's objectives, strategies and financial recourses, enable the selection of the right policy to be made.

Vehicle Scheduling

The objective of scheduling is to achieve optimum vehicle utilisation by operating vehicles at maximum load and at minimum cost. In carrying out this objective the fleet manager will wish to ensure that the fleet is used efficiently and vehicles are available when required. Similarly the manager needs to ensure that the most suitable vehicle for particular loads and journeys is used.

Constraints

In scheduling and routing vehicles the fleet manager must have regard to a number of constraints imposed by the law, the company's resources and the needs of the customer. Among these are:

- The legal permitted driving hours.
- The need for drivers to have days off.
- Speed restrictions.
- The maintenance and servicing requirements of vehicles, which involve vehicles being off the road.
- The number of vehicles available at any one time.
- The types of vehicles available, since this will govern capacity available.
- Where the company's depots are located, and the number of depots.
- The types of traffic involved; parcel traffic will be different from heavy haulage, when schedules are prepared.
- The number of calls to be made and their distance from each other.
- The time involved in loading or unloading at each call.
- If an urban area or a rural area is involved.
- Any special requirements of the trade involved, or of customers.
- Such matters as public holidays, industrial holidays of customers, and local holidays, not forgetting early closing days, if in the retail trade.
- The type of roads used (motorways, dual carriage ways and so on).
- Temporary restrictions caused by road works, building operations and similar work.
- Certain loads may require special routes, to avoid obstructions, or bridges with weight limits and the like.

How to Choose the Route

Whilst there are a number of (expensive) software packages available, this is a considerable problem since, as we have seen, there are many factors to consider. Several ways of selecting vehicle routes and loads for vehicles on that route may be used. These include:

- *Pigeon Hole Method:* this is probably the simplest method and is widely used for this reason. Delivery points are grouped together into geographical areas that have been adopted on the loading deck, usually in special bays. Thus, one would see bays for London, West Midlands, South East and so forth. When the goods for each area are known a detailed schedule is worked out, and a vehicle allocated. This method is most suitable where the number of areas and delivery points are limited.

- *String Diagram:* another simple method is the use of string diagrams to select the best routes. A good map is required, showing your transport depots, and customer delivery points, the map will of course be to a known scale enabling distances to be read easily. A pin is fastened to each depot location, and also at each delivery point. A piece of string is fastened to a depot and taken to each delivery point in the sequence that appears to be the best route. In this way it is possible to show a number of alternative routes, and the distances involved can be measured. The best route or routes can then be selected. In practice the maps will be mounted on board and coloured strings used to show alternative routes more clearly.

- *Distance Saving:* this means selection of the optimum routes by first selecting the worst route. This would normally be by making an individual call each time to one customer, next trying to link the two nearest delivery points together to see what the savings would be. The next nearest point would then be linked up, and this would continue until an acceptable route emerged.

- *Travelling Sales Representatives:* this is sometimes used, and means visiting each customer by the shortest route and returning to the depot. It has a limited use in practice.

- *Linear Programming:* this is an operational research technique developed to show how limited resources can be used to their optimum. As the title suggests, linear is proportional, and assumes that if for instance we have more time we can produce more goods. The basic method used in linear programming is to locate an extreme point of a feasible region, examine each boundary edge intersecting at this point and see if any overmen along any edge would increase the value of the objective function. If this is so, move along the edge to the adjacent extreme point. Repeat to the value of the objective function on longer increases.

If, for example, we assume that a company has depots and stock as follows:

Depots	Stock
Anytown	30
Hightown	32
Northborough	22
Westborough	26
	110

Customer orders are:

Customer	Order Quantity
Smith	34
Brown	40
Jones	36

The transport costs from each depot to each customer will be assumed in this case to be:

	Anytown	Hightown	Northborough	Westborough
Smith	16	18	12	6-1
Brown	12	22	10	20
Jones	6-1	16	14	18

We are now in a position to select the best routes, for there are a number of alternative solutions available. One may be for stock to be allocated as below:

Customer	Qty	Depot Route	Qty	Depot Route
Smith	8-	Northborough(1)	26	Westborough (2)
Brown	26	Anytown	14	Northborough (4)
Jones	4-1	Anytown	32	Hightown (6)

The cost of doing it this way is:

Delivery Route	Cost/Item	Qty	Cost
1	12	8	96
2	6	26	156
3	12	26	312
4	10	14	140
5	6	4	24
6	16	32	512
		TOTAL COST	**1240**

This, of course, only gives us the cost of using one method. We need to repeat this exercise for each possible method and so by a process of elimination discover the most economic route. This appears to present a system of trial and error but linear programming is a planned method of trying all alternatives until the best solution is found. In our example the allocations and costs are:

Customers	Depots						
	Anytown		**Hightown**		**Northborough**	**Westborough**	
Smith		16		18	8	12	26	6
Brown	26	12		22	14	10		20
Jones	4	6	32	16		14		18

An alternative is for Smith to take one from the Anytown depot. However, if we do this we must re-allocate issues from other depots. The whole exercise must then be calculated to see what the difference in cost in the revised method is, against the original. In this case:

Customers	Depots						
	Anytown		**Hightown**		**Northborough**	**Westborough**	
Smith	+1	16		18	8-1	12	6
Brown	26-1	12		22	7-1	10	20
Jones	4	6	32	16		14	18

So in cost terms we have: Cost of Anytown to Smith 16, less Smith to Northborough 12 - an increase of 4. Northborough to Brown 10, less Anytown to Brown 12 – a decrease of 2. In this case a net increase of 2 in cost. This is repeated for each unused route.

Supervisors should monitor and evaluate the effectiveness of their own distribution planning by measuring their performance against targets set either by themselves or by their line managers. They should analyse any variances between the planned and actual performance, to assess whether these have been caused by deficiencies in their planning (such as setting unrealistic schedules, or failing to take account of external changes). This will then enable them to improve their planning in the future.

Maintenance and Security

These are two factors to which all transport managers must give considerable attention. Road safety is constantly receiving attention in Parliament and the press, and rightly so. Road vehicles carry the majority of goods in transit and so naturally there are many attractive loads being moved about the country in this way. Therefore, security is a major function of transport management.

Facilities for Maintenance

A very high degree of maintenance is required to keep a modern transport fleet on the road, maintained properly and according to law. Accordingly any firm operating vehicles must consider how it is going to maintain and service its vehicles. Methods available are:

- *Company Garage and Workshops:* this requires properly equipped premises with all necessary facilities to service and repair vehicles. It also means employing qualified fitters, vehicle electricians and other staff. This method is convenient as there is complete control over maintenance programmes. Repairs can be carried out to suit the operating schedules. It gives a great deal of flexibility. On the other hand it is expensive to maintain these facilities, and is therefore uneconomic for many operators with small fleets.
- *Contact Maintenance:* this is the method which must be adopted if circumstances do not justify having one's own workshop facilities. Most commercial garages will be willing to enter into a contract

for the servicing and maintenance of vehicle fleets. The types of contracts available are too numerous to be dealt with here and in any case need to be considered in detail. However, the contract may cover regular planned maintenance or simply servicing when required. Vehicle manufacturers often have schemes whereby contract maintenance and servicing is carried out through their agents. In the UK, Ford and Bedford are among the manufacturers who offer this facility.

Quality Control

This is a major aspect of vehicle servicing and maintenance, since there is little point in arranging for maintenance to be carried out, whether in your own garage or under contract, if it is not to the required standard. A mixture of road transport publications mixed with a little common sense suggests:

- Positive checks should be made at pre-determined intervals of time or mileage on items that affect the safety of the vehicles.
- Staff carrying out servicing and repairing of vehicles must be aware of the significance of defects.
- Any vehicle inspector or other staff whose duty it is to inspect vehicles must have authority to have defects rectified and to take unsafe vehicles off the road.
- Written records must be kept showing when and by whom inspections are carried out, the results of the inspections, and when and by whom remedial work is done and details of the work.
- Under-vehicle inspection facilities should be provided.
- A system whereby drivers can report defects must be provided, and these reports must be in writing. The clearance of the defect should also be recorded.
- The mechanical condition of hired vehicles and trailers is the direct responsibility of the user. (This is the employer of the driver). Documents that are required to ensure an effective system of maintenance are service sheets for the pre-determined time/mileage checks, inspection check lists, drivers defect report, vehicles history record, job cards and planning sheets.

Proper planning maintenance is essential if the vehicles are to be kept on the road and there are a number of aids to the planning needed. It is interesting to note that the Freight Transport Association have a quality control scheme, enforced by inspectors employed by them. They check vehicles on behalf of members, whether they are maintained by company workshops or on contract.

Security

One has only to think for a moment of the wide variety of goods moved by road to realise how desirable many of these loads are to thieves. Insurance companies as well as operators of fleets are concerned that security should be effective. In fact insurance companies often require certain precautions to be taken by the operator as a condition of providing insurance.

Security is an attitude of mind that must be cultivated to ensure that everyone is aware of the problem and the elementary safeguards necessary. The advice of the insurance companies is always available, and so is that of the police. The police have crime prevention officers whose job it is to advise companies on security matters. The Road Haulage Association is also concerned about vehicle and load security and has produced a guide for the use of its members. Among the points mentioned are:

- Recruitment of staff: references should be checked over the last five years and any gaps investigated. Beware of telephone numbers for references, it may be an accomplice. If a new driver is engaged do not let the vehicle be taken out until you have their P45 and other documents. They also advise using the Association's engagement form.
- Alarms and immobilisers should be fitted; models which provide protection without the driver getting out of the vehicle are available. The devices should be checked frequently.
- If a driver has a valuable loads he or she should be instructed not to get out of the cab if stopped. If the police stop him or her they should offer to go to the nearest police station. As an anti-hijack measure, bolts should be fitted to the inside of doors.
- Vehicles should not be left unattended, especially at night.
- Keys should never be left in the vehicle. Numbers should be removed from security locks, starter and ignition keys or switches. If a key is lost, change all locks and switches.

- Drivers should be asked to change their routine by not visiting the same cafes at regular times.
- When a vehicle is sold, remove the company name.
- A cash bonus is suggested, payable if the drivers observe security rules.

Security is also important for the long-term future of the business, since if a company gets a reputation for bad security, customers may withdraw their trade.

Containers, Unitisation and Palletisation

It is an obvious advantage if a consignor can load goods in some way at his premises, such that they can be transported and delivered to the consignee without the necessity of unpacking and handling individual items in transit. The above mentioned aids enable this to be done, as they are all methods of providing a unit from one mode of transport to another. There is, therefore, no interference with the load in transit.

Containers

A container is now a major piece of transport equipment, and since its purpose is to ensure that a load is transported without interference to the consignor, it is important that it can be moved across national boundaries. It would be a major problem if containers were of different sizes and aptness in various countries. Therefore the International Standards Organisation (ISO) have made recommendations for freight containers. These recommendations are accepted generally by national standards bodies, and also by Lloyds Register of Shipping. Lloyds also operate a system of certifying containers that meet these requirements.

The ISO say that general purpose freight containers are of a rectangular shape, weatherproof for transporting and storing a number of unit loads, packages or bulk materials; they confine and protect the contents from loss or damage and can be separated from the means of transport, handled as unit loads and transhipped without rehandling the contents. The ISO gives a detailed definition of what a container is, which is well worth remembering. They state that a freight container is an article of transport equipment:

- of a permanent character and accordingly strong enough for repeated use;

- specially designed to facilitate the carriage of goods by one or more modes of transport, without intermediate reloading;
- fitted with devices permitting its ready handling, particularly its transfer from one mode of transport to another;
- so designed as to be easy to fill and empty;
- have an internal volume of one metre or more.

The freight container does not include vehicles or conventional packaging. ISO standard container sizes are based upon a module of 2.4m x 2.4m (8ft x 8ft), and will take the following loads:

- 10 ft long = 10 long tons
- 20 ft long = 20 long tons
- 30 ft long = 25 long tons
- 40 ft long = 30 long tons

Types of Container

It is important to remember than an ISO standard, while a valuable one, is not going to meet all requirements and many companies will wish to design their own containers to suit their needs. Floors may be required to be strong enough for fork lift trucks to enter when loading or unloading. Sides and posts may be required to be suitable for use with special lifting devices. Many types of containers are available. Among them are:

- High capacity box
- Demountable tank (for bulk liquids)
- Ordinary box
- Insulated
- Curtain-sided

The companies despatching by these methods may own the containers, which will be painted in their colours, and have an advertising value. Alternatively they may be hired.

Continental Operation

If companies are regularly sending goods across Europe, it will be an advantage to have Transport Internationaux Routier (TIR) Registration, which enables containers to cross customs frontiers easily. A point worth noting is that, for tax purposes, the container is not part of the unladen weight of the vehicle.

Unitisation

This means assembling a number of small packages into one large package, or unit load. It will be appreciated that this makes handling much easier and when loading or unloading will:

- reduce the amount of labour required;
- enable mechanical handling to be used;
- reduce vehicle turn round time;
- make loading and stowage easier;
- allow safer working practice to be used;
- reduce damage and pilferage;
- permit marking and labelling of consignments to be simplified.

All this means reduced handling and transportation costs. In the case of air freight these advantages are very important, since speed is the main reason for using this method of transport. Unitisation means a much speedier method of loading is possible, as against handling loose items of cargo. The customer can share in the reduced costs, since airlines offer special rates for bulk unitisation cargos.

Standard Packaging

Many companies have a range of standard packs, taking certain quantities of each product. Therefore when an order is received it is known at once which standard outer pack will be suitable. This not only takes advantage of unitisation principles, but means that the air or shipping space can be booked right away.

Palletisation

We are not concerned here with the description of pallets and their construction but in palletisation to facilitate transport loading. As with unitisation the advantages gained from palletisation can be summed up as the reduction in handling and transportation costs, and the particular advantages are also similar, namely:

- enables mechanical handling to be used;
- reduces road vehicle turn round time;
- makes loading and stowage easier;
- reduces damage and pilferage.

The savings possible by the use of amplest are considerable, since goods can be picked up by forklift truck, and taken aboard ship or into container and stowed. Many port authorities (for example Rotterdam and Oslo) have published details of savings through palletisation, which you can look up if you wish to study the matter further. At this point it is worthwhile reminding ourselves of what a pallet is, and for this purpose we chose the definition of the European Convention of Customs Treatment of Pallets used in International Transport:

> A device on the deck of which a quantity of goods can be assembled to form a unit load for the purpose of transporting it, or of handling or stacking it with the assistance of mechanical appliances. This device is made up of two decks separated by bearers, or of a single deck supported by feet; its overall height is reduced to a minimum compatible with handling by fork lift trucks and pallet trucks; it may or may not have a superstructure.

Two variations of pallet are shown at Figure 41.

Figure 41: Typical Pallets

Semi-Bulk Pallet

Roll Pallet

Ownership and Return of Pallets

This represents a considerable problem, since everyone using pallets has his own, and the cost of having them returned can be considerable. One solution is to use "low-cost, non-returnable pallets" known as LCNR pallets. The difficulty is to have them strong enough to support loads and stand forklift trucks moving them, at a low cost. In practice they are usually reinforced with plastic.

Another solution is to use a pallet pool, where all users contribute to the pool and use pallets accordingly, but this does not seem to have got off the ground. One exception is the scheme operated by the European Railways, but the UK is not a party to the scheme. Why have these schemes not been taken up more widely? Why have pallets not been as universally adopted, as was once thought they would be? The reason, I suggest, is the drawbacks that pallets have when compared with containers. Among these are:

- The pallet offers only limited protection to goods.
- It still requires a reasonable amount of labour to handle pallets.
- The pallet loads cannot be transported under bond as they cannot be sealed.
- A single pallet load is not an economic unit of transport.

In addition there has been a failure to agree among countries on a standard for pallets. For example the United States, the UK and Western Germany have different standards.

Mechanical Aids to Loading and Off-Loading

The time spent loading and unloading vehicles can be considerable and can be costly in terms of vehicle time. Any aid to make this operation more efficient will reduce these costs, and speed vehicles turnround.

There are types of equipment available which are suitable for most purposes, and the problem is to select that equipment which is most suitable in particular circumstances. To decide on the correct equipment we must consider:

- Weights of materials to be handled.
- Quantities of materials to be handled.

- Nature of goods involved.
- Handling characteristics of the goods.
- Frequency of loading.
- Customer's needs.

We have to consider that while, in many cases, vehicles are unloaded or loaded by equipment mounted on the loading bays, circumstances often require the ability of the vehicle itself to load and off-load. Accordingly we shall look at equipment used in both circumstances.

Equipment for Loading and Unloading Bays

Automatic dock levellers, or elevating platforms, are almost essential on loading bays, since vehicle platforms are of varying heights. These levellers enable forklift trucks, barrows and the like to be driven from dock into the vehicle. These may be built into the bay or be of the portable type. Forklift trucks are widely used and a wide range of models is available with an even wider range of fittings and adoptions (for example fitting for handling drums, coils, clamps for certain loads, crane hooks, etc). Pallet loads are of course intended for forklift truck movement, and it is therefore an advantage if loads are palletised.

Cranes also have a wide range of uses in loading and unloading. They are particularly useful where large and heavy loads are involved, but are unable to deal with large volumes. The cost of installing cranes is high and the amount of goods traffic to be unloaded must justify the high capital cost involved. Cranes have freedom of movement within a certain area. There are several types of crane available the main ones being:

- *Fixed Jib:* which is a single mast in a fixed position so, naturally, the area where it can operate is limited.
- *Gantry Type:* this comprises load-bearing girders supported at each end and running on rails which gives the gantry the means of movement. On the girders is a trolley housing, the lifting mechanism which provides the traverse movement. Traverse is therefore possible in all directions. Control is by a suspended cabin or a remote control switch.
- *Wheeled Type:* when a crane is mounted on road wheels, it is a useful and mobile piece of apparatus. There are several types available for purchase or hire.

- *Rail-Mounted Cranes:* these are limited to areas where rails are laid.
- *Pully Blocks and Hoists:* in a sense these are types of cranes but are smaller, and can usually be fixed where required for a particular job. Awkward and cumbersome loads can be unloaded with these. There are many types available varying from traditional "rape-blocks", to the pull-lift type using a roller chain.
- *Telphers* are another type of crane useful for particular operations. They are cub-operated and run over a certain area on a mono or single overhead rail. Movement is, therefore, restricted to one direction only. When fitted with grabs they are often used for loading loose materials such as sand, gravel or coal.
- *Pneumatic Tubes* handle loose materials in powder form and are often used for flour, sand and similar materials. The tubes are laid from the loading bay to where the material is produced and the material sucked along the tube.
- *Pipelines* are needed where liquids are involved.
- *Conveyors* are widely used in loading and off-loading materials, since they are particularly suited to high-volume loads as movement is continuous and comparatively cheap. Conveyors may use gravity or be powered. They may also be fixed or moveable. A fixed conveyor taken up considerable space and for unloading purposed portable conveyors are often found more useful. Care must be taken in handling conveyors as they are vulnerable to damage. There are types of conveyors available to suit a wide range of materials, for example flat belt, toughened belt, slatted, filler and so on.

In many circumstances, such as vehicles delivering to retail shops or scattered depots, handling aids are unlikely to be available at the site of unloading or loading. Therefore we have to consider aids that are available for use on vehicles.

Loading and Unloading Equipment Available on Vehicles

Tail lifts are provided on a wide range of vehicles. Lifts are also available for the side of the vehicle, so loads can be transferred to the pavement easily. A tail lift is on the rear of the vehicle and forms a platform on which goods can be lowered to ground level by power. The vehicle must have a chassis and framework strong enough to support the mechanism. Rollers may be provided in floor of the vehicle allowing loads to be moved easily inside the vehicle. Where they are provided they may be retractable below the floor to prevent the load moving. Cranes are available for mounting onto vehicles. A specially strengthened floor and chassis is required. Various types are available to suit particular purposes. Tankers are normally fitted with pumps permitting them to discharge their loads into the customers' tanks or wherever required.

Special equipment is also available for many purposes and we have not got the time to study every aspect, but if you have a special problem in this area, investigation among suppliers of vehicle equipment will probably be worthwhile. One, for instance, will build a conveyor inside the van body.

Road Vehicle Design and Road Planning

As goods vehicles are costly to buy and maintain it is essential that the fleet is operated efficiently; this includes ensuring that the vehicles are those most suitable for their intended purpose. In deciding the type of vehicle for a particular use, we must consider the following factors:

- The goods or materials to be carried.
- The goods we may wish to transport in the future.
- Our distribution area.
- Number of journeys made.
- Potential changes in distribution patterns.
- The expected life of vehicles.
- Any relevant government legislation.
- Any advantages offered in terms of cost, customer relations or turnround time in using special purpose vehicles, or particular design modifications.
- What our competitors or independent haulers are likely to do.

One of the first decisions to be taken is whether to use a standard vehicle available from vehicle manufacturers or to have the vehicle, at least as far as the body is concerned, specially made.

Standard Vehicle Bodies

Manufacturers of road haulage vehicles have a large range of these available "off the shelf". A study of what is available will be well worthwhile, since a standard body will be much cheaper than a specially designed one. Indeed, in the light van class (and most other vehicles up to about six tons) it is doubtful if it is worth having a custom-designed van body. Manufacturers also have available a number of engine sizes and various axle ratios.

Custom-Built Vehicles

The main reasons for choosing to have a vehicle body built to your own specifications are:

- To obtain more economic distribution because vehicles can be designed to carry greater loads.
- Vehicles can be designed to facilitate materials handling.
- Vehicles can be designed to suit your routes.
- A specially designed body may minimise damage to goods.

Disadvantages may be that a specialised vehicle has a lower resale value, flexibility of operations reduced and if the nature of your goods change, new vehicles may be needed.

Motor Vehicle (Construction and Use) Regulations

These regulations apply to commercial vehicles and trailers, and must be observed by all operators. Therefore anyone considering designing their own vehicle body should understand them. The items covered include such matters as:

Maximum Weight in Relation to Wheelbase.

- Length and width of chassis
- Brakes
- Tyres
- Lighting equipment
- Mirrors

There is a choice of vehicle bodies available, and the most common types are:

- The bon van, widely used where goods need protecting during transit, often used for clothing, foodstuffs and general parcels traffic.

- The main general purpose vehicle is the platform truck which comes in two basic forms. Firstly, the flat platform which has no sides can carry most goods, which are protected by tarpaulin and ropes. Secondly a platform with sides: this is often used for loose material such as coal, sand, soil and the like. It may be fitted with tipping gear to facilitate unloading.
- Swap or de-mountable bodies are an attempt to combine the advantages of the bon van with the flexibility of the platform vehicle. The bon van is this case is a separate unit, which is lifted onto the platform vehicle, or off it as required. This gives the effect of a dual purpose vehicle, for when the bon body is not mounted a flat platform vehicle is available when it is needed. The bodies can be built to suit the needs of the operator.
- Articulated vehicles are now used extensively for the transport of goods, and the variety available is considerable. Basically, however, they are either flat platform or bon type. They consist of a separate towing unit and vehicle body. The towing or tractor unit comprises the cab and power unit, to which can be coupled various bodies. Therefore a towing unit can take a load to a customer, detach the body, couple up another body and return with it to its depot. This greatly assists loading and unloading, more important probably is the quicker turnround time that can be achieved by this method of operation.
- Many other types of vehicle are available and if money is no object almost anything can be built on a chassis. However, the most commonly used categories are special containers or skips used by scrap dealers for collecting swarf or similar materials, tankers for liquids (from milk to oil), special vehicles for ready mixed concrete, and refrigerated units.

Road Planning

The economic use of the vehicle is the objective, and this is likely to be better achieved if the vehicle is designed to suit particular needs. If it is decided to go ahead with custom-built vehicles, to facilitate economic loading, the manufacturers of the vehicles should be consulted. Factors to be considered in deciding size and type of body include:

- Nature and weight of loads.
- Method of packing, size of pallets, unitisation and use of containers.
- Nature of the goods and method of distribution.

A study of these factors will enable decisions to be made on such matters as:

- Type of body and of chassis required.
- Which loads will require a bon van, or platform vehicle, etc.
- Methods of loading, for example rear loading, side loading, etc.

Accessibility is an important feature when planning vehicles. Those delivering goods to high street shops will have different requirements to the lorry delivering heavy machinery. Among matters to be taken into account are the platform height of the vehicle and the need for rear doors, roller shutters, side doors or curtain sides.

Methods of Construction

A vehicle must be suitable for its purpose, but at the same time have durability, strength and lightness. A wide variety of materials is available in the construction of vehicle bodies, all with advantages and disadvantages. Among these are steel and its alloys, strong but liable to corrosion. Aluminium alloys are of course not liable to corrosion. All metal panels can be beaten out. Plastic which is durable, including glass fibre, cannot be repaired easily if damaged.

The purpose and use of the vehicle will enable the most suitable combination of materials for body construction to be decided. Often in large vans, roof lights are put in to assist loading. Loading aids were mentioned earlier, and it is cheaper if these are fitted at the time of manufacture. In addition, other interior fittings may also be considered desirable and should be considered at the construction strange. Such items may include tie rails, shoving bars, rubbing rails and damage bags. The cab is an important part of any vehicle, but this is not strictly within the scope of body construction. However, we shall achieve our objective more easily if strain on the driver is minimised. Therefore comfort and safety is important. Such items as seats, air conditioning, radio and so on must be considered. Good instrumentation and warning systems are also an essential aid to good driving

The law relating to the safe carriage of goods in general is contained in the Motor Vehicle Construction and Use Regulations and the various Transport Acts. These cover the mechanical condition of vehicles, and their safe driving. Codes of practice also exist in relation to the securing of loads of sheeting and roping, and by the use of shoring bars and webbing restraints similar to car seat belts. The carriage of dangerous goods is covered by separate regulations regarding the design and construction of petrol tankers, for example, and the labelling of such vehicles to indicate the nature of their contents to other road users and the emergency services who may be called out to deal with any incident.

Distribution and Marshalling

The pattern of distribution must be studied and such factors as the following taken into account.

- Urban and rural routes.
- Delivery of goods to a large number of individual customers.
- Bulk deliveries.
- Number of special loads (such as heavy machinery).
- Collections.
- Vehicles needed for each load.

Suitable arrangements must be made for marshalling goods for distribution. This will usually mean:

- Planning of loads according to geographical location, and the need to make up a full load.
- Planning loading, so that goods are in order of delivery.
- A separate marshalling area will be required with, perhaps, separate "pens" for each route.

There will usually be part loads or parcels which will not justify sending a vehicle, in which case it is usual to use public haulers.

Road Haulage

The advantages of road transport are as follows:

- Flexibility: HGVs can go almost anywhere and can carry almost anything.
- Door-to-door delivery from consignee to consignor.
- Speedy delivery.

- Capital investment in movement of goods can be low, as one vehicle can often carry a variety of goods over many routes.
- Special or elaborate packing is not usually needed.

If a company decides to distribute goods by road, it may choose either to send them by a public haulier, or to purchase or hire a fleet and operate it themselves. The advantages of using a public haulier to include the following:

- As the company does not operate any vehicles of its own, it has no responsibilities or problems in the area of transport when a load or consignment is available.
- A particular type of vehicle can be used to suit particular needs.
- All costs are known in advance (the rates charged), the most competitive charges selected, and plans made accordingly.
- Transport facilities, such as garages, workshops and so on, do not have to be provided.

Charges

Charges for sending goods by the public haulier are based upon weight of consignment and the distance carried. Full loads and specials are also charged on a similar basis. The charge is based upon either a weight of one ton or, if the load is bulky, 80 cubic feet is taken to equal one ton.

General Parcels Traffic

Often called "smalls", most haulers issue a set scale of charges for small parcels. This scale is made up of a set of charges and the country is divided for this purpose. There would, for instance, be a set of charges for parcels collected in, say, the Birmingham area and delivered in the London area, and a further list of charges for traffic between North Wales and Tyneside. These scales are subject to various modifications according to particular circumstances. For example, there will be extras for collections and perhaps a reduction if parcels are delivered to a depot only. There are minimum charges levied by most carriers. Also, if vehicles are detained for a long time extra charges may be incurred.

Where a company, such as a mail order company, deals with large volumes of parcels, special contract arrangements can be made with the haulier. A typical contract agreement would be based on the number of parcels despatched over a period, the delivery areas, and the availability of vehicles and result in a flat-rate scale for all parcels delivered anywhere in the UK.

Contract Hire

In many cases companies feel that for reasons of operating convenience and prestige it is necessary to run their own fleet. A method of doing so without spending large sums in capital expenditure for purchase is to hire a fleet of vehicles. Some of the advantages offered are:

- The company has complete control of operating the vehicles, and in respect of the drivers.
- There is considerable flexibility since, the vehicles are under the company's control.
- Vehicles are normally painted in the hiring company's livery, and so advertising and prestige are gained.
- The hirer is usually responsible for servicing and maintenance, licenses and other charges.
- The agreement will usually provide for replacement vehicles if any are off the road for any length of time.
- Costs are known in advance, and can therefore be allowed for in budgets.

The disadvantages of contract hire include the following:

- Costs may be incurred as the vehicles are limited to carrying goods for the hirer, and return loads may be difficult to obtain. This means that vehicles may sometimes be running empty.
- Charges will continue regardless of the use made of the vehicles.
- Transport facilities, such as garages, offices and loading and routing staff will have to be provided, and will be a cost upon the company, in addition to hire charges.
- At the end of the contract period, the vehicles will revert to the company from whom they were hired.

Basis of Charges

In each case there will be a detailed contract between the hire company and the hiring company, which must be negotiated to suit each particular circumstance. Typical agreements might be:

- *Heavy Haulage:* a fixed annual charge plus a charge per mile, or a high annual charge but the mileage charge operating after a specified mileage. Period of hire might be for five years.
- *Light Vans:* a fixed annual charge up to a specified mileage, and a mileage charge when this is exceeded. Again the hire period may be for five years.

The agreement must be studied carefully to make sure that it meets requirements and the costs you intend to be covered are in fact covered. Points to check are:

- Do charges cover maintenance and license charges?
- Is replacement provided if a vehicle is off the road?
- Are any advance charges required?
- Is insurance cover adequate for your requirements?
- What are the conditions under which replacement vehicles are supplied?
- Are you sure that mileage charges are reasonable?

Own Fleet

Many companies prefer to own and operate their own vehicles, since this gives maximum control and flexibility, and may well be cheaper than other methods. The advantage is that the company has complete control over vehicles and drivers, which gives maximum flexibility in operation. Similarly the vehicles can be used to project the company's image by its livery and for advertising particular products. A company operating its own fleet will have to provide a transport management function, and the necessary supporting organisation. Workshop and garage facilities for maintenance and facilities for storing and issuing fuel are required along with facilities for drivers and mates. There are of course disadvantages which include:

- Provision of capital sums to acquire and replace vehicles.
- Difficulty in assessing exact costs of providing own fleet since some costs will be hidden in general overheads (wages and salaries department, etc).
- Vehicles are licensed for your use only, and cannot be used for anyone else (ie hired out).

- Charges are incurred whether vehicles are used or not.
- Problem of unbalanced loads, vehicles may run empty due to difficulty in obtaining return loads.
- Tendency to use vehicles without regard to cost, "as they belong to the company anyway".

Operating Costs of Own Fleet

All the charges which are involved in the organisation of a transport undertaking and the costs which are incurred in either the movement of passengers or of goods are covered by the term operating costs, and for the sake of convenience these are divided into standing charges and running costs.

Standing Charges

Immediately a business is commenced and vehicles obtained, certain expenses will be incurred whether or not the vehicles are operated on the road; such charges are not related to the number of miles run of the number of hours worked. These charges are as follows:

- Interest on capital, if allowed, at 1 per cent or 2 per cent above minimum lending rate.
- Depreciation on cost price of vehicle, less residual value and cost of tyres.
- Revenue licences: annual cost.
- Road service licence and certificate of fitness.
- Licence: annual cost.
- Insurance: comprehensive policy including third party, fire, and so on. Employer's liability, goods-in transit insurance, and so on.
- General administrative charges.
- Garage expenses.
- Wages.

Each one of these components which together form the standing charges of an undertaking will now be considered separately.

Interest on Capital

It has been contended that operators should include in their standing charges a sum equal to that which they would receive if the capital had been invested in government or other high-class securities, instead of being invested in vehicles; that the interest on capital should therefore be an element in standing charges. There seems no logical reason why this should be done, for it is not the general practice for trading companies to allow interest on fixed assets in assessing costs of production. This should be absorbed by the item allowed for profit. It may be found, therefore, that some operators will allow for interest on capital, while other operators ignore this item completely and rely on the percentage of profit added to cost.

Depreciation

Depreciation is due to three causes: wear and tear, depreciation in value due to fall in market price and obsolescence due to the constant improvement in design. Wear and tear is the common cause of depreciation in value, and for this reason there are those who contend that the charge under this heading should be included in running charges; even if a vehicle remained stationary all the time it would depreciate in market value, and in the end become obsolete, therefore inclusion of depreciation in standing charges is the general practice.

The cost of tyres must be deducted from the purchase price of the vehicle. As several sets of tyres will be fitted to the vehicle during the course of its useful life, it is thought proper that these should form an element of the running costs.

Finally, in estimating the amount to be written off for depreciation, the operator must assess the value that is expected to be obtained from the vehicle upon sale at the end of its useful life. Many operators sell and buy new vehicles, rather than arrange for extensive refits which would make the vehicle mechanically should for several more years. This value on sale or scrap value must be allowed in providing for depreciation.

The charge for depreciation is therefore based on cost of vehicle, less cost of tyres, less residual value. The resultant sum is the amount to be provided for depreciation, before distribution of profits, during the expected life of the vehicle. There are several methods of arranging for this.

The necessity for the allowance has previously been explained. If this were not charged, it would be equivalent to returning a proportion of the capital each year to the shareholders.

Insurance

Adequate insurance against all risks is necessary in any business, while third party risk insurance on vehicles is made compulsory by law. Further insurance must be taken out according to the nature of the business and the work undertaken. For the purpose of costing, insurance is included as a standing charge, for it is incurred whether the vehicles are on the road or in the garage. It may be reduced on the vehicle if it is taken out of commission for the considerable time.

Licences

This item covers both the revenue licence and also the licences which are necessary by virtue of the provisions of the Road Traffic Acts. The charges paid for these licences are fixed, but the cost of the revenue licence varies with the unladen weight of a goods vehicle or the seating capacity of a passenger service vehicle. This item must therefore be allocated in accordance with the amount paid for each vehicle. With licences issued under the Road Traffic Acts, these are at a fixed rate per annum, and consequently the cost is divided proportionately among all vehicles of the fleet.

General Administrative Charges

General administrative charges include the salaries of office staff and managers, directors' fees, rents, rates, taxes, lighting and heating of offices, postage, telephones, stationery, time-keepers and watchmen, garage and depot staff and other essential expenses which are incurred for the benefit of the business as a whole, and which cannot be allocated to any particular vehicle. These items can only be included among the standing charges, and as such are assessed on a time basis. Such charges could be allocated to a vehicle in accordance with mileage run, but it would be very difficult to allocate the item precisely.

Garage Expenses

The wages of garage and depot staff may be included under this heading instead of the previous one, together with all other expenses relating to the upkeep of the garage: rents, trades, taxes, lighting, heating and so on. It may be noted that the repair shop is usually treated separately in order that the cost of this may be allocated over the repairs to the vehicles. Day-to-day maintenance may be detailed to carry out duties in the garage, and the proportion of wages for time so spent should be allocated to garage expenses.

Wages

This item covers the wages of drivers and of statutory attendants or mates in the case of goods vehicles. With road hauliers, drivers usually have charge of one vehicle, and their wages can therefore be charged to that vehicle; but where the driver's time is spent on two or more vehicles, then the time must be ascertained and the wage split up accordingly. It must also be borne in mind that drivers are entitled to an annual holiday, and this must be allowed for in making up costs either by charging it up against the driver's own vehicle, or spreading the item over the whole fleet. Wages must be included with the running costs.

The above items form the total cost of standing charges. With road hauliers it is usual to find the standing cost for each vehicle, and it is essential to divide some of the items in accordance with the varying tonnage of the vehicle.

Running Costs

Under this heading are included the following charges:

- Petrol or other fuel lubricants: quantity used, worked out to a fraction of a penny per mile.
- Tyres: actual issues.
- Maintenance and repairs: cost, or a fixed weekly sum.
- Sundries: cost.

Fuel

The quantity issued to each vehicle must be ascertained and charged to that vehicle, and the mileage for each vehicle must be obtained for each gallon or unit of fuel consumed, and also for lubricating oil.

Tyres

The wear on tyres in accordance with the mileage and the charge under this item must be assessed accordingly; the manufacturer's assessment of life must be taken until the operator has sufficient experience upon which to base his own calculations. Some operators include this item under maintenance.

Maintenance and Repairs

The cost under this heading varies from week to week, and in accordance with the life of the vehicle. Experience has to be the guiding factor in this connection, for a weekly sum must be charged to each vehicle, based on usage, to cover the item, and by this means something in the nature of a sinking fund is built up. The total of the weekly charge is credited to this account, and the actual cost of repairs debited thereto.

Sundries

There are many small expenses which cannot conveniently be included under any of the above headings, and must be charged out to each vehicle, or allocated proportionately among all vehicles.

Rail Freight

Railways have certain advantages when arranging for the movement of goods. Among these are:

- A reliable and speedy service between main cities.
- Collection and delivery to customers can be arranged if this is required.
- Special contracts for the movement of large regular consignments are possible.

On the other hand there may be problems in using rail, including:

- Good and secure packaging is required.
- Delivery times may be lengthy if customers are not on the main line.
- Danger of pilferage.

There are a number of services offered by British Rail.

Ordinary Goods Service

Single consignments which may be delivered or collected from the station. Alternatively the railways collect goods for despatch, and deliver to consignee.

Passenger Express Parcels Service

Goods are carried on normal passenger services. This is intended for parcel traffic, and parcels may be handed in at any station. It is also possible to arrange for parcels to be collected and delivered by the railway.

Freight Sundries

British Rail operate this service, which is a door-to-door one. They collect from the consignor and deliver to the consignee by road. There is a weight limit of three tons on consignments.

Priority, Express Passenger Service (Red Star)

This Red Star service gives priority from station to station. Parcels can be despatched on stated trains by request. Special charges apply to this service.

Use of Containers by Rail

Containers offer many advantages in the despatch of goods; we shall look at these in detail, but at the moment is is sufficient to know that there are many types of various sizes available. This means that a container is available to suit many types of goods. Containers can be loaded by the consignor, transported by road to the railway, and afterwards taken by road to the consignee. These services are operated by Freightliners Limited, who have a number of Freightliner Depots throughout the UK. Containers are delivered to a depot by road, transported by Freightliner train to a depot near the consignee, off-loaded to road vehicles and delivered to the consignee. Freightliners are on a regular schedule timetable.

Special Arrangements for Large Regular Consignments

British Rail offer special facilities to anyone who has large quantities of goods to move on a regular basis. Examples of the type of goods are minerals such as iron ore, coal, oil, cement and even motor cars, which are moved to distributors in this way. Anyone who has travelled by rail will have seen trains made up of oil tankers or car transporters; these are company trains operated by British Rail to suit the needs of particular companies. To take advantage of this service it is better if the companies have their own rail sidings, connected to the British Rail system.

Rail Charges

At one time the railway operated an inflexible, rather complicated rate-charging system. This has now been abandoned. Many customers today are very large organisations placing substantial amounts of business, and making individual contracts with British Rail. Examples are:

- Mail order or other companies with a large amount of parcel traffic may arrange a special price per parcel irrespective of distance or parcel weight.
- Large organisations operating "company trains", for example motor car manufacturers, cement manufacturers and similar bodies with bulk contracts, will negotiate special contract prices.
- Freightliners also negotiate individual rates with customers for hire or lease of containers, as well as for the transport by Freightliner from door to door.
- National Carriers also operate a system of national distribution in association with the railway operators.

Air Freight

Modern travel means air transport. We now travel by air as a matter of course for holidays and for business. Air freight is now as important as passenger travel, and is as convenient when wishing to send goods from one place to another.

There are disadvantages of air freight when compared to other methods of transport, and these include:

- Higher cost of transport.
- Restriction in size and weight of materials to be sent by air.
- Prohibition of certain items.
- Possible delays and diversions due to weather.

We must consider against these the advantages of despatching by air.

- Speed of delivery.
- Reduction in standard of packing is possible.
- Lower insurance rates may be obtained.
- Greater security of goods
- Marketing flexibility is obtained.

When one considers the advantages and disadvantages of air freight it becomes clear that in the following circumstances air freight is fully justified.

- Where goods are urgently required, for example medical supplies or a part required for plant that is broken down.
- Where the nature of the goods make it imperative that they are delivered quickly, for example daily newspapers, fresh flowers and similar items.
- Where the value is high compared with weight or size, for example precious stones, modern transistorised electronic equipment.

Regulation of Air Freight

This is carried out by an international body on which are represented various member countries, who have international air lines. It is known as the International Air Transport Association (IATA). This organisation fixes rates, and makes regulations observed by all airlines. Among the more important are:

- *The Cabotage Principle:* this states that all air freight within a country's boundaries must be carried by that country's airlines. This prevents foreign competition on domestic routes. In the case of the UK, it also applies to traffic to and from the colonies and dependent territories; note that special non-international rates may apply in the case of UK cabotage.
- *Determination of Cargo Rates:* air cargo is always calculated per kilogramme gross weight or, in bulky material, per volume equivalent. Air freight rates are decided by IATA on the above basis, and are from airport to airport.
- *Minimum Charges:* these apply for small consignments irrespective of actual weight or volume. They take precedence over charges that would be make if the general cargo rate were applied.
- *General Cargo Rate:* this applies to all goods not in a specific rate grouping. These consist of minimum charges (m), usual rate (n), and quantity rate (q) at various brake points.
- *Specific Commodity Rate:* this applies to specifically designated commodities carried between two specified points, for consignments at fixed minimum rates. It is lower than the general freight rate.

- *Class Rates:* these apply to specifically designated classes of goods for carriage between points in a specified area or areas. There is a percentage reduction on surcharge based upon the under 100kg general freight rate for consignments to which minimum charges apply.
- *Special Bulk Unitisation Charges:* where goods are shipped in IATA registered and standardised containers, special rates are available. Most routes use pallets and containers, and freight companies will be pleased to discuss the method of transport with customers.
- *Documentation:* the most important document is the consignment note or airway bill. This note is a standardised IATA document and is in two forms: one for use on domestic routes and one for use on international routes. It is prepared by the consignor in a number of copies, one of which he or she retains, a copy goes to the airline, and also accompanies the goods. It is evidence of a contract and a receipt for the goods. Unlike the bill of lading used when goods are sent by sea, it is not a negotiable instrument (that is to say ownership cannot be changed by endorsing the bill), nor is it required in order to obtain the goods.
- *Declaration of Value:* the value of the consignment must always be stated, although the statement "no value declared" is allowed. Valuation charges are made on a weight or volume basis; below this value no charge is made.
- *Valuable Items:* where valuable items are to be sent by air, quantity rates do not apply. They are charged at the under 45kg rate plus 100 per cent although this may vary with the item value/type and indeed the air carrier.
- *Hazardous Goods:* certain items are classed as hazardous, and will not be accepted for air freight. Among these are explosives, compressed gases and inflammable liquids. Full details are given in the IATA "Restricted Articles Regulation Manual".
- *Other Matters Dealt with by the IATA:* these are many but include uniform labelling of consignments, making advance arrangements when necessary, tracing consignments, arranging transfers and so forth.

Other Documentation Required

In order to prepare the IATA airway bill and generally to make the necessary arrangements for despatch by air, the following are needed:

- Export license (if applicable).
- Commercial invoices (in several copies).
- Packing lists.
- Certificate of origin.
- Instruction for despatch goods form, or a similar method of giving despatch instructions.

If receiving goods by air, the following documents will usually be required:

- Import licence (if applicable).
- Commercial invoices.
- Packing lists.
- Certificate of origin.
- Customs declaration forms.

Food for Thought

Trading organisations, when deciding on whether to own and operate their own vehicles or to use the services of contractors, should employ classic make-or-buy purchasing decision techniques. In the particular case of transport, organisations should be aware of the marketing techniques employed by contractors (such as emphasising the immediate cash flow benefits from the sale of the existing vehicle fleet, which may have the effect of turning the whole exercise into a very expensive form of borrowing for short-term gain).

The future prospects for door-to-door parcels delivery services in most countries are stimulated by the globalisation of business and the growth of mail order retailing. Other factors include the legal environment (for example the abandonment of state-run monopolies and the provision of the necessary transport infrastructure).

The objectives of the supervisor when making decisions about the day-to-day allocation of vehicles to routes and loads should be to satisfy customer requirements at the lowest overall cost. These should be related to performance targets and budgets, but should include long-term as well as short-term goals. (As an example, many companies try to ensure that the same driver delivers to each customer daily so as to build up good working and marketing relationships between them.)

The current trend in the FMCG (fast moving consumer goods) sector towards large centralised supply points can be explained by the drive for cost-effectiveness and the increased efficiency of road transport which enables 24-hour delivery to be achieved throughout a country from a single supply point.

Case Study

The Problem: Vacuum Generators, who were a division of Fisons Instruments, manufacture a range of specialised scientific equipment. With users throughout Europe demanding rapid delivery of components, Vacuum Generators decided that their sales growth depended largely on the level of customer service provided. Market research showed that no single supplier had a particular competitive edge but that guaranteed delivery times could significantly improve a supplier's market share. The question was, could distribution be improved to provide a quicker guaranteed service whilst, at the same time, reducing costs?

When the Logistics Business examined the distribution network it became clear that there was considerable scope for reducing stocks and cutting lead times by eliminating the locally held stock and shipping directly from Vacuum Generators' warehouse in Hastings. However, this had been tried in the past and discounted by Vacuum Generators on the basis that it was too expensive to ship the many small, low-value items which customers required. Therefore, in order to confirm the view and assess the overall viability of a new strategy they needed to put together a detailed analysis of all goods ordered and shipped over a six-month period. With efforts concentrated on Germany (by far the largest market) every order despatched was analysed and compared with alternative shipment methods.

The Solution: it became apparent that there were significant benefits to be gained from holding the stock centrally and shipping to customers' "on demand" using one of the global parcel carriers such as DHL or TNT. What is more, when the costs were analysed, it proved to be cheaper to deliver overnight than on a two to three day delivery service. This was due to the fact that for overnight delivery airfreight is used and this favours the lightweight packages which made up most of the Vacuum Generators deliveries. Hence it was decided to offer customers a guaranteed two to three day delivery service but to use the overnight service of the carriers, thus being confident of achieving high standards of performance.

The Success: Delivery times have been reduced from more than a week to less than three days. Service performance has greatly improved. Overall delivery costs have been reduced. Stock is now held at one location and total inventory is lower.

Details of other cases and service provided by the Logistics Business Organisation can be obtained from: The Logistics Business Limited, Aston Science Park, Birmingham, B7 4BJ, United Kingdom. Tel: 0121 333 6303. Fax: 0121 333 6407. E-Mail: HYPERLINK mailto:Info@logistics.co.uk Info@logistics.co.uk. http://www.logistics/co.uk

CHAPTER 11

Physical Distribution

We have, so far, looked at the operation of stores and stockyards, transport operation and the various samples of legislation with which the stores manager must comply. We need now to consider the methods of achieving effective planning and control of the distribution of goods, to customers, stores and warehouses by a road fleet.

Distribution

The development of distribution facilities and techniques is increasingly evident in the attention given to this area of company activities, taking into account the need to co-ordinate

- transport: vehicles and routes;
- warehousing: central and local;
- production: batch size and lead time;
- customer service: appropriate level;
- finance: capital investment.

In practice, the optimum distribution system may result from trade-off agreements within the organisation, combining individual cost advantages and disadvantages to obtain an overall cost benefit to the company and a satisfactory customer service level.

The growing interest in the contribution which an efficient distribution system can make to company objectives has been recognised by the formation of the Centre for Physical Distribution Management sponsored by the British Institute of Management.

It is interesting to note that, organisationally, the concept of a totally co-ordinated distribution system at senior management or director level is complementary to the materials management development of a "linked" system of procurement of supplies, storage and inventory control, and production control to obtain the benefits of a total supplies system and access to the early stages of design and development in choice of materials.

Distribution Planning

A number of factors must be considered in planning a distribution system, the first and most important being the needs of the customer. However, it would clearly be impossible to send a vehicle every time a customer required an item and we have to balance the customers' needs against the cost of providing that service. There are a number of distribution channels by which a product or service reaches a customer and these are illustrated in Figure 42.

Figure 42 Channels of Distribution

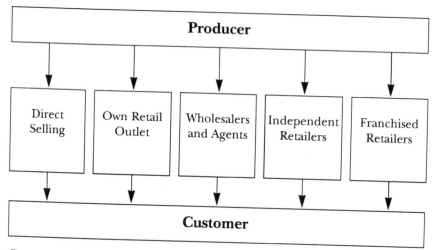

Customers' needs will be very varied and we must decide the type of transport organisation and distribution system best suited for a particular customer. In many trades a weekly delivery is required, and this is not difficult to plan, but it is as well to remember that people expect a delivery on a particular day, and this should be taken note of and adhered to if possible. In many cases weekly deliveries must be on specified days. There are trades where daily deliveries are required. Suppliers of drugs and medical supplies are one example; fresh foods such as bread and cakes are another.

In some cases goods are sent out when a full load is made up, but this is unusual since most businesses are based upon a regular delivery service. This is true of deliveries made from central stores to sub-stores and depots. Special loads of the type we see taking machinery to a plant with police escort are, of course, one-offs and need very careful planning.

Loads

The type of load and the quantity and/or volume are important factors that must be taken account of when planning the distribution system. The nature of the goods must also be considered. Perishable goods must be delivered right away and will require particular methods of handling. Petroleum spirit and other inflammable or toxic substances will be subject to special regulations. Corrosive loads will need special precautions. If any of these goods with special handling problems are to be carried, arrangements must be made when distribution is being planned.

The Organisation Required

The above factors, together with the volume of traffic involved, will give the basis for deciding the type of organisation best suited for our purpose. A decision must be made on centralising or having a decentralised method of operating. Where the work is mainly of a local character, it is probably sensible to operate on a decentralised basis. This means vehicles operating from a depot in each area where there are customers or stores, each depot having its own manager and organisation. This method has the advantage of direct control by local management and it is flexible. However, where a company has a number of vehicle depots, it may be costly, since a number of vehicles must be carried at each depot, some of which may be underutilised. Where a company is operating on a national basis, it is more likely that a national centralised system will be adopted. This will make maximum utilisation of transport easier, since central planning is possible. It also makes it uneconomical to use management aids, such as computers, for vehicle scheduling and loading. Support services such as owned workshops are also possible with centralisation.

We must also consider the method operating and the type of service, for this will influence the organisation of the transport service. The company that provides a delivery service to each customer will need more detailed planing than a company that does not provide this service. Many large organisations find it economical to have depots or collection centres at each regional location (London, Birmingham, Bristol, Manchester and so on). This enables them to use large vehicles which when fully-loaded are more economical to operate than small vehicles involved in the same traffic. This method is often known as "trunking", and is popular where the volume of traffic justifies it, as a large vehicle can take a load from one depot to another, and return with a load back to its depot. It is, of course, also necessary to provide a local service, either by your own transport or by using local haulier on a sub-contract basis. If operated by your own company, a local management organisation will be needed. If the job is sub-contracted this is avoided, but you will have lost direct control of delivery to your customers. Where the traffic is only serving factories or depots within a company or group, the local factories or depots may collect form a central depot in the region at regular times.

There are often localities that have to be served which present special problems. The north of Scotland and the Shetlands are examples of such areas, as well as areas of the UK which, while not remote, may have only a solitary manufacturing unit or customer. It would clearly be uneconomical to send a vehicle on this type of journey and to incorporate in the plan provision for the use of commercial carriers for this traffic is essential.

Warehouses and Depots

The provision of warehouses and depots will obviously affect the planning of a distribution system. This first point to consider is whether warehouses are necessary. Two factors have, in recent years, altered the basis of providing warehouses. The first is the provision of the modern motorway system, which makes it possible to supply a very wide area from a central warehouse. Consider the area that can be serviced from a central warehouse in West Bromwich which is adjacent to the M5, M6 and M1. The second factor is the recent development of large vehicles which make it economical to move large loads, via the motorway network. Nevertheless there may well be a case for warehouses to be provided, based upon:

- *Types of Goods Being Transported:* perishable goods may require local storage where goods are regional (only sold in some areas).
- *Cost of Vehicle Operation:* it may be that vehicle mileage is sufficiently reduced by providing a local warehouse to make it an economical proposition. Better vehicle utilisation may also be possible.
- *Customers Needs:* if customers can be better served by having a local warehouse, or they request such a service, then there are reasonable grounds for providing such a facility.

Among factors that should be considered are the:

- cost of order processing;
- stockholding costs;
- lead time for the customer;
- time taken to process orders.

The Management of the Function

This will depend upon the needs of the organisation, and there is no general pattern. The needs of the company, the nature of the traffic, the customer and the market must all be studied. It is common to have a distribution manager but in some companies this function may come under the marketing director or indeed a logistics director.

Logistics and Delivery Planning

In its original meaning logistics referred to the means of moving and quartering troops and of supplying their needs. Today it is also used as a general term for planning the movement of all kinds of materials. It is the means of deciding the best way of doing this that we are now to consider. The objective of planning a delivery service is to organise the types of vehicles and the routes to be used in order to achieve the highest mileage at the highest loading. If this can be done the transport cost per load or item will be the lowest possible. This is important since, as noted earlier, transport adds to the cost but not to the value of goods.

Now, having our objective clearly in mind we can plan to reach it. Planning decisions however must be based on realistic facts established by research and investigation. This investigation must include:

- Operating costs of transport vehicles.
- The distribution and location of customers and collection points. There is a need to list the towns, districts and areas which have customers or collection points and mark their location on a map or by some other convenient means.
- Loads to be carried, size and weight and also the nature of the goods to be carried.
- Individual customer's methods of ordering and their requirements. If collections are to be made, these too must be studied.
- The number of vehicles available, their type and size.
- Maintenance and planned servicing requirements.

As a result of investigations into the above-mentioned factors, the actual planning of deliveries can be made and routes decided on the basis of where customers are and the goods required, customers' particular requirements, and the vehicles available. In practice this means establishing a routine which will mean the provision of a loading bank.

A Goods Loading Bank

Generally, it is found that operators of parcels services maintain loading banks; but a small loading bank will often be of advantage to the general carrier, for there are occasions when goods have to be off-loaded from a vehicle upon which repairs must be effected, and the use of a loading bank will then make transference easier. It is not unusual for one vehicle to be backed against another for transfer of goods to be carried out, and although this may be effective for certain loads, it has disadvantages. Again, where goods have been collected and sent to a distant point and it is found that delivery cannot be performed immediately as, for example, during a holiday it may be an advantage for an operator to off-load and store the goods temporarily, thus releasing the carrying vehicle for further service. A simple storage media is shown in Figure 43.

The first point to be considered before constructing a loading bank is the flow of traffic, and this must be considered in relation to the services given by the operator. It is possible that several vehicles will be engaged each day between main towns, so that the time goods remain on hand before being placed on the on-carrying vehicle is very small. On the other hand, the services of the operator may extend over a large rural area, where a vehicle operates over a certain route on alternative days, twice weekly, or even fives times per weekly service. In such cases parcels must remain on hand and be stored temporarily, and the size of the bank must provide for this temporary storage. One operator may deal with many more packages than another, and yet the need for a large loading bank may not be so great.

Figure 43: A Typical Storage Platform

Other operators, again, accept goods in bulk from rail and arrange for delivery to outlying districts on receipt of instructions from suppliers; the size of the loading bank must therefore be extended to cope with the temporary storage necessary, or an upper storey added to the building for this purpose. The question of the flow of traffic, or the speed with which it can be cleared must receive first consideration in determining the size of a loading bank.

Siting, Construction and Lay-Out of Depots

The quantity of traffic to be handled and the speed with which it is to be cleared must, therefore affect the size of the depot. In deciding upon the site for a depot, several factors must be borne in mind. The depot must be situated near the principal sources of traffic in order to eliminate empty running as much as possible, for this is entirely unremunerative. It must be so placed that easy entrance and exit is available for all types of vehicle likely to be used; a side road for instance would be better for this purpose than a main road; the ground space should allow for further development, and for a marshalling yard in addition to the space to be occupied by buildings. It must also be decided whether vehicles are to be undercover during the night, or left in the open, as this affects the amount of covered space required.

Upon deciding these points, one may then consider the lay-out of the premises which must conform, to an extent, to the shape of the plot. Within the depot must be placed the loading bank, or banks, for the transfer of goods and, in a separate part of the buildings, the repair shops, stores, rest room, and so on. The size of the repair shops will be considered in relation to the work to be carried out, for it may be day-to-day maintenance only, or the repair shops may cater for all repairs to chassis, engine and transmission, and body.

Site and lay-out having been determined, the operator can then make plans for construction and, apart from this having a pleasing appearance, the main points to be considered in connection with it are lighting, heating and ventilation, and the provision of the essential services. Buildings must conform to local bye-laws, and so all plans will need to be passed by the local authority.

There are very few operators of goods transport vehicles who have depot facilities which compare with the operators of road passenger transport. If you look over any goods operator's building (or passenger garage) this difference will be very apparent. The buildings may, however be adequate for the goods operator's business. If possible, inspect a large goods depot, and also a passenger operator's garage, and from them consider the question of siting, lay-out and construction.

A loading bank may be single-sided or double-sided, or a number of bays may be constructed in order to make the maximum use of the space available. The advantage of a double-sided bay is that reception of goods can be more easily controlled where a large number of vehicles are engaged; the work of sorting is performed without interruption and goods stacked in the delivery section. The height of a loading bank must be similar to the platform height of the vehicles, in order to avoid the use of labour unnecessarily in off-loading. Bays containing large unit loads using powered mobile storage are quite common; an illustration is shown at Figure 44.

Figure 44: End-view of Powered Mobile Pallet Racks

Static end rack

Receiving and Despatching Goods at Depots and Warehouses

Normally it is to be expected that collecting vehicles will return to the depot in the evening after making collection rounds, and delivering vehicles will leave on their rounds in the morning, so that a large amount of the sorting work and reloading is done in the late afternoon, and the balance the following morning. There will be some movement of manufacturers goods awaiting suppliers' instructions for delivery and sorting will be carried out during the day. The question of the amount of labour to be engaged on sorting and checking must be conditioned by the flow of traffic, some early and some late turns being essential.

In order to facilitate sorting, the delivery section of the bank must bear indication boards, plainly visible, showing the various sections of the bank allocated to various delivery points, and as the work of off-loading proceeds the goods are immediately transferred to the section of the bank appropriate to the destination.

Within each section of the bay allocated to traffic for delivery there may, or may not, be a further sorting required. If goods are to be placed on a trunking vehicle no further sorting is necessary, but where delivery is to be performed goods must be placed on the vehicle in such a manner that the driver has not to search the vehicle for a particular parcel. Goods must be so loaded that the first deliveries must be at the rear of the vehicle; the last goods to be delivered must be the first to be loaded. This involves sorting out the goods in the order in which delivery is to be carried out either by first examining and sorting out the consignment notes, if these are available, or by reading the labels on the goods in the stack and making out a delivery sheet or loading list.

Lock-Up

Some of the goods dealt with will be of high value and so need special care; other goods may be on hand for which delivery cannot be made due to insufficient address, or the refusal of the consignee to accept delivery. All such goods must be removed from the loading banks and transferred to a lock-up until such time as the manner of disposal has been decided upon.

Supervision

Much of the successful working of a depot depends upon the manager in charge. He or she will receive instructions from the depot manager and ensure that they are carried out and will supervise the checkers and sorters to ensure that the work allocated to them is properly done. The safety of goods whilst lying on hand in the depot are also his or her responsibility, and all steps must be taken to reduce damage to goods by handling, and loss through pilferage. The key of the lock-up must be in the manager's possession, and no unauthorised person must have access to it. The order in which waiting vehicles must be off-loaded, and the manner of loading vehicles is under his or her control. The manager must be experienced in the handling of the various classes of goods dealt with, and the use of the various appliances which are available for the movement of goods, and must be satisfied that traffic is securely stowed on vehicles before leaving the depot.

Checking of Goods

The objects of checking goods are, first, to see that they agree with the details on the collection or delivery sheets or on the consignment notes which may be either prepared by the sender or in the carrier's office; second, to ensure that only goods covered by consignment notes or load waybills are placed on forwarding vehicles; and third, that the goods are in apparent sound condition, properly packed and labelled. When vehicles enter the depot after making collections, the drivers will report to the manager, who will allocate a discharging standard and instruct a checker and sorters to deal with each vehicle. The driver of each vehicle will hand all consignment notes to the checker, who, as the unloading of the vehicle proceeds, will mark off the note that the package or packages have been inspected and are in order for forwarding. Should the checker find any package apparently inadequately addressed, or not properly packed, or suspect that a package contains damaged goods, it should be placed on one side. Instructions should be obtained from the foreman in charge, or from the office, as to the action to be taken. In many cases it will be necessary to communicate with the sender to clear up any point of doubt. Should no consignment note have been obtained from the sender, a note must be taken of the goods and this note must be handed to the office so that the necessary documents can be prepared. The fleet number of the in-carrying vehicle may be placed on the consignment note as a record for future use, if required. When the off-loading of a vehicle has been completed, all consignment notes should be handed into the office for inspection to enable the loads for the out-going vehicles to be made up.

The work of checking out-going vehicles is similar. The consignment notes making up the load will be received from the office, and the checker will see that these are placed in delivery order. He or she will then supervise the actual stowing of the goods on the vehicle and again may put the fleet number of the out-carrying vehicle on the consignment note. In many undertakings, a waybill is prepared, especially for use on trunk journeys, to which the consignment notes are attached. When loading is complete, the checker should initial the waybill or loading sheet.

Incoming vehicles from other depots must be checked when off-loading as carefully as other vehicles. The waybill should be handed to the checker for marking off and any discrepancy between the waybill and the goods received should be noted on the waybill.

We must never of course be satisfied with the method of delivery and routing we are using; one method of ensuring that we are still operating efficiently is to review operations. Here it will mean taking each vehicle, the routes used, and recording such factors as:

- Total mileage per trip.
- Mileage to each delivery point and between delivery points.
- The number of deliveries or collections.
- Time leaving and returning to depot .
- Time at each collection or delivery point.
- Details of loads, such as weights, handling problems and other relevant information.

As a result of the analysis of this information, improved operations can be developed. Points to look for include such indicators as routes which always take longer than expected; hold ups when loading or unloading at the depot or at customers premises; in fact anything which is not normal!

Budgetary Control in Distribution

The master budget of a business is the method by which the performance desired is achieved. It is a method of management control as it is a method of determining standards in each area of performance, measuring actual performance and comparing results. A company budget is normally based upon the sales forecast which, after any adjustments for stocks and capacity, becomes the production programme. The cost of meeting this programme is calculated and becomes the production budget. The production budget is in turn broken down into its component parts, such as materials budget, plant budget and labour budgets.

In a similar way the sales forecast is translated into the sales budget. In order to achieve this level of performance it is necessary for each department to operate at a certain level. This will only be possible at a certain cost, which will become that department's budget. The distribution budget will be one of the departmental budgets which combined with all others will become the overall budget. The objectives of this overall budget are:

- To control the performance at each level of the business and to ensure that company objectives are attained.
- To co-ordinate the various activities in pursuit of the common objective.
- To allow "management by exception" and therefore allow management to concentrate upon areas of deviation from standards.

The Budget Period

For convenience the budgetary period is usually one year, broken down into twelve monthly "mini-budgets". As the period of control is monthly, if the actual expenditure exceeds, or is less than, budgeted, action can be taken quickly, certainly within a short time of the monthly figure being produced.

The Distribution Budget

The factors contributing to this budget will be:

- Warehouse rent and rates.
- Warehouse wages and labour charges.
- Warehouse salaries.
- Warehouse heating and lighting.
- Warehouse maintenance.
- Drivers' wages and other related costs.
- Vehicle costs.
- Garage and workshop costs.
- Fuel costs (petrol and diesel oil), and lubricants.
- Any incidental charges.

Care must be taken to ensure that the budgeted figures are realistic, being based on known facts, and anticipated increases in costs during the budget period.

Cost Centres

The distribution budget will be broken down into cost centres. This is to enable standards to be fixed for each depot, garage or stores, whichever breakdown of operations is most convenient to control the department effectively. In this manner the cost of operating a depot or stores can be known each month, and compared with the budget. Action can be taken where there is a difference between the two figures. This is the real meaning of "management by exception"; the management needs only to look at those instances where the actual figure is different from the budget. The majority of cases where the figures are the same need not be looked at any further.

In a similar way stocks can be controlled by valuation. A cost centre can be a particular stores or warehouse, and if required can be further broken down into material classifications. Thus it is possible to see the value of stock in a warehouse and also the value of, say, steel or types in that location. Thus if labour charges or fuel costs are high at a certain garage, they can be investigated and corrected.

Making sure that products reach customers cannot be regarded by marketing managers as simply the concern of someone else. This distribution activity is as much part of the company's marketing mix as are product, pricing and promotion decisions. In fact, in some markets, the impact of the distribution element on sales can exceed that of the other mix elements. Seen in this light, the means whereby the product reaches the customer assumes a vital importance in marketing strategy. The implications of this view of distribution's marketing role are therefore far-reaching, and can involve a considerable reappraisal of attitudes as well as of the means of distribution used. Moreover, since the average European manufacturing company spends 15 per cent of its sales revenue on distribution-related activities, it is not difficult to contemplate the benefits of such a reappraisal.

Although place is a convenient shorthand description used to define of the quartet of "Ps" which go to make up the marketing mix, it represents the means whereby the needs of the market and the offering of the company are physically matched. As such it provides the addition of time and place utility to the product. Without this added value the product is worthless. Without effective planning and control there may be no products to physically distribute. There is in essence a chain and this is shown in Figure 45.

Figure 45: Transport & Distribution Links in the Chain

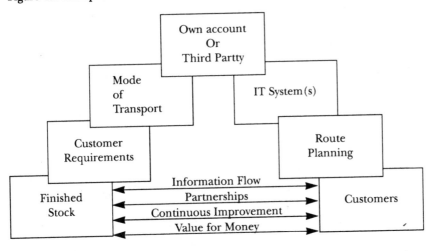

Again each link should be reviewed and assessed in order to develop the full strength of the chain.

Food for Thought

Forklift trucks are often taken for granted. A daily check should be undertaken and cover:

- Levels of hydraulic and engine oils, fuel, battery and coolant where applicable.
- No leaking from any of the above nor from lift cylinders
- All controls are functioning correctly: handbrake, hand and foot controls, hydraulic lines, steering.
- Cab and safety frame, wheels and tyres are satisfactory.

Forklift trucks can be multi-purpose but there are different types and should be used properly which, for example:

- *Counterbalance:* the most popular type of truck for lifting or stacking operations where the load is carried on forks projecting forward of the front wheels and which can move vertically only.
- *Reach:* here the forks are accommodated within the wheelbase while goods are in transit but projected forward when lifting the load so no heavy counterbalancing is required and the truck can turn easily in confined spaces.

- *Side-loading:* similar to the reach truck but the mast and forks are projected from the side which is particularly useful when lengths of material such as piping and timber are to be carried and/or stocked alongside aisles in the stores.

The use of materials handling equipment may frequently be abused. Examples of good use include:

- *Narrow Aisle Forklift Trucks:* quick in operation and can reach greater heights than conventional trucks so useful when ready access to all levels is required.
- *Overhead Travelling Crane with Fork Attachment:* can complement the normal crane by handling pallets in loading and/or unloading circumstances.
- *Pallet Conveyors:* moving pallet loads along permanent routes by hand. When powered they can cover long distances with minimum manpower with possible stopping points to allow operations as weighing, collation and strapping.
- *Pedestrian Stacker:* manually operated and can lift moderate loads to a limited height but, although very manoeuvrable, can only move as fast as the operator walks.
- *Chutes:* used for moving goods from upper to lower levels and particularly useful for loose materials, robust packages and items not liable to damage.

It would not be unusual if an organisation ran out of space. If this happens it may be that there is a lack of capital to build or extend storage, no further space on site, seasonal fluctuations in sales patterns requiring additional stocks or simply temporary stock increases to cover exceptional circumstances. When discussing the terms for hiring temporary accommodation, consider the following aspects:

- Is the complete building, or only part, required?
- Is it a purely temporary arrangement or is there any possibility of a long-term hire?
- What is the period of letting at first and length of notice required for termination?
- Whose responsibility for heating and lighting?
- Whose responsibility for insurance to cover buildings and/or stock?

- Who is responsible for general maintenance?
- Is there adequate access for type of transport that could be used for deliveries and/or dispatch? You would be surprised how many people forget transport access!

Case Study

The Problem: in recent years growth, both internal and through acquisition, resulted in sales trebling. This has been accommodated through the use of a number of short-term fixes and support from a variety of third-party distributors. To reduce costs and improve control the company was keen to develop a new distribution strategy.

The Logistics Business was invited to undertake a programme of data analysis (difficult in this case due to the rate of change reflected in the raw data collected) and develop plans for the future. Data dumps were taken from the client's computer systems to provide details of all sales orders over a two-month period. From this both peak and average activity levels could be assessed and projected into the future based on the general business forecasts. Part of the project involved helping to develop a distribution strategy to cover all of Scottish Power's stores in both Scotland and England. From the data collected it was possible to model distribution patterns through the country and find a solution to make best use of the existing infrastructure. From this and other data it was possible to develop a statement of the business requirement.

The Solution: these included plans for extending and greatly improving the performance of one distribution centre and layouts for a completely new distribution centre. Both warehouses were designed around a mix of narrow aisle trucks with separate picking and replenishment aisles, and gravity conveyor based pick faces for both pallets and cartons, block stack and shelving. Product lines were then assigned to particular picking and storage areas depending on throughput, physical size, stock volume and product type. Recommendations for computerised warehouse management were also made.

The Success: by basing the analysis on raw data it was possible to ensure far greater accuracy in the analysis. The analysis of products using a number of different measures enable products with different characteristics to be grouped and optimised around those specific characteristics. At the end of the project Scottish Power had a clear set of costed plans for a distribution network to meet the future needs of the business.

For details of similar cases and their solutions the Logistics Business Organisation may be contacted at: The Logistics Business Limited, Aston Science Park, Birmingham, B7 4BJ, United Kingdom. Tel: 0121 333 6303. Fax: 0121 333 6407. E-Mail:- HYPERLINK mailto:Info@logistics.co.uk   Info@logistics.co.uk. http://www.logistics.co.uk.

CHAPTER 12

Electronic Data Interchange (EDI) and Electronic Procurement

A Definition of Electronic Data Interchange (EDI)

In its broadest definition electronic data interchange (EDI) is the exchange of information between two difference computer systems. For the purpose of this chapter however we shall use the most commonly used definition of EDI.

During the 1980s, the introduction of information technology into companies has enabled significant change within the business: change in working practices, change in organisational structure and change to business strategies bringing improved efficiency, management control and customer service, and with them, a bottom line.

Technologies such as the introduction of the personal computer (PC), local area networks (LANs) and latterly, more widely based corporate networks have been adopted. Within the organisation this has enabled the application (for example a material requirements planning system) to be brought closer to the end user and has facilitated the sharing of information between applications across common databases. This implementation of technology has brought with it real business benefits to the organisation.

There is, however, a further dimension to the implementation of information technology which has emerged over the last seven years in particular. This is the electronic exchange of information between the applications of different organisations' electronic data interchange (EDI). The business requirement for EDI is clear.

Whatever the business, organisations need to trade in order to survive. To achieve this documents such as orders, delivery instructions and invoices must be interchanged and processed. Furthermore, because market conditions can change rapidly, these communications must be fast and accurate, with administrative processes minimised to ensure that, at all times, market opportunities are exploited and profits are maximised. In other words, the organisation needs to communicate effectively with all of its trading partners, whatever their function in the supply chain, whatever their size and wherever they are.

Electronic data interchange (EDI) services allow the exchange of trading data, such as orders and invoices directly from one computer system to another, regardless of its make, size or location and without the need for manual intervention. As such, the consequential benefits to be obtained from the use of EDI are very significant. In the ordering process alone, the speed of movement of information means the supply chain can work together to ensure the right stock is in the right place; that the order is delivered on time; to make sure the market opportunity has been captured and to minimise working capital in the process. In short it gives competitive advantage in competitive markets.

The winners of the 1990s will be those organisations that not only implement but exploit information technology and particularly EDI more creatively, more efficiently and more successfully than their competitors. They will be those companies that form much closer working relationships with their trading partners, customers and suppliers alike and as a result EDI will be a key enabler in this process.

The Fundamentals of EDI

There are many different ways in which two businesses can communicate with one another: face-to-face meetings; paper transactions; telephone conversations; the telex or the fax; and, more recently, electronic mail. In each of these cases an "operator" is required within each organisation for the communication to be completed. In essence they are all forms of person-to-person communications.

In addition to personal communications, information technology has allowed organisations to offer trading partners access to their computer systems by a variety of communication methods. These include airline reservation systems and insurance quotation systems. Whilst one "operator" becomes a computer system, it is still in essence being interrogated by a person at the other end. Hence we also have person-to-computer communications.

EDI takes this one step further, being a dialogue between two computer applications without the need for any personal intervention. EDI transactions are designed to be generated by a computer application, not a person. Likewise an EDI transaction coming into a company is not designed to be printed and read, but rather be entered directly into a computer application. The basic functions are shown in Figure 46.

Figure 46 Basic EDI Network.

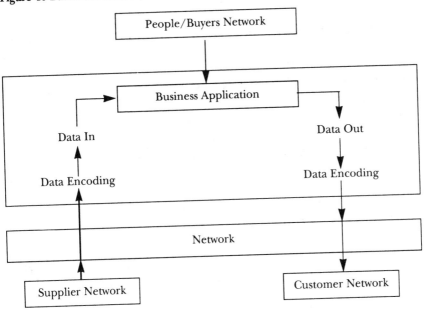

Adapted from Parfett M (1998) High Level EDI Overview.

EDI has two main components outlined briefly below.

Data Standards

If organisations are to exchange commercial data such as orders and invoices with trading partners, there needs to be some formal explicit definition of the document. This enables the sender to know what information to send in what order, and the computer receiving the transactions knows exactly what is contained within the transaction and therefore how to process the information.

As EDI has developed over the years in different parts of the globe there are, understandably, many different data standards available.

In the UK there are only three widely acceptable standards, namely TRADACOMS, ODETTE and EDIFACT. The standard to choose depends on the standard used by the trading community. In an industrial sector where there is no accepted standard established, the choice will depend on the business requirements of the sector, for example if international in nature this would favour the new international EDIFACT standards.

Communication

There are many different ways in which data can be exchanged between computers without the need for manual rekeying. Computer diskettes or magnetic tape, for example, can be used to exchange data, but they still rely on some kind of courier service to relay them between trading partners, which obviously has time-delay implications.

Discounting these options, therefore, the choices are point-to-point connections or leased lines between organisations, packet-switching services usually offered by the public telephone service providers (commonly known as the PTTs), or value added network service providers (VANs).

Whilst all three options are used in the UK, most of the inter-organisation EDI is conducted using the services of VANs. With respect to communications, the main reason for this is that the EDI services deal with the differences in computer protocols of different trading partners and provide store and forward facilities, so that a data exchange does not have to be scheduled for when both partners have their computer systems available for the task.

Why Use EDI?

External and Internal Pressures

There are two sets of triggers driving EDI which can work independently or together. One group is external, the other internal. The major pressure driving organisations into EDI is external pressure from major customers. Some are building EDI capability into conditions of contract, others are imposing financial penalties for each paper document submitted. The other external driver is competition. Needing to match or stay ahead of the competition, particularly in servicing customers' leads to the introduction of EDI.

Internal pressures are much more diverse. Organisations seeking to reduce the cost of purchase are attracted to the cost savings EDI delivers. Inventory reduction programmes, support for Just-in-time (JIT) programmes, order-cycle and lead-time reductions and the need for greater productivity are all supported by EDI.

EDI Benefits

EDI offers substantial benefits for improving the efficiency and effectiveness of the purchasing and logistics functions. Most organisations focus on the cost saving aspects of EDI. These include:

- stationery;
- postage;
- mail handling;
- data entry and correction;
- inventory reductions.

The speed of EDI transactions also beings benefits. Reduced purchase and delivery cycle times contribute to reduced lead times with a subsequent reduction in inventory.

EDI Activity in the UK

There are over 5,000 organisations across some 40 major industry sectors in the UK currently involved in electronic data interchange through open third-party clearing house services. Many other organisations also use EDI both within their organisations and with their major trading partners using direct telecommunications connections (for example permanent/leased lines).

Industry Sectors currently active with EDI include:

Aerospace	Brewing & Leisure	Builders' Merchants
Chemicals	Clothing	Construction
CTNs/Newsagents	Distribution	DIY
Education	Electrical	Electronics
Engineering	Energy/Oil	Export/Transport
Food/Grocery	Garden Products	Healthcare
Home Shopping	Household	Local Government
Manufacturing	Motor Manufacturing	Motor Parts Dist'n

Office Products	Pharmaceuticals	Publishing
Retail Chemists	Retail Department/	White Goods
Stationery	Variety Stores	
	Sound & Vision	

The largest of these industry communities are food/grocery, DIY and motor manufacturing, each with EDI communities ranging in size from 300-500 organisations. Organisations involved across the 40 sectors range from the UK's largest multi-nationals (approximately 75 of the *Times* Top 100) to firms employing only one or two people. They come from all parts of the industry supply chain: retailers, distributors, wholesalers, importers, manufacturers and transportation firms.

Legal Issues

The information being exchanged in the EDI chain is, in some instances, part of a legal process. Purchase orders, invoices and some freight documents have legal as well as business purposes. If nothing else, EDI eliminates the battle of the forms. Documents with terms and conditions referenced now disappear. The legal structure and rules, however, are built to serve a paper-based trade system. It has not caught up with the technology.

In the UK there are no restrictions on the use of EDI in the legal code, save for the requirement that land and bond purchasing be effected under seal. No one has yet found a way of applying a seal to an EDI message. The 1981 Finance Act was changed at the request of the EDI lobby to amend clauses which would have outlawed EDI-based invoices. Whilst there are no significant restrictions on EDI, it must be pointed out that, to date, EDI has not been tested in the courts. When selecting EDI software and services satisfy yourself that full audit trials are provided.

To help remove the uncertainty by this lack of legal precedence, the UK-based EDI Association (EDIA) has produced a model interchange agreement. The agreement is designed to supplement existing terms and conditions of contract when EDI is used. It includes clauses covering security and integrity of data, use of intermediaries (EDI service providers) and disputes.

Whether the EDIA or another interchange agreement is used, it is important to review existing terms and conditions of trade. Many include references to paper and postal systems which will have to be removed. As most EDI transactions relate to term contracts, contract negotiation is not an integral part of the transaction, terms and conditions having been agreed upfront.

Organisations seeking to use EDI in an international arena will need to be particularly careful. The legal status of EDI differs, even within the European Union. The United Nations has produced guidelines (the UNCID rules) to help draft interchange agreements. The European Commission is currently trying to harmonise the Union's legal position on EDI but that work is not yet completed.

Finally, to pull all of the above into context, it must be said that the UK now has a community in excess of 5,000 organisations clearly demonstrating that legal issues have not restricted the growth in its use.

Degree of Integration

Supply chain operations involve vast quantities of information. Efficiency in supply chains demands efficient means of handling this information. Information technology has been, and is, used extensively in certain sectors of the supply chain: inventory control, logistics manufacturing planning, distribution, purchasing, and sales order processing are commonplace. In some organisations, these functionally-based systems have been integrated to reflect more accurately internal supply chain operations. With EDI it can be seen that this integration expands across organisations, continuing the trend of directing IT investments to facilitate greater degrees of integration.

EDI will significantly improve the efficiency of information across the supply chain, bringing great benefits to purchasing and logistics operations. By creating a link between business processes in different organisations (or disparate parts of the same company) EDI will result in significant changes. Not since the introduction of Just-in-time (JIT) has a concept been devised which will have such far reaching implications, and for once, the West leads Japan.

Electronic Procurement and Commerce

All around the world, purchasing and supply management (P&SM) professionals are now advocating harnessing purchasing as a strategic function to increase profit margins. Many organisations are waking up to the fact that every dollar saved in P&SM contributes directly to the bottom line. Some of the tactics used in this transformation process are volume purchase, buying from approved supplier, selecting the right supplier, awarding business based on performance, improving quality of buy and reducing paper work and administrative cost (Chin Nam, 1998).

As a rule of thumb, about 20 per cent of an organisation's purchases constitute 80 per cent of the total purchase value. To reap quick returns from purchasing, the organisation spares no effort on improving the effectiveness of high-value and big-volume purchases. This approach requires purchasing personnel to perform functions like consolidate buy, buy only from approved source, improve quality of existing suppliers, do contract negotiation and form partnership with suppliers. This in turn causes purchasing personnel to spend a lot of time and effort on upstream procurement activities such as qualifying suppliers, building rapport with strategic suppliers and carrying out supplier evaluation and certification.

It is also common to hear purchasing people complaining they expend 80 per cent of their time on 20 per cent of the total purchase value. A high percentage of this time is spent on non-value-added activities such as performing data entry, correcting errors in paperwork, expediting delivery or solving quality problems. As such, they do not have sufficient time to put their full attention to upstream activities. Organisations then try to redress this balance by implementing new purchasing policies and ISO9000 procedures. However, all of them face the uphill task of enforcement because these structured procedures require more work and time to execute.

What many organisations fail to understand is that a fundamental change in their internal processes must be effected to maximise the full benefits of such a move. The two critical success factors which most organisations overlook are to cut down the number of routine tasks and to reduce the overall programme cycle through the use of appropriate technology.

The latest technological trend is to get on the high-speed information technology highway. For the purchasing industry, electronic procurement is an IT-enabler for procurement; a tremendously powerful tool that will revolutionise the purchasing climate and beef up the organisation's bottom line. It automates and streamlines the laborious routine of the purchasing function, thus freeing up purchasing professionals to focus on more strategic purchases.

Chin Nam (1998) argues the advantages of electronic procurement to be:

- Reducing purchasing cycle time and cost.
- Enhancing budgetary control.
- Eliminating administrative errors.
- Increasing buyers' productivity.
- Lowering prices through product standardisation and consolidation of buy.
- Better information management; for example supplier's information and pricing information.
- Improving the payment process.

Implementing electronic procurement is equivalent to installing a host of time-saving perks such as the elimination of manual information tracking from separate sources. These labour-saving tactics free up time for value-added activities such as supplier qualification, quotation award and negotiation. The ability to electronically generate documents and track the status of approvals on-line dramatically reduces the cycle time from the initiation to fulfilment of a buy. Indeed Parfett (1998) suggests the cost of information processed by EDI is 20 per cent of the equivalent paper costs, 20 per cent reduction in cost of processing a purchase order, 25 per cent stock reduction, reduced lead times and reduced working capital.

Up to 50 million people now have access to the Internet throughout the world, of whom the majority are increasingly connecting from their workplace. Despite inception and most developments occurring in the US, it is Germany and the UK that are now the fastest growing countries on the Internet. In fact eight of the top 12 fastest growing countries, in terms of Internet hosts, are European. The global growth rate has more than doubled each year for the last four years and thousands continue to connect every month.

Globally the number of host computers on the Internet has grown from just a few in 1989 to 9.5 million in January 1996, connecting over 150 countries. Projections by the Internet Society put the number of hosts at nearly 109 million by the year 2000.

The Internet is forecast to grow and develop at substantial rates from its current position. Although research organisations provide conflicting statistics, there is universal agreement that the Internet will help shape large changes in general computing usage and how information is portrayed, displayed and accessed in the future. There has certainly been a mass influx of commercial representation, and utilisation of the Internet in the last 24 months. Parfett (1998) estimated that 95 per cent of businesses have expressed the intention to develop some Internet usage by the end of 1996.

Some people use the terms electronic commerce (EC) and information superhighway interchangeably but EC is a particular subset that deals with commercial transactions and the surrounding processes. There are many more uses for the information superhighway than just EC.

Most EDI product and service suppliers now use the term EC rather than EDI as it indicates that EDI is just one facet of the overall electronic trading environment. It is the integration of the enabling technologies, not in a technical sense but in respect of the support of trading activities which make EC "different".

The interest in and subsequent use of EC will vary amongst the user and supplier community. Some advanced users may well have intelligent gateways which can decide which particular enabling technology is required for a particular business function and automatically select and invoke the technology. The use of intelligent agents, software based on artificial intelligence, to support such activities is not too far away. Others may manually select the technologies required which could cover the whole spectrum or specific specialist area such as the electronic catalogue.

In most organisations, the business vision applicable before and after the introduction of EC is very similar. In essence, EC has resulted in few changes to accepted methods of working although trading documents may arrive or be sent in an electronic form rather rather on paper. There is little doubt however, that as electronic commerce gains momentum, EDI solutions using Internet look set to play a key role (Attwood 1998).

References

Ammer, D (1974) *Materials Management,* 3rd edition. Irwin, Homewood, Illinois.

Atlas, M (11998) "New Trends in Internet Commerce" *Journal of Internet Purchasing,* July.

Attwood, R (1998) "E-com Coming" *Supply Management,* 30 July, pp. 37-39.

Audit Commission (1984) "Reducing the Cost of Local Government Purchases" HMSO, London.

Bailey, P (1983) Purchasing *Systems and Records* Gower Publishing, Aldershot.

Baily, P (1991) *Purchasing and Supply Management,* 5th edition, Prentice Hall, London.

Baily, P and Farmer, D (1985) *Purchasing Principles and Management* Pitman, London.

Bain, J S (1959) *Industrial Organisation* Wiley, New York.

Bauer, P T and Yamey, B S (1968) *Markets, Market Control and Market Reform* Weidenfeld and Nicholson, London.

Black, G (1996) "Critical Information" *Financial Times,* 15 October.

Bolton, J F (1972) Small firms, Cmnd 4811, HMSO, London.

Boulding, K E (1956) "General System Theory - the skeleton of science" *Management Science* Vol 2 pp 197-208.

Branwell Report (1964) *The placing and management of contracts for building and civil engineering works* HMSO, London.

BS5750/ISO 9000 (1987) *A positive contribution to better business* BSI, London.

Buckner, H (1967) *How British Industry Buys* Hutchinson, London.

Cavinato, J L (1992) "A total cost/value model for supply chain competitiveness" *Journal of Business Logistics* Vol 13 No 2 pp 285-301.

CIPS (1997) "Supply Chain Management" *Technical Services Guide* Chartered Institute of Purchasing & Supply, Easton.

Clothier, K (1998). "The Role of Systems Integrators in Electronic Commerce" *Journal of Internet Purchasing*, March.

Compton, K & Jessop, D (1995) "Dictionary of Purchasing & Supply", CIPS, Easton.

Croell, R C (1977) "Measuring purchasing effectiveness" *Journal of Purchasing and Materials Management*, 13 (1), 3-4.

Crosby, P (1979) "Quality is Free". McGraw Hill, London.

Cross, R & Leonard, P (1994) "Benchmarking A Strategic and Tactical Perspective" *Managing Quality* ed. Dale, B G, Second Edition, Prentice-Hall.

Cyert, R M and March, J G (1963) *A Behavioural Theory of the Firm* Prentice-Hall, Englewood Cliffs, New Jersey.

Deming, W E (1988) "Quality, Productivity and Competitive Position" MIT Study. Massachusetts pp 29-30

Dickie, H F (1951) "ABC Analysis shoots for dollars not pennies" *Factory Management and Maintenance*, July.

Dobler, D W (1990) "Purchasing and Materials Management Text and Cases" 5th Edition. McGraw Hill, New York

Dooley, K (1995) "Purchasing and Supply An Opportunity for OR?" *OR Insight* Vol 8 No 3 pp 21-25.

Economist Intelligence Unit (1986) *Retail Business*, April, No 338, London.

Edwards, R S and Townsend, H (1985) *Business Enterprise, its Growth and Organisation* Macmillan, London.

Elliott-Shircore, T & Steele, P (1985) "Procurement Planning Overview" *Purchasing and Supply Management*. December pp23-26.

Ellram, L (1990) "Supplier Selection in Strategic Partnerships" *Journal of Purchasing and Material Management* Fall pp8-14.

Farmer, D H (1972) "Source decision-making in the multi-national company" *Journal of Purchasing* 8(1), 5-18.

Fearon, H E (1961) *Purchasing research in American business* PhD thesis, Michigan State University.

Gattorna, J (1990) *The Gower Handbook of Logistics and Distribution* 4th edition, Gower Publishing, Aldershot.

Heinritz, S F and Farrell, P V (1981) *Purchasing: Principles and Applications* Prentice-Hall, Englewood Cliffs, New Jersey.

Hendry, J (1995) "Culture, Community and Networks: The Hidden

Cost of Outsourcing" *European Management Journal* Vol 13 No 2 pp 193-200.

Hoffman, M (1998) "The Future of Interbusiness Commerce" *Journal of Internet Purchasing*, March.

Institute of Purchasing & Supply (1990) *Electronic Data Interchange*, IPS, Easton.

Institute of Purchasing & Supply (1990) *Just In Time: The Purchasing Viewpoint* IPS, Easton.

Johnson, G and Scholes K (1992) *Exploring Corporate Strategy Text and Cases* Prentice Hall, London.

Kavanegh, J (1998) "The Logistics Chain: Electronic Data Interchange Fresh Enthusiasm" *Financial Times*, 06 March

Kostishack, J D and South, J C (1973) "The composition of industrial buyer performance" *Journal of Purchasing* 9(3), 50-63.

Kotler, P and Balachandrian, V (1975) "Strategic remarketing, the preferred response to shortages and inflation" *Sloan Management Review*, August.

Kotler, P and Levy, S J (1973) "Buying is marketing too" *Journal of Marketing*, January.

Lamming, R (1993) "Beyond Partnership: Strategies for Innovation and Lean Supply". Prentice Hall, Hemel Hempstead.

Lauer, S (1967) "Westinghouse Plant X." In *Purchasing Problems* (eds Baily and Farmer) POA, London.

Lee, L and Dobler D (1977) *Purchasing and Materials Management* McGraw-Hill, New York.

Leenders, M R (1965) *Improving Purchasing Effectiveness through Supplier Development* Harvard University Press, Cambridge, Mass.

Lewis, C D (1970) *Scientific Inventory Control* Butterworth, London.

Little, D and Barclay, I (1986) "Materials Management: the technologist's role in controlling materials costs" *Purchasing and Supply Management*, January. IPS Easton.

Macbeth, D Ferguson, N Neil, G & Baxter, L (1989) "Not Purchasing but Supply Chain Management" *Purchasing and Supply Management* November pp30-32.

Meopham, B (1985) ICE *Conditions of Contract – a Commercial Manual* Waterlow Publishers, London.

Moos, S (1971) *Research Report 13*, Committee of Enquiry on Small Firms, HMSO, London.

Muhlenmann, A, Oakland, J and Lockyer, K (1992) *Production and Operations Management* Pitman, London.

Myer, R (1989) "Suppliers - Manage Your Customers" *Harvard Business Review* Vol 89 No 6 pp 160-168.

Nam, C C (1998). "Increase your profit margin through electronic procurement" *Journal of Internet Purchasing.* July.

New, S J (1994) "Supply chains: some doubts". Proceedings of the IPSERA Conference Cardiff pp 345-362.

New, S J (1997) "The Scope of Supply Chain Management Research" *Supply Chain Management* Vol 2 No 1 pp 15-22.

Newing, R (1996). "Software moves to meet supply chain needs", *Financial Times*, 10 February.

Newman, R G (1985) "Validation of Contract Compliance under Systems Contracting" *Journal of Purchasing and Materials Management*, Summer.

Parfett, M (1998) "What is EDI?", Electronic Commerce Innovation Centre, University of Cardiff.

Parfett, M (1998) "An Introduction to Electronic Commerce". Electronic Commerce Innovation Centre. University of Cardiff.

Parfett, M (1998). "High Level EDI Overview". Electronic Commerce Innovation Centre. University of Cardiff.

Parfett, M (1998) *The Internet* Electronic Commerce Innovation Centre. University of Cardiff.

Porter, M E (1979) "How competitive forces shape strategy" *Harvard Business Review* March-April.

Porter, M E (1982) "Competitive Advantage of Nations". Prentice Hall, New York.

Quayle, M (1991) "Prime Contractorship", *Purchasing and Supply Management* April, IPS, Easton.

Quayle, M (1992) "Developing Industrial Purchasing Policy" *Purchasing and Supply Management* February, IPS, Easton.

Quayle, M (1996) "Supply Chain Management and the Factors Affecting Sourcing Decisions", Proceedings of the Chartered Institute of Marketing Eastern Region Conference: Focus on Customers, Getting Them and Keeping Them. Imperial War Museum.

Quayle, M (1997) "Purchasing in UK and Switzerland: An Empirical Study of Sourcing Decisions", Proceedings of an International Purchasing and Supply Education Research Association (IPSERA) Workshop Purchasing Decisions, University of Twente, Enschede, The Netherlands.

Quayle, M (1997) "The Supply Chain: Organisation Impact of Factors Affecting Sourcing Decisions", Proceedings of International Research Symposium Effective Organisations, University of Bournemouth, Bournemouth.

Quayle, M (1998) "Supplier Development for High Technology Small Firms in UK", Proceedings of 6th Annual High Technology Small Firms Conference. University of Twente, Enschede, The Netherlands.

Quayle, M (1998) "Industrial Procurement: Factors Affecting Sourcing Decisions, *European Journal of Purchasing & Supply Management* Elsevier Science, Vol 4 No 2.4., Oxford.

Quayle, M (1998) "The Impact of Strategic Procurement in the UK Government Sector", Proceedings of 7th International Purchasing & Supply Education and Research Association (IPSERA) Conference, London.

Quayle, M (1998) "The Impact of Strategic Procurement in the UK Government Sector", *International Journal of Public Sector Management* MCB University Press, Vol. 11, No. 2.4., Oxford.

Rees, G (1969) *St Michael, A History of Marks and Spencer* Weidenfeld and Nicholson, London.

Rook, A (1972) *Transfer Pricing*, British Institute of Management, London.

Rowe, D and Alexander, I (1968) *Selling Industrial Products*, Hutchinson, London.

Saunders, M. (1994) "Strategic Purchasing and Supply Chain Management". Pitman, London.

Schonberger, R J (1986) "World Class Manufacturing: the Lessons of Simplicity Applied". Free Press London.

Strauss, G (1962) "Tactics of lateral relationships: the purchasing agent" *Administrative Science Quarterly* 7 September.

Tse, K K (1985) *Marks and Spencer* Pergamon Press, Oxford.

Van Weele, A J and Rozemeijer, F A (1996) "Revolution in Purchasing" *European Journal of Purchasing and Supply Management* Vol 2 No 4 pp 153-160.

Webster, F E and Wind, Y (1972) *Organisational Buying Behaviour* Prentice-Hall, Englewood Cliffs, New Jersey.

Welford, R and Prescott, K (1992) *European Business An issue-based approach* Pitman, London.

Williams, F (1997) "EDI data exchange spreads its wings" *Financial Times*, 21 March.

Womack, J P, Jones, D R and Roos, D (1991) *"The Machine that changed the World"* Harper Perennial, New York.

Index

Industrial Marketing management